Palgrave Studies in Compromise after Conflict

Series Editor

John Brewer
Queen's University Belfast
United Kingdom

This series aims to bring together in one series scholars from around the world who are researching the dynamics of post-conflict transformation in societies emerging from communal conflict and collective violence. The series welcomes studies of particular transitional societies emerging from conflict, comparative work that is cross-national, and theoretical and conceptual contributions that focus on some of the key processes in post-conflict transformation. The series is purposely interdisciplinary and addresses the range of issues involved in compromise, reconciliation and societal healing. It focuses on interpersonal and institutional questions, and the connections between them.

More information about this series at
http://www.springer.com/series/14641

Azrini Wahidin

Ex-Combatants, Gender and Peace in Northern Ireland

Women, Political Protest and the Prison Experience

palgrave
macmillan

Azrini Wahidin
Nottingham Trent University
Nottingham, United Kingdom

Palgrave Studies in Compromise after Conflict
ISBN 978-1-137-36329-9   ISBN 978-1-137-36330-5   (eBook)
DOI 10.1057/978-1-137-36330-5

Library of Congress Control Number: 2016942452

Cover illustration: Wall mural on Ascaill Ard na bhFeá/Beechmount Avenue, Belfast, by Danny Devenny and Marty Lyons. Photo by Brid McKernon

Printed on acid-free paper

This Palgrave Macmillan imprint is published by Springer Nature
The registered company is Macmillan Publishers Ltd. London

'A strong woman is a woman determined to do something others are determined not to be done'.
'Strong is what we make together'[1].

To all those whose experiences have made this book possible but in particular I would like to acknowledge:

Che Mah Wahidin

Evelyn Brady

Kate McKinney

Eibhlín Glenhomes

---

[1] Piercy, M (2013) For Strong women in Moon Is Always Female, New York: Knopf Doubleday Publishing Group.

Series Editor's Preface

Compromise is a much used but little understood term. There is a sense in which it describes a set of feelings (the so-called 'spirit' of compromise) that involve reciprocity, representing the agreement to make mutual concessions toward each other from now on: no matter what we did to each other in the past, we will act toward each other in the future differently as set out in the agreement between us. The compromise settlement can be a spit and a handshake, much beloved in folk lore, or a legally binding statute with hundreds of clauses.

As such, it is clear that compromise enters into conflict transformation at two distinct phases. The first is during the conflict resolution process itself, where compromise represents a willingness amongst parties to negotiate a peace agreement that represents a second-best preference in which they give up their first preference (victory) in order to cut a deal. A great deal of literature has been produced in Peace Studies and International Relations on the dynamics of the negotiation process and the institutional and governance structures necessary to consolidate the agreement afterwards. Just as important, however, is compromise in the second phase, when compromise is part of post-conflict reconstruction, in which protagonists come to learn to live together despite their former enmity and in face of the atrocities perpetrated during the conflict itself.

In the first phase, compromise describes reciprocal agreements between parties to the negotiations in order to make political concessions sufficient to end conflict; in the second phase, compromise involves victims and perpetrators developing ways of living together in which concessions are made as part of shared social life. The first is about compromises between political groups and the state in the process of state-building (or re-building) after the political upheavals of communal conflict; the second is about compromises between individuals and communities in the process of social healing after the cultural trauma provoked by the conflict.

This book series primarily concerns itself with the second process, the often messy and difficult job of reconciliation, restoration and repair in social and cultural relations following communal conflict. Communal conflicts and civil wars tend to suffer from the narcissism of minor differences, to coin Freud's phrase, leaving little to be split halfway and compromise on, and thus are usually especially bitter. The series therefore addresses itself to the meaning, manufacture and management of compromise in one of its most difficult settings. The book series is cross-national and cross-disciplinary, with attention paid to inter-personal reconciliation at the level of everyday life, as well as culturally between social groups, and the many sorts of institutional, inter-personal, psychological, sociological, anthropological and cultural factors that assist and inhibit societal healing in all post-conflict societies, historically and in the present. It focuses on what compromise means when people have to come to terms with past enmity and the memories of the conflict itself, and relate to former protagonists in ways that consolidate the wider political agreement.

This sort of focus has special resonance and significance, for peace agreements are usually very fragile. Societies emerging out of conflict are subject to ongoing violence from spoiler groups who are reluctant to give up on first preferences, constant threats from the outbreak of renewed violence, institutional instability, weakened economies, and a wealth of problems around transitional justice, memory, truth recovery and victimhood, amongst others. Not surprisingly therefore, reconciliation and healing in social and cultural relations is difficult to achieve, not least because inter-personal compromise between erstwhile enemies is difficult.

Lay discourse picks up on the ambivalent nature of compromise after conflict. It is talked about in common sense in one of two ways, in which compromise is either a virtue or a vice, taking its place among the angels or in Hades. One form of lay discourse likens concessions to former protagonists with the idea of restoration of broken relationships and societal and cultural reconciliation, in which there is a sense of becoming (or returning) to wholeness and completeness. The other form of lay discourse invokes ideas of appeasement, of being *compromised* by the concessions, which constitute a form of surrender and reproduce (or disguise) continued brokenness and division. People feel they continue to be beaten by the sticks which the concessions have allowed others to keep; with restoration, however, weapons are turned truly in ploughshares. Lay discourse suggests, therefore, that there are issues that the *Palgrave Studies in Compromise after Conflict* series must begin to problematize, so that the process of societal healing is better understood and can be assisted and facilitated by public policy and intervention.

In this contribution to the series, we return again to one of the important groups in any process of post-conflict social reconstruction, recovery and reconciliation; namely, ex-combatants. Of course, ex-combatants compete for centrality with other stakeholders, such as victims, the state, and international and regional powers, but the importance of ex-combatants is recognised in the growth of an extensive literature on ex-political prisoners in post-conflict societies. The issues this literature raises range from the various disarmament, demobilisation and reintegration (DDR) policies in the post-conflict state, the mental health and well-being concerns they often face, their social marginalisation and risk of high levels of unemployment, questions of atonement and reparation, and, in Northern Ireland in particular, the positive contribution they make to community development and the peace process more generally. A striking feature of this literature, however, is its attention to men. This is partly because combatants were mostly male but, even so, this literature neglects the combatant role of women and the gendered experiences of women ex-combatants in prison, as well as the contribution that women ex-prisoners made to establishing and building the peace when outside jail. These issues form the central theme of Professor Azrini Wahidin's excellent analysis of Republican women ex-prisoners in Northern Ireland.

These women's voices have largely gone unheard and the book is important for articulating them with such rigour and insight.

The ethnographic richness and depth of the interview data is fascinating and the author is fully on top of the historical and political detail of her case study. Wahidin recognises the combatant role of Republican women and captures their experiences in prison, which are often neglected due to the attention given to Republican men, but Wahidin rightly gives focus to the positive role women played inside the jails in giving their imprimatur to the Good Friday Agreement and their support to Sinn Fein's peace strategy on the outside.

The irony of the book is that it serves to identify a lacuna in that a similar analysis is sorely needed of Loyalist women. Gender and peace-building is an important field, mostly for the recognition it affords to the principle of gender justice and the need for broader gender mainstreaming as a strategic response to facilitate social transformation after conflict. Post-conflict societies that do not simultaneously address issues of injustice, unfairness and inequality will always experience their conflict transformation as fragile and vulnerable. Gender justice forms part of the social transformation that post-conflict societies need to consolidate the peace. Regretfully, the issue of women combatants and ex-combatants does not feature as a topic in the field of gender and peace-building, and this book in the Palgrave series can be seen as a call to other researchers to begin to address the gendered experiences of prison for women ex-combatants and the contribution women ex-combatants can make to post-conflict recovery. As Editor, I warmly welcome this book to the *Palgrave Studies in Compromise after Conflict* Series.

John D. Brewer
Belfast, UK
January 2016

Acknowledgments

My first acknowledgment is to Evelyn Brady, Eibhlín Glenhomes and Kate McKinney who have contributed enormously to this project and have joined me on this journey. They have my deepest gratitude and respect.

I extend my thanks to the 48 women and men whose voices fill these pages and without whom this book could not have been written.

Ex-Combatants, Gender and Peace in Northern Ireland: Women, Political Protest and the Prison Experience was conceived while I was establishing the first undergraduate Criminology programme at Queen's University, Belfast. It became more than just an idea due to a conversation that occurred between myself, Deena Haydon and Phil Scraton, for which I am grateful. I would also like to thank in particular John Brewer, for creating the intellectual home to develop this book.

So many people, directly and indirectly, have contributed to my work over the years. This book, then, is the result of a collaborative venture and one that has evolved over many years. In writing this book, friendships have been formed and consolidated with people who, personally and intellectually, have been so supportive. My thanks go to Una Convery, (Sean, the Convery family—in particular, JJ and Matthew), Deena Haydon, Linda Moore (Henry, Annie and Alex), Bob Miller, Phil Scraton and Margrit Shildrick.

Voices: Republican Women Ex-prisoners Group, Tar Anall and Coiste na n-Iarchimí,[1] has been instrumental in locating respondents willing to be interviewed. Many thanks go to Roddy Hegarty, based at the Cardinal Tomas O'Fiaich Library; staff at the Linen Hall Library; *An Phoblacht*; and the Special Collection Queen's University, Belfast. I would like to thank Martina Anderson, Caitríona Glenholmes, Bobbie Hanvey, Bik McFarlane, Jim McGiven, Billy McKee, Jim McIlmurray, Jim McVeigh, Brenda Murphy, Monsignor Raymond Murray, Pauline Prior, Pat Sheehan, Clara O'Reilly, the National Graves Association, Belfast (Cumann Uaigheann na Laocradh Gaedheal, Béal Feirste), Eva Patterson, Nuala Perry, Pauline Prior, David Torrans and the Féile Women's Choir.

I have been supported by my colleagues, in particular Ron Aday, Yvonne Barnett, Michelle Burman, Maureen Cain, Pat Carlen, Malcom Cowburn, Bernie Christian, Pam Davies, Robert Dingwall, Michele Devlin, Bill Dixon, Feargal Mac Ionnrachtaigh, Yvonne Galligan, Loraine Gelsthorpe, Claire Hackett, Paddy Hillyard, Ruth Jamieson, Helen Jones, Simon Holdaway, Shadd Maruna, Kathie Moore, Judith Phillips, Ian O'Donnell, Ella O'Dwyer, Denis O' Hearn, Eoin O'Sullivan, Kieran McEvoy, Laurence McKeown, Gill McIvor, Fergus McNeill, Aogán Mulcahy, Laura Piacentini, Mary Rogan, Bill Rolston, Joe Sim, Mike Tomlinson, Sarah Vickerstaff, Julia Twigg and Sally Wheeler. Also, the Law School at Queen's University, the Centre for Transitional Justice and the Criminology Department at the University of Ulster have been intellectually stimulating homes.

On a more personal note, I would particularly like to thank Evelyn Brady, Una Convery, Laurence Cairns, Paul Dunleavy, Bríd McKernon, Kate McKinney, Linda Moore, Úna Mulgrew and Marie Quiery who, on our cycle rides and walks, have endured my attempts at An Ghaeilge and have listened to various stages of this book. They have supported me with a friendship to which words fail to do justice. This sentiment is extended to my friends in England: Chris Crowther-Dowey, Esha Sarkar

---

[1] Voices: Republican Women Ex-prisoners Group, Tar Anall Coiste na n-Iarchimí, is a network of Republican ex-prisoner organisations based in both Northern Ireland and the Republic of Ireland. Their work includes providing various services and a range of support to Republican ex-prisoners and their families.

Sandie Hope-Forest, Terry Gillespie, Gail Heath, Ellen Robottom, Alex Sporidou and Shirley Tate.

I benefited greatly from visiting scholarships from Melbourne University, The School of Social and Political Sciences and the University of Sydney, where I spent eight months writing this book and two edited collections. My thanks go to Kit Carson, Natalie Hanley, Fiona Haines, Steve James and Alison Young, for making my visit a memorable and a productive one.

Particular thanks go to John Brewer, Dominic Walker and Jules Willan, for their supportive and insightful comments as the manuscript developed.

Finally, and as ever, my thanks and love goes to my mother and sister, Che Mah and Wan-Nita Wahidin.

A Chairde, Ba mhaith liom mo bhuíochas a ghabháil le Mná Ard Mhacha as an chuidiú ar fad. Go raibh míle maith agaibh. Tiocfaidh ár lá.

All royalties from the book will be shared between the Voices: Republican Women Ex-prisoners Group, Tar Anall and Coiste na n-Iarchimí.

Contents

List of Tables

1

Introduction

Irish women are every bit as revolutionary as Irish men and their resistance is every bit as fierce, be they IRA, Sinn Féin activists or campaign organisers and protesters. (*An Glór Gafa/The Captive Voice* 1990)

The aim of this chapter is to contextualise by way of background the ghostly shadow of the past through examining political protest, discriminatory prison policy, and how both female and male Volunteers in the Irish Republican Army found ways of resisting the brutality of the state forces (see Punch 2012). What this chapter clearly shows is the complexity of the political situation in Northern Ireland[1] and how this has impacted on the lives of female ex-combatants.

This chapter sets out the method used to access the experiences of the ex-combatants. The subsequent chapters focus on particular aspects of women's experience as activists, as combatants, as prisoners and as participants in the peace process, in order to build an account of the

---

[1] The term 'Northern Ireland' is contentious but it will be used in this book interchangeably with the North of Ireland as it is used by both communities and is internationally recognised.

© The Editor(s) (if applicable) and The Author(s) 2016

A. Wahidin, *Ex-Combatants, Gender and Peace in Northern Ireland*,
DOI 10.1057/978-1-137-36330-5_1

significant but under-explored role of the construction and experience of gender under conditions of struggle.

Researching Political Imprisonment

This research was a personal and political journey where the questions were reformulated over time through formal and informal discussions with former politically motivated prisoners/ex-combatants. This research started off with a question, which was fluid and open to contestation. As Taylor states, 'we shall find that its terms are transformed, so that in the end we will answer a question which we could not properly conceive at the beginning'. The initial question was to disrupt the silence surrounding women's involvement in the IRA and their experiences of political protest, struggle and imprisonment. The subject and nature of the study was one that was about struggle and, hence, it was important to reflect the voices of the women and interrupt the silence surrounding their involvement as Volunteers/soldiers in an Army. This book is about their experience of political protest and the role they, as women, played in configuring the pathway to peace.

Community activists and ex-prisoner groups provided contacts on the basis of which a snowballing approach was used to locate further interviewees. The main ex-combatant group had a database of contacts for former male politically motivated prisoners but there was no equivalent for women. In the process of gaining access, I was in contact with Voices: Republican Women Ex-prisoners Group, Tar Anall and Coiste na nIachmí. The latter responded in a positive way but felt that it would be difficult to find women who would speak about their experience. It was through the other two organisations and with the support of three particular women that access was facilitated to female and male former ex-combatants/Volunteers who would otherwise be difficult to reach. The 28 women and 20 men interviewed in the course of this research came from across Ireland; some came from cities and others came from rural areas. Some had spent time in British prisons and others had served time in the Republic of Ireland or in the North of Ireland. Many had experienced being on the run and all attested to levels of brutality at the hands of the state. Focus groups were held with female and male ex-combatants, who had the opportunity to read, amend and comment on the process. They were provided with the questions and an envelope beforehand, and were asked to make changes and incorporate areas that they thought were missing. They were also given the opportunity to read the transcripts and make changes. They were given the chapter content to comment on, and also the draft manuscript. The aim was to create a participatory process that involved cooperation and collaboration, thereby transgressing traditional power relationships between those who are researched and those conducting the research. It allowed ex-combatants as much ownership as possible of the material, so that 'the issue of what [was to] be disclosed [remained] under the control of the interviewee' (Jamieson and Grounds 2002, p. 10). It enabled a priori assumptions to be challenged reflecting the participants' experiences, rather than an imposition of my own preconceptions as to what would emerge as significant. Full and informed consent was given and participation was voluntary: it was stressed to participants that they were free to withdraw at any time during the study. Such an approach was important with regard to validating the nature of the research with a group that was hard to reach (Grounds and Jamieson 2003).

This study applied a life-course approach to the involvement of women in the Irish Republican Army and examines the experiences of being criminalised from arrest to imprisonment and life almost twenty years later. The youngest participant was in her 40s at the time of interview and the oldest was 80.

The participants represented different ethnicities and sexualities; some were widowed, some were grandparents and some had remained single. A number of the participants had doctorates, some were Members of the Legislative Assembly (MLAs), some were community workers, writers or film directors, and all had at one time been involved at various levels of the Irish Republican Army structure both inside and outside of prison. Their stories are testimonies of the pain they endured as politically motivated, as mothers, daughters, partners, sisters, fathers, brothers and soldiers. Their stories are illustrative of the violence the state used to maintain a system of inequality. Both women and men had been subjected to prolonged periods of interrogation and degrading treatment, and had faced uncertain lengths of imprisonment, possible loss of life, divorce, penury, lone parenthood and, in some cases, having their children taken into care. These are just some examples of the impact the Conflict[2] had on the lives of the women and men in this study. But what this research clearly shows through the narratives of the women and men which form the focus of this book is their resilience, resistance and political transformation in the face of war and terror. The voices in this book disturb and interrupt the silence surrounding their experiences as former politically motivated prisoners and question the impunity of the British state in the transition from conflict to peace.

In this book, all the names of the ex-combatants and any identifying variables have been changed in agreement with the participants of the study unless they have chosen otherwise.

The remainder of the Introduction provides an outline of the book, indicating the focus of each of the following chapters as they chart the journey of women's involvement and examine how they took the struggle from the home and the streets to beyond the wire: the prison.

Overview

The book examines the gendered experiences of imprisonment, how the women Volunteers placed femininity in dissent, by drawing out the ways in which (contested) conceptions of gender were brought into play in the course of the struggle and, at times, became a site and focus of punishment and of resistance. It is only by interrogating how femininity was inscribed on the body of the female ex-combatant that one begins to tease out the contradictions that emerged not only through the attitudes of

---

[2] The use of the term 'Conflict' rather than 'The Troubles' will be used to refer to the period of armed conflict involving state and non-state groups. The Conflict involved the suspension of normal powers of law enforcement and the due process of the law, and the internment and incarceration of politically affiliated prisoners. Eventual ceasefires and the initiation of the Peace Process led to the 1998 Good Friday (Belfast) Agreement and political devolution to the Northern Ireland Assembly. The British and Irish governments established a commitment to democratic and peaceful means of resolving political issues. The term denotes the protracted and symbolic nature of the 'long war'.

fellow comrades, but also through the way the state forces responded to women's involvement in political protest in Northern Ireland.

It is by listening to the voices of women and male Volunteers that their experiences of being part of a wider struggle that continues to sustain the momentum of the peace process comes to the fore in spite of attempts made by groups (ie. Unionists, Dissident Republicans) who wish to derail the journey of change. The overall aim of this book is to address the lacuna surrounding the role women played in the IRA and their experience of the criminal justice system, and to question why women remain marginal in a society that is transitioning from war to peace. In this movement of transition, new spaces are being created that have the potential to develop new possibilities for a different type of society.

The book is therefore innovative on several levels. It challenges the cultural stereotypes by recognising the combatant role played by women, a stereotype that pervades cultural perspectives of women as 'natural peacemakers' and which seriously neglects the role they have played in war. It builds on the extensive literature on ex-combatants in post-conflict societies (for example, McMullin 2013) by taking a gendered approach in order to bring voice to female ex-combatants who are usually overlooked in what is a dominant focus on male ex-prisoners. It also builds on the growing literature in Northern Ireland on ex-combatants' contribution to the peace process (for example, Shirlow et al. 2010) by showing that the imprimatur of women prisoners was also important, inside and outside of prison. In this respect, it directly engages with the women's attitude towards the Good Friday Agreement and their involvement in post-conflict politics. Finally, it explores the same transition made by ex-combatants from a military to a political strategy in Northern Ireland addressed by Brewer et al. (2013), but brings a gender perspective by considerably expanding on the number of female ex-combatant respondents whose narratives of transition are analysed and addressed. We hear the stories of women directly involved in war and peace—and, largely, for the first time.

Chapter 2 explores the debates surrounding peace, war and gender. The chapter will begin by contextualising the discussion with reference to some of the literature on peace and war. It will then place the discussion within a feminist framework to facilitate the deconstruction of masculinity and femininity and, in particular, examine the role of gender constructs during times of war.

Chapter 3 explores the landscape of Conflict in Northern Ireland and provides the context of key moments of political action; that is, women taking to the streets and challenging the authority of the state. The chapter contextualises and examines the turning points in penal policy and prison resistance. It then discusses the gendered nature of warfare and how women's bodies became a tool in the weaponry of the British state.

Chapter 4 examines the rise of women's involvement in relation to direct action. This chapter focuses on how and why women became involved in the Irish Republican Army (IRA). The chapter demonstrates how women organised themselves to counteract military power on their street, in their homes and in their communities, by organising bin lid patrols as an effective warning system that alerted members of the IRA of the presence of the British Army.

Chapter 5 explores the historical development of women's involvement in the IRA by focusing on the rise and fall of the women's Republican organisation Cumann na mBan. It charts the growing involvement of women and the challenges women faced in demanding to be treated as equals in the IRA. It is argued that, throughout the twentieth century, women have played crucial roles operationally, behind the scenes and on the front line. The second part of this chapter focuses on the motivations for, and experiences of, becoming an active Volunteer, and how gender and the constructions of femininity either facilitated or presented obstacles to women's involvement within the IRA.

Chapter 6 focuses primarily on women's experiences of Armagh prison, charting the initial reactions of the women to Armagh prison: the reception process; their reactions to their cells, and how political prisoners were organised within the confines of the prison walls.

Chapter 7 contextualises and illustrates techniques of resistance utilised by the women political prisoners by drawing on a key moment for the women in prison—*The Great Escape*. By using this act of resistance as a case study, the chapter illustrates agency and resistance, the modalities of prison power and the power to punish. In their attempt to destabilise the authority of the prison the women, demonstrated the continued struggle that occurred behind the prison walls.

Chapter 8 examines the events of 7 February 1980 in Armagh Prison (also known as Black February). The chapter explores the subjective experiences of the women on the no wash protest and how the act of defilement created new spaces and new ways of controlling the prison gaze. This chapter also details how the women placed their femininity in dissent by challenging expectations around cleanliness of the female body and how the gendered body was used by the prison authorities to increase feelings of vulnerability that were fuelled by the prospect of further violence towards the women.

Chapter 9 examines the policy and practice of strip searching of the women of Armagh and the events leading to the mass strip search at HMP Maghaberry. The chapter examines how the women responded and experienced this particular type of gendered punishment. It demonstrates that the role of strip searching was primarily to control, punish, humiliate and discipline the bodies of politically motivated prisoners and thus calls into question the government's claim that strip searching was necessary for the purpose of security.

Chapter 10 explores the nature of the negotiated peace process and details the transition from war to a post-conflict society. The chapter provides an account of the need to move from a situation of conflict to a situation of peace—albeit a fragile one. It discusses the far-reaching consequences of the failure to offer full amnesty to prisoners under the Good Friday Agreement. An air of silence still surrounds the accounts of those who were directly involved in political protest, who experienced imprisonment and who are still living with the trauma and pain of the Conflict—for many, their voices remain unheard.

Chapter 11 explores the complexities of disarmament, demobilisation and reintegration (DDR) in Northern Ireland. This chapter examines not only the salient role ex-combatants played in the process of DDR, but also the difficulties facing ex-combatants as they move into a demilitarised phase of the struggle while reconciling the legacy of the past with a society transitioning from conflict to peace. It explores how female ex-combatants are making peace with the past in Northern Ireland and reflects on their central contribution to the peace process.

References

An Glór Gafa/The Captive Voice. (1990). Vol. 2, No. 2, Summer, Belfast.

Brewer, J. D., Mitchell, D., & Leavey, G. (2013). *Ex-Combatants, Religion and Peace in Northern Ireland: The Role of Religion in Transitional Justice.* Palgrave Macmillan.

Grounds A.T. & Jamieson R. (2003) No Sense of an Ending: Researching the experience of imprisonment and release among Republican ex-prisoners. *Theoretical Criminology* 7: 347–362.

Jamieson, R., & Grounds, A. (2002). *No sense of an ending: The effects of long term imprisonment amongst republican prisoners and their families.* Monaghan: Ex-Prisoners Assistance Committee.

McMullin, J. (2013). *Ex-combatants and the post-conflict state: Challenges of reintegration.* Basingstoke: Palgrave Macmillan.

Punch, M. (2012). *State violence, collusion and the troubles.* London: Pluto.

Shirlow, P., Tonge, J., MccAuley, J., & McGlynn, C. (2010). *Abandoning historical conflict? former political prisoners and reconciliation in Northern Ireland.* Manchester: Manchester University Press.

2

Women, War and Peace

Numerically, women were smaller. I also don't think that people are quite comfortable with the thought of a woman with a gun. The stereotypical picture of Ireland is Mother Ireland and her sons will protect her. Well, didn't she have any daughters? Because they were there for her too. But I think it's just that romanticism of the image of a stereotypical freedom fighter—Che Guevara[1] rather than ... and it plays with people's minds. Don't get me wrong, women prisoners had a lot of support and sympathy from people when they were in jail. But when they were out, those same people may not have been so keen to support them because they felt there was something not quite right about a woman with a gun, much less a woman with a gun who had *used* it. It challenged this image of the Irish Colleen,[2] who was always supposed to be a victim but was never supposed to stand up for herself and say *no more*. (Emphasis in original)

---

[1] Che Guevara allied with Fidel Castro and was a key member in the revolutionary movement that disposed of the Bolivian Batista regime in 1959.

[2] Colleen: Gaelic for a girl or young woman.

© The Editor(s) (if applicable) and The Author(s) 2016
A. Wahidin, *Ex-Combatants, Gender and Peace in Northern Ireland*,
DOI 10.1057/978-1-137-36330-5_2

Introduction

The scholarly literature on women and war is limited and the narratives of female ex-combatants detailing experiences of state violence during the Conflict in Northern Ireland have until recently been conspicuously absent, although there are some exceptions (see Aretxaga 1997; Brady et al. 2011; Corcoran 2006a, 2006b; Darragh 2012). Women's experiences have been relegated to the shadows of more 'significant' historical events during the Conflict.

In understanding the causes, motivations and conditions of war, one also has to reflect on the nature of peace. The aim of this chapter is to provide a general context for the book by alerting the reader to the debates surrounding peace, war and gender.

Defining 'Peace'

A common understanding of peace is that it is the absence of war, violence or conflict. More legalistic definitions imply that peace is a condition that comes: 'from a civil or divine source that keeps the peace through contractual relations' (Anderson 2004, p. 102). Brock-Utne (1989), a Norwegian feminist scholar and peace activist, described peace as the presence of justice and respect for human rights. UNESCO[3] declared that: 'peace is more than an absence of war. It means justice and equity for all as the basis for living together in harmony and free from violence' (Matsuura 2002, p. 2). These ideas reflect expressions of peace from cultures that see peace in positive terms as including particular characteristics. For example, the Hebrew and Arabic words *shalom* and *salaam* are both derivatives of *shalev*, which means 'whole and undivided'. The Sanskrit terms *shanti* and *chaina* are words for peace that refer to inner peace and mental calmness. The Chinese characters for peace represent harmony in balance, and the Japanese characters represent harmony, simplicity and quietness (Anderson 2004).

---

[3] UNESCO: United Nations Educational, Scientific and Cultural Organisation.

All too often, peace can be understood narrowly to mean the ending of violence and fails to address wider issues of justice and the conditions which make peace sustainable. The wish for the killing to stop is natural enough. However, peace incorporates well-being, and more limited notions of peace can ignore the range of issues of social justice, such as social redistribution of wealth, the introduction or restoration of equality and fairness in the allocation of scarce resources, and the opening up of life opportunities that were once closed to some groups. There are emotional dynamics that need to be managed and negotiated, including the feelings of affected communities toward both 'peace' and 'justice'; from which follows the requirement to persuade people to value equally a non-violent state and the social redistribution of resources.[4]

The Gendering of War

Eisenstein wrote:

> The patriarchal nature of most social and political systems often provides barriers to women's involvement in the formal political process, a place in which women could effect significant change. It's the classic opposition, dualist and hierarchical. Man/woman automatically infers great/small, superior/inferior.

> In fact, every theory of culture, every theory of society ... everything spoken, organised as discourse, art, religion, the family, language ... it is all ordered around hierarchical oppositions that come back to the man/woman opposition, an opposition that can only be sustained by means of a difference posed by cultural discourse as *natural* ... The opposition is founded on the *couple*. A couple poised in opposition, tension, conflict ... To be aware of the couple ... is also to point to the fact that it's on the couple that we have to work if we are to deconstruct and transform culture (1981, p. 44; emphasis in original).

---

[4] These definition issues are addressed further in Brewer (2010) and Brewer et al. (2011).

Among the enduring stereotypes encountered in the analyses of the roles of women and men during times of conflict are that women are essentially 'peace-orientated' while men are 'war-oriented'. Cynthia Cockburn puts the relationship between men and women that now defines most social and political structures into a broad historical perspective: 'what is clear is that from around the beginning of the third millennium before the Christian era all societies have been patriarchal. That is to say, men have dominated women, in the family and by extension in all significant social institutions' (2004, p. 52). She also notes that, as Europe moved from a feudal system to capitalism, one of the shifts was from a 'literal rule of the father' to, more simply, 'the rule of men' (Cockburn 2007). Governments, education systems, businesses, the military, religious orders, all organised by men, effectively left women out of the decision-making/power structures. The next section will examine the construction of women as peace-makers and challenge the essentialist discourses that posit women's activity as purely peace-making.

The 'Women and Peace' Stereotype

In her book *In a Different Voice*, Carol Gilligan argues that women think differently, primarily as a result of socialisation:

> From the different dynamics of separation and attachment in their gender identity formation through the divergence of identity and intimacy that marks their experience in the adolescent years, male and female voices typically speak of the importance of different truths, the former of the role of separation as it defines and empowers the self, the latter of the ongoing process of attachment that creates and sustains the human community. (1982, p. 156)

Others have subsequently argued 'that women, more than men, are socialised in "relational thinking", to think more about human relationships and the social consequences of actions' (Brock-Utne 1989, p. 15). In relation to activities of war and peace, Reardon and Snauwaert (2015), Brock-Utne (1989) and others have argued that women are generally more peace-orientated in terms of 'nurturing international understanding', 'building consensus through cooperative efforts', 'open and regular communication', 'reducing military budgets' and desiring a more equitable distribution of resources (see Brock-Utne 1989, p. 1). It has been argued that 'attitude studies consistently show that women are more peaceful than men'. Tickner further argues that 'since women have not identified with state institutions, due to being "situated far from seats of power", women are less likely to support war as an instrument of state policy', and to focus more clearly on structural violence at the national and international levels (2001, pp. 50–51).

What the above indicates is the pervasive nature of traditional stereotypical evocations of femininity which are incompatible with the idea that women are as capable as men of being violent. An increasing body of scholarship has begun to challenge the dualistic construction of gender and the a priori association between violence and masculinity (Hatty 2000). These works argue that many studies reify, rather than challenge, the association between masculinity and violence. These configurations of gender and the a priori association of violence with masculinity therefore fail to acknowledge the wide variation in female and male behaviour. By framing males as violent and females as passive and natural peace-makers, the complexity of human behaviour is vastly simplified. Because post-modern theories posit a post-socially sexed body (that sexual difference is created, rather than emerges from some innate origin), these theorists are concerned to analyse how we understand gender and the mechanisms through which gender is performed (Butler 1990). They suggest that the 'essence' of meaning is no more than the very establishment and maintenance of binary opposites. Thus, we can only know what 'man' is through its *opposition* to 'woman'. The female is everything that is absent from the male and vice versa. Gender difference is sustained through a play of absence and presence. Post-modern theories of gender argue that gender identity is assembled, fragmentary and shifting, and that individuals 'practice' gender through a variety of mechanisms (Rose 1999).

In terms of gender, our modern condition of self-knowledge necessitates that women and men both comprehend and accept bifurcated characteristics (O'Neill and Hird 2001). Precisely because gender is neither immutable nor static, women and men are obliged constantly to reflect on gender practice. Gender, as with all other symbols involved with identity, must be interpreted and, even on a superficial level, this interpretation requires a social actor. As Brittan expresses it, 'men are not simply the passive embodiments of the masculine ideology' (1989, p. 68). Thus, a particular power–knowledge nexus produces the 'truth' about gender: gender and power are wholly co-implicated. Brittan's comment reflects the view that not only does gender have to be interpreted by a subject, but also that gendered behaviour is an outcome of an interplay of accommodations, enactments, contestations and partial refusals or re-workings of 'permissible' and expected behaviours by both women and men, in which intention and agency operates. This book clearly demonstrates that the women act within and against both the received notions of womanhood and the material/political constraints of their situation.

Cultural norms governing traditional gender roles have another impact on combatant women. In as much as they challenge the stereotype of women as carers, reconcilers and nurturers, those who uphold these norms criticise combatant women for their militancy because they are supposedly denying their essential femininity. This may result both in male combatants resisting the participation of women in fighting, and also in the wider cultural criticism levied against women combatants when they infringe social mores by engaging in armed militancy. By explaining women's peace-making as being due to their femininity, this reduces their public roles to an extension of their private ones. Not only is this disparaging, it is exclusionary. It assists in the political marginalisation of women by encouraging the retort that women would be better returning to their 'natural' domain (the home) and leaving the business of war to men. Evidence shows, however, that women can be as violent as men in communal conflicts. It was estimated that one third of the women who were involved with rebel and government forces in Sierra Leone were in active combat roles (Mazurana and Carlson 2004), and that just over 16% of the rebel Revolutionary United Front were women (McKay and Mazurana 2004, p. 92; on the reintegration problems faced by young girl ex-soldiers, see McKay 2004).

In Northern Ireland, women combatants were subject to particular vilification by the media, especially when assassinated (for example, Márie Drumm) or killed on active service (for example, Mairéad Farrell), or for participating in the no wash protest 'compared to their male combatants'. An extension of this sort of gendered criticism is found in the negative portrayals of women combatants in films and popular culture. Women combatants, therefore, struggle not only against the state or regime to which they object, but also against unreconstructed gender roles that undervalue their militancy and agency.

Haleh Afshar writes:

> Conflicts can both empower and disempower women, since women can be at the same time included in practice and yet excluded ideologically, or they may be both victims and agents of change—though they often have no effective choice in these matters. (Afshar 2004, p. 2)

Women may opt to fight or take action, or they may choose to do nothing. Regardless of which they choose, they will not be untouched or unscathed by conflict around them. This does not preclude women political activists from taking positions and roles that are more overtly political. For example, in Northern Ireland, women participated in statutory commissions, such as the Parades Commission and the District Policing Partnerships as well as the Human Rights Commission, all overtly political positions that allowed them to address broader political issues head on.

Situations of conflict can also cause women to move beyond those traditional roles and take on new ones. As Donna Pankhurst notes, in some cases the circumstances of war and conflict have resulted in 'moments of liberation from the old social order. As the need arose for them [women] to take on men's roles in their absence, so they had to shake off the restrictions of their culture and live in a new way' (2000, p. 20). In fact, what this means is that, whether they wanted to or not, women were often thrust from the private realm into the public, and many found it not only liberating but life-changing. It is the political and social empowerment that can take place during conflict that emboldens women to take political action not only during the conflict, but also subsequently. Considering these historically situated shifts, the binary divide between the private and the public spheres is not so clear-cut. Rather, the public and private spheres can be understood as a continuum, with women crossing these spheres.

As the female ex-combatants in this study show, the nature of the Conflict propelled them to play a more visible role. Utilising a gendered analysis, feminist International Relations scholarship provides a challenge to traditional International Relations to examine the ways that 'gender differences permeate all facets of public and private life' (Tickner 1997, p. 621). As Giles and Hyndman state, 'feminists have long argued that private/public distinctions serve to de-politicise the private domestic spaces of "home" compared to more public domains' (2004, p. 4). Such scholars have shown that, despite the fact that women are often marginalised politically (because women are primarily located in the 'private' sphere), the symbolism of woman becomes essential to the survival of the state and the nation. Women are constructed as being in need of being *defended* and *protected*, and it is men who are viewed as the protectors, thereby prompting men to support the call to war. In such a context, the control of the 'private' sphere and the identities formed within it become all the more intense, as masculine and feminine identities are 'co-opted' whether by the state (as seen clearly in the First World War propaganda exhorting women not only to 'keep the home-fires burning', but also to vilify male non-combatants through overt attacks on their 'masculinity'), or by communities defined by resistance, thus perpetuating the pattern. Even when women enter the public sphere, the mechanisms of patriarchy are in operation and women's participation in numerical terms is smaller.

Women have long struggled with issues of citizenship and identity, and the challenge to be recognised as equal members of society. The same society that values and reveres women as symbols used to create national identity ('mother country') as well as for their responsibility for producing the next generation also diminishes or minimises the role that women play as productive contributors to society. This duality that surrounds the perception of women is often exaggerated in times of war and conflict where the symbolism or myths of womanhood are essential to the very survival of the country. Yet, the political reality is such that the decisions regarding war and conflict are generally made by men within the political system from which women are excluded.

Women ex-combatants, as we will see from this study, are not just symbols of group identity; they also support, and often actively participate in, political activism. Whether in the form of direct involvement and leadership of the armed campaign or of military activities, or engaged in a supportive role to feed and clothe combatants, women have been involved in all aspects of the political struggle and Conflict in Northern Ireland. Although women's involvement in the Conflict is bound by patriarchal discourses, the Conflict in Northern Ireland created a space for new opportunities for women to learn new skills and to take on new responsibilities normally reserved for men. What will be highlighted throughout this book is the convergence of the traditionally public and private realms. This, in turn, raises a series of questions regarding the political options that are available to women who are affected by conflict but who are also removed from the political decision-making process that led to the conflict in the first place. Depending on the circumstances, women in the study have referred to the four main options available to them to respond to their situation of conflict: (1) to do nothing, (2) to become politically active to help resolve the conflict, (3) to participate actively in the conflict as belligerents engaged in violence, or (4) to flee the fighting. Regardless of which option is ultimately selected, women are forced to deal with the situation in some way that requires a conscious choice. And, in responding, women demonstrate agency.

It is clear that women were affected by the Conflict at every stage, from the actual outbreak of violence to participating in the process of resolving the Conflict. Often, the roles that women played or were placed into prior to or during the Conflict had a direct effect on the options available to them during and after the Conflict.

This book demonstrates, as Jacoby (2008, p. 29) attests, that in the case of Northern Ireland 'women mobilised alongside their men, to liberate their society from colonial or post-colonial oppression, campaigning for national self-determination'. But the nature of this Conflict also meant that women's territory was no longer off limits and that women were thrust into the centre of the Conflict, whether they wanted to be or not. Furthermore, as the Conflict escalated, women's involvement increased but what noticeably did *not* change was that women were still under-represented in the decision-making process. It is important to note that this does not mean that 'women's issues' were omitted from consideration by the dominant political parties connected with the paramilitary organisations. For example, the Sinn Féin Manifesto on Women, believed to date from 1989, begins by stating: 'women face significant difficulties in their daily lives as a result of years of discrimination and injustice against them. This repression is deep-rooted, not merely, nor even primarily, legislative. We must all work to explore the manner in which legislation is used to oppress women, and highlight the way in which our own attitudes add to this oppression'. Despite this acknowledgement that discrimination exists against women, women are still under-represented in the political decision-making hierarchy of Sinn Féin (Hackett 1985; Ward 2000).

In looking at women's political activism prior to the outbreak of the Conflict, during the Conflict and through the transitional stage from war to peace, it is important to remember that the process is a dynamic one. In this study, women have often become politicised to participate in activities as Volunteers and, as a direct result, many are now participating politically to avert further conflict in this propitious move towards peace.

Conclusion

The conclusion to emerge here is that femininity as such is not inherently peaceful. Women can be equally war-prone and can act as the preventers of peace as much as men—and, most likely, men can be equally as peace-loving as women. The lack of recognition of women's involvement as combatants indicates how the Conflict in Northern Ireland has assumed a masculine character in which women Volunteers have been perceived as 'outwith' femininity (see Carlen 1983). This demonstrates how women's agency is still based on gender-specific assumptions about women's role in society. This way of thinking ensures that women's behaviour is evaluated specifically in relation to their sex and not in terms of their capabilities. Furthermore, it gives rise to a gendered specificity in the forms of violence and punishment endured by women and men, and produces the female body itself as a central site of punishment and of struggle and resistance.

The recognition of women's involvement over the last 40 years in the IRA is slowly coming to the fore and is producing a body of experience and a range of innovative responses which inform approaches to the Disarmament, Demobilisation and Reintegration programmes

(Brewer et al. 2001). In relation to periods of conflict, the Fourth World Conference on Women, held in Beijing in 1995, brought to the attention of world leaders the specific impact of war on women's lives.[5] Five years later, the United Nations Security Council Resolution (UNSCR) was adopted (Bushra-El 2007). Resolution 1325 has become a powerful tool for those advocating for gender equality (gender balancing) and sensitivity to gender issues during and after times of war. What this book illustrates is that the essential discourses of femininity serves only to silence and make invisible the important role women played not as passive victims but, rather, as combatants and activists during Republican and after the Conflict.

Chapter 3 contextualises the history of the Conflict in Northern Ireland and how legislation and penal policy was adapted in response to the increase in violence.

References

Afshar, H. (2004). War and peace: What do women contribute? In H. Afshar & D. Eade (Eds.), *Development, women and war: Feminists perspectives*. Oxford: Oxfarm.

Anderson, R. (2004). A definition of peace. *Peace and Conflict: Journal of Peace Psychology, 10*.

Aretxaga, B. (1997). *Shattering the silence: Women, nationalism and political subjectivity in Northern Ireland*. Princeton, NJ: Princeton University Press.

Brady, E., Patterson, E., McKinney, K., Hamill, R., & Jackson, P. (2011). *The footsteps of Anne: Stories of republican women ex-prisoners*. Belfast. Shanway Press

Brewer, D. J. (2010). *Peace processes: A sociological approach*. Cambridge, UK: Polity.

Brewer, D. J., Bishop, K., & Higgins, G. (2001). *Peacemaking among protestants and Catholics*. Belfast: Centre for the Social Study of Religion, Queen's University of Belfast.

Brewer, D. J., Higgins, G. I., & Teeney, F. (2011). *Religion, civil society and peace in Northern Ireland*. Oxford: Oxford University Press.

---

[5] Until 1995 the global conference on women had focused on economic developmental issues.

Brittan, A. (1989). *Masculinity and power*. New York: Blackwell.

Brock-Utne, B. (1989). *Feminist perspectives on peace and peace education*. London: Pergamon Press.

Bushra-El, J. (2007). Feminism, gender, and women's peace activism. *Development and Change, 38*(1), 131–147.

Butler, J. (1990). *Gender trouble: Feminism and the subversion of identity*. New York: Routledge.

Carlen, P. (1983). *Women's imprisonment: A study in social control*. Routledge and Kegan and Paul.

Cockburn, C. (2004). The continuum of violence: A gender perspective on war and peace. In W. Giles & J. Hyndman (Eds.), *Sites of violence: Gender and conflict zones*. Los Angeles: University of California.

Cockburn, C. (2007). *From where we stand: War, women's activism and feminist analysis*. London: Zed Books.

Corcoran, M. (2006a). *Out of order: The political imprisonment of women in Northern Ireland, 1972–1998*. Cullompton: Willan.

Corcoran, M. (2006b). Talking about resistance: Women political prisoners and the dynamics of prison conflict, Northern Ireland. In A. Barton, K. Corteen, D. Scott, & D. Whyte (Eds.), *Expanding the criminological imagination: Critical readings in criminology*. Willan: Devon.

Darragh, S. (2012). *'John's Lennon Dead': Stories of protest, hunger strikes and resistance*. Belfast: Beyond the Pale.

Eisenstein, Z. R. (1981). *The radical future of liberal feminism*. New York: Longman.

Giles, W., & Hyndman, J. (2004). Introduction: Gender and conflict in a global context. In W. Giles & J. Hyndman (Eds.), *Sites of violence: Gender and conflict zones*. Berkeley and Los Angeles: University of California Press.

Gilligan, C. (1982). *'In a Different Voice': Psychological theory and women's development*. Cambridge, Massachusetts, USA: Harvard University Press.

Hackett, C. (1985). *Sinn Féin and Feminism 1979–1984*. MSC thesis, Queen's University, Belfast.

Hatty, S. (2000). *Masculinities, violence and culture*. London: Sage.

Jacoby, T. A. (2008). *Understanding conflict and violence: Theoretical and interdisciplinary approaches*. London: Routledge.

Matsuura, J. (2002). *Security, rights and liabilities in e-commerce*. Norwood, MA: Artech House.

Mazurana, D., & Carlson, K. (2004). *From combat to community: Women and girls of Sierra Leone*. Washington, DC. Women Waging Peace.

McKay, S (2004), Women, Human Security and Peace –building: A Feminist Analysis. IPSHU English Research Report. Series No. 19: Conflict and Human Security: A search for new approaches of peace-building. Chapter 7, pp 152–175.

McKay, S., & Mazurana, D. (2004). *Where are the girls? Girls fighting forces Northern Uganda, Sierra Leone and Mozambique: Their lives after the war.* Montreal: Canada International Centre for Human Rights and Democratic Development. 92.

O'Neill, T., & Hird, M. (2001). Double damnation: Gay disabled men and the negotiation of masculinity. In K. Backett-Milburn & L. McKie (Eds.), *Constructing gendered bodies.* Palgrave Macmillan: Basingstoke.

Pankhurst, D. (2000). *Women, gender and peace-building* (Working Paper No. 5). Bradford: Centre for Conflict Resolution, Bradford University Press.

Reardon, B., & Snauwaert, D. (2015). *Key texts in gender and peace.* New York: Springer.

Rose, N. (1999). *Governing the soul: Shaping the private self.* London: Free Association Press.

Tickner, A. J. (1997). You just don't understand: Troubled engagement between feminist international relation theorists. *International Studies Quarterly, 41*(4), 611–632.

Tickner, A. J. (2001). *Gendering world politics: Issues and approaches in the post-cold war era.* New York: Columbia University Press.

Ward, M. (2000). The Northern Ireland Assembly and Women: assessing the gender deficit, Democratic Dialogue December. Belfast: Northern Ireland http://cain.ulst.ac.uk/dd/papers/women-assembly.htm

3

An Cogadh Fada: The Legacy of Conflict in Northern Ireland

Background to the Conflict

The causes or sources of conflict between individuals and groups cannot be separated from the totality of relationships, and the environmental conditions that promote relationships. (Burton 1990, p. 47)

In national conflicts, law, order and justice are not issues that happen to arise from other causes. National conflicts, once they are fully developed, revolve around these issues. (Wright, cited in McGarry and O'Leary 1993, p. 3)

Definition: Politically Motivated Prisoners[1]

From 1972, 'terrorism' was defined in successive pieces of Emergency Legislation (relating to both Northern Ireland and Britain), and the

---

An Cogadh Fada is Irish for a long war.

[1] The women are viewed as agents making their own choices, through acting within multiple hierarchical structures and specific contexts. The ex-combatants investigated were non-conscripted. They were non-state ex-members who had engaged in combat or were trained and prepared to do so. 'Combat' is conceptualised broadly to include terrorist tactics such as bomb-making and assassinations, as well as more conventional forms of battle.

© The Editor(s) (if applicable) and The Author(s) 2016

A. Wahidin, *Ex-Combatants, Gender and Peace in Northern Ireland,*
DOI 10.1057/978-1-137-36330-5_3

official definition of terrorism is given in section 31 of the Emergency Provisions (NI) Act. The term 'terrorist'[2] was defined as 'a person who is or has been concerned in the commission or attempted commission of any act of terrorism or in directing, organising or training persons for the purpose of terrorism'.[3] Political prisoners[4] are those convicted of offences listed in Schedule 4 of the Northern Ireland (Emergency Provisions) Act 1978 and, subsequently, 'imprisoned for their role in acts related to the Conflict' (Shirlow et al. 2005, p. 22).

From 1973, in Northern Ireland the distinction between scheduled and non-scheduled offences was that cases went before the non-jury Diplock Courts[5] with amended rules of evidence to deal with persons charged with a suspected terrorist offence (Jackson and Doran 1995).[6] It must be noted that those convicted of scheduled offences may not have had paramilitary connections (Boyle et al. 1980 [1975], p. 81). Indeed, Walsh (1983, pp. 80–82) has argued that the vast majority of armed robberies (which were treated as scheduled offences) were not

---

[2] The use of the phrase 'political violence' as defined in Section 31 of the Emergency Provision Acts (Northern Ireland) 1978 and 1987 is as follows: 'Terrorism means the use of violence for political ends and includes any use of violence for the purpose of putting the public or any section of the public in fear'. The use of the word 'terrorist' in quotation marks reflects the processes of criminalisation and the de-legitimation of which I write. (For a more detailed discussion of the difficulties of terminology, see Gearty (1991).

[3] The original definition was taken from the legislation which introduced Internment, the Detention of Terrorists (NI) Order 1972, Article 3, and from versions of the Emergency Provision Acts and the Prevention of Terrorism Act. The current definition of terrorism defined in the Terrorism Act 2000, includes a wider range of activities and where: 'the use of threat is designed to influence the government or to intimidate the public or a section of the public, and the use or threat is made for the purpose of advancing a political, religious or ideological cause', Terrorism Act 2000, S 1 (1) and (2).

[4] In this book 'political prisoners' will be defined as those convicted of offences listed in Schedule 4 of the Northern Ireland (Emergency Provisions) Act 1978, so-called 'scheduled offences'. The distinction between scheduled and non-scheduled offences was first introduced in 1973, when the non-jury Diplock Courts were established to deal with politically motivated offenders (Jamieson and McEvoy 2005). Drawing on the article by Boyle et al. (1980 [1975], p. 81), the writers note that some of those convicted of scheduled offences had no paramilitary connections. Indeed, Walsh (1983, pp. 80–82), has argued that the vast majority of armed robberies (which are automatically treated as scheduled offences) are not political in nature (see Rolston and Tomlinson 1986).

[5] Diplock Courts were established in 1973 to deal with scheduled (conflict-related) offences.

[6] Scheduled offences are those normally associated with the commission of terrorist acts (for example, murder, manslaughter, explosions, and so on) and are listed as an appendix to the Emergency Legislation.

political in nature. Similarly, a few people convicted of non-scheduled offences were politically motivated; for example, those sent to prison for non-payment of fines arising from protests against the Hillsborough Agreement.[7] The legal definition discussed above serves to erase the 'political'/'politically motivated' element of the offenders' actions. The term 'terrorist' holds pejorative connotations (Goodwin 2006) and lacks a definitive meaning and conceptual clarity (Gearty and Tomkins 1996; Schafer 1974). Many scholars who have worked in this field have adopted a more neutral term of politically motivated prisoner (e.g. Gormally and McEvoy 1995; McEvoy 2001) and it is for this reason that 'politically motivated prisoner' rather than 'terrorist' will be used in this book.

Context of the Conflict

In 1964, *The Campaign for Social Justice* was formed to address the discriminatory practices against Catholics in the form of employment, housing allocation, electoral boundaries and the over-use of 'stop and search' on the Catholic population. For example, the 1991 census showed that the unemployment rate for men was 2.2 times higher for Catholics than Protestants; and for women it was 1.8 (see Cormack and Osborne 1991). A number of protest marches began to take place seeking to reform the existing state, not to overthrow it. The Royal Ulster Constabulary (RUC) and 'B' Special Reservists reacted to the demonstrations in a hostile way and, in response to heightening tensions, the British government agreed to the deployment of troops in 1969[8] (see Farrell 1980). Between 1969 and 1999, 3,636 people died in the Conflict, 2,037 of whom were civilians (McKittrick et al. 1999,

---

[7] The Hillsborough Agreement (Agreement at Hillsborough Castle, 5 February 2010) established priorities for a devolved criminal justice system. The agreement promised to provide a 'comprehensive strategy for the management of offenders'; 'consideration of a woman's prison, which is fit for purpose' and meets international standards for best practice; and a 'review of how children and young people are processed at all stages of the criminal justice system'. Available at: http://www.nio.gov.uk/agreement_at_hillsborough_castle_5_February_2010.pdf (accessed 26 November 2014).

[8] Violence and Civil disturbances in Northern Ireland in 1969, Report of a Tribunal of Inquiry (1972; Cmnd 566; Chair, Mr Justice Scarman) Para. 20.1 (The Scarman Report).

p. 1477; Ruane and Todd 1996, p. 1), 247 women have been killed since 1969 by bomb explosions and gun attacks,[9] and 36,807 people were seriously injured.[10] Twenty-nine prison staff members were killed and scores more were injured (CAJ 2010) Approximately, one in ten of those killed during the Conflict were direct victims of state violence' (White 2015, p. 9). During that period, Northern Ireland's population was approximately 1.5 million. Hayes and McAllister (2001, p. 901), record that one in seven of the population has had a direct experience of violence, one in five has had a family member killed or injured and one in four has been caught up in an explosion. A 2003 household survey on poverty and social exclusion found that half of those interviewed knew someone who had been killed. An estimated 88,000 households were affected by the loss of a close relative and 50,000 households contained at least one resident who was injured. Approximately 28,000 people were forced to leave work and 54,000 households were compelled to relocate through intimidation, threats or harassment (Hillyard et al. 2005, p. 6). Approximately 80,000 men, women and young people were imprisoned (ibid., p. 8). If we take Hayes and McAllister (2001, p. 901) recorded figures they report that one in seven of the population has had a direct experience of violence, one in five has had a family member killed or injured and one in four has been caught up in an explosion. To contexualise these figures, if one were to take the population size of the USA it would mean more than the number of those Americans who died in the Second World War and nine times more than the Americans who died in Vietnam (Hayes and McAllister 2001, p. 902). Although, the true extent of the damage of the Conflict is contested, some have argued that the scale of the Conflict in Northern Ireland has been relatively low when compared with the 700 Palestinians killed during the two-year Intifada or the 65,000 killed in one decade in El Salvador (Ditch and Morrissey 1992). However, there are two significant features which have made the

---

[9] Royal Ulster Constabulary Statistics Unit (Belfast, Northern Ireland Office, October 1994).

[10] Royal Ulster Constabulary Statistics Unit (Belfast: Northern Ireland Office, October 1994). The injuries figure dates from 1968, while the first death attributed to the political situation occurred in 1969.

situation distinctive; first, is the length of time over which the Conflict has been sustained and, second, is the relatively small size of the country (Amnesty International 1994). Until the recent ceasefires (see key moments leading up to the ceasefires: 31 August 1994, 20 July 1997, May 2000) the 'Troubles'[11] have continued unabated since 1969, when armed troops were called to respond to the escalating violence (Adams 1986; Bowyer Bell 1991; McKearney 2011). When this is added to the population count, which totals 1.5 million, it means that there are few areas in Northern Ireland which have been left unscathed.

Most notably, the Civil Rights March of 1968 in Derry organised by the People's Democracy was attacked by Loyalists and the RUC. It has been documented widely that: 'At the bridge at Burntollet the marchers were attacked by over 200 Loyalists armed with sticks, bricks and iron bars' (Brady et al. 2011, p. 30; Devlin 1971), and 12 months later saw tensions between Catholics, Protestants, the police and the British Army erupt into what became known as the battle of Bogside. Widespread rioting occurred. This led to an aggressive response by the Army and the police/RUC. Catholic communities in Belfast felt targeted and victimised by the British Army and the police (Bernard 1989; Challis 1999). The effects had devastating consequences where 'three-fifths of the houses on Bombay Street were destroyed by fire. Of 63 houses on Bombay Street, '38 needed to be demolished, 5 required major repairs and 10 required minor repairs' (Gillespie 2008, p. 21). By contrast, few houses were damaged in Protestant areas. Over 3,500 people were driven from their homes, with over 3,000 coming from the Nationalist and Republican community (Lee 1989, p. 421). Pogroms had taken place in previous generations under the Unionist regime.[12] In August 1969, however, in a departure from previous policy, the British government made a direct intervention with the deployment of 10,000 British Army troops (Dewar 1996; Farrell 1976). The Catholic community's first reaction to the British troops was to welcome them. This changed within a few months, once it became clear that the British Army was there to support the status quo. In July 1970, the British

---

[11] See Chapter 1: Footnote 2
[12] See Chap. 2.

Army (using helicopter-borne loudspeakers), imposed a week-long curfew on Belfast's Lower Falls[13] area, barring movement within and from this area, but the boundaries were initially unclear.[14] People were required to clear the streets, house raids were intensified, there was a prohibition of movement at certain times and there were widespread arrests (Ó Fearghail 1970). The quotes below taken from the participants clearly convey the violent nature of the dawn raids.

House Raids

It's usually the dawn raids before six. What they [the British Army] did was batter down the door and all sweep in. Everybody was put in one room and then they just tore the house apart searching. This happened on a regular basis.[15]

Another woman recalls her experience of the raids:

It's hard to describe it to anyone who's never been through it. The entire community was swamped by the British Army. They [the British Army] were raiding our house and my brother was interned in Long Kesh.[16] The only people in our house were three young women, aged 12, 15 and 17, so that was me and my two elder sisters and my mother and father. So they were raiding our house. They were raiding our house on the pretext that we had arms and ammunition, but when they were raiding our house they were probably raiding another house up the street and raiding two houses in the next street and two houses in the next street. They didn't do it in isolation.

---

[13] The Lower Falls Road area is the main road through West Belfast in Northern Ireland.

[14] The journalist Tony Geraghty escaped conviction on the basis that he could show he was arrested outside the strict curfew area. See 'Newsman in Curfew Case Cleared', *Irish News*, 28 July 1970.

[15] Any names, if used throughout, are fictitious and the lack of names is used not to depersonalise the characters involved but, rather, to protect the identity of individuals in the study and to ensure anonymity, unless the women and men stated otherwise.

[16] 'Long Kesh' is also known as the 'Kesh', 'the Lazy K', '*Ceis fada*' (the literal Gaelic translation meaning 'long bog'). Hereafter, in this book, the Maze will be referred to as Long Kesh/the Maze.

It was part of organised terror by the British state. It was part of the British systematic intent to put down the Nationalist people. To put fear into the Nationalist people, and when they came to raid they literally wrecked everything and they [the British Army], left us with nothing. We had nothing. The [British Army] came in and they destroyed everything, and then they wondered why kids were out on the streets, stoning them and some of them obviously wanted a gun in their hand to shoot them.

The Falls Curfew: The Bread and Milk March

According to the *Irish News* (4 July 1970), at 10:20 pm on 3 July 'a helicopter with a loud speaker circled low over the rooftops and announced that a curfew was being imposed on the area and anyone caught out of doors would be arrested. Saracen armoured vehicles lined along the Falls Road'.

An armed force of 1,500 surrounded the 'area of a population of 10,000 citizens' (Aretxaga 1997, p. 56). During what became known as the 'Falls Curfew', the British Army killed four people who were widely believed to be innocent civilians (McKittrick et al. 1999), fired 1,500 live rounds, made 337 arrests and fired CS tear gas.[17]

'Young men were beaten, forced to lie flat on their faces on the street or to kneel with their hands at the back of their heads while being interrogated' (*Sunday Times* Insight Team [STIT] 1972).

Rather than quelling disorder, it fuelled further animosity against the British state. English (2003, p. 136) argues that the Falls curfew, 'was also instrumental in heightening tensions further, and was arguably decisive in terms of worsening relations between the British Army and the Catholic working class', especially after the introduction of internment without

---

[17] For military-based accounts, see Hamill (1985), pp. 36–39, and Barzilay (1977), pp. 11–16. See also Ó Fearghail (1970). CS gas stands for chlorobenzylidene malononitrile-anti personnel riot gas.

trial (1971)[18] and the Bloody Sunday killings in 1972.[19] The curfew was suspended temporarily to permit shopping for food for two hours on Saturday afternoon (within the perimeters of the curfew), and on Sunday morning to allow for Sunday Mass. By Sunday afternoon, women from outside of the curfew area marched into the barricade with bread and milk and broke the curfew (Ashe 2006, 2008). This was the first visible direct action taken and organised *by* and *for* women. On the evening of 3 July, the women returned with more rations and, by this stage, 3,000 women had gathered to help them in their efforts. This march broke the Falls Road Curfew. This example of resistance shows also how working-class women identified with each other. The mutual concern for each other's families created a strong feeling of solidarity; the additional incentive of defying the British Army may have been nothing more than that (Edgerton 1986; *Irish News* 1970).

The wire barricades in working-class districts of West Belfast transformed these estates into 'no-go areas', cutting them off from the outside world. The soldiers at the barricades were taken by surprise by the chanting and singing of women. The women marched down the Falls Road waving shopping bags, carrying bottles of milk and loaves of bread. An Army spokesman said later that they had 'looked the other way' during the march. Many of the women carried placards with the words 'British Army worse than the Black and Tans, women beaters and child beaters' (O'Keefe 2013, p. 26)

This has become known as 'the Bread and Milk March' (Taylor 2001; Pickering 2002). The gendered significance of this protest was that 'women not men organised themselves into a march; women were accompanied by their children, and women carried the food' (Aretxaga 1997, p. 59). What the above shows is not only how political identities were constituted through struggle, but also how both subjectivities and

---

[18] See page 11.

[19] 'Bloody Sunday' refers to the events that took place in Derry on the afternoon of Sunday 30 January 1972. A Northern Ireland Civil Rights Association (NICRA) march had been organised to protest against the continuation of internment without trial in Northern Ireland. Between 10,000 and 20,000 men, women and children took part in the march in a 'carnival atmosphere'. Soldiers of the Parachute Regiment, an elite regiment of the British Army, moved into the Bogside in an arrest operation. During the next 30 minutes, these soldiers shot dead 13 men (and shot and injured a further 13 people), mainly by single shots to the head and trunk (Purdie 1990).

struggles were constituted spatially. This form of resistance challenged the occupation and domination of space by the British Army.

The Army's response to the Bread and Milk March, the events that led to Bloody Sunday, is an example of the extended use of emergency powers that not only intensified social disorder, but also mobilised new recruits for Republican paramilitaries in the early 1970s (Coogan 2000; Farrell 1980, p. 283).[20] Adams recounts, 'the Falls Road curfew in July 1970 made popular opposition to the British Army absolute in Belfast … After that recruitment to the IRA was massive' (1986, p. 55).

Moreover, this imposition of a curfew had no statutory authority (see Campell and Connolly 2003). The Ministry of Defence (MOD) issued a statement denying that a formal curfew was imposed. It was stated that:

> No formal curfew was imposed … Restrictions on movement were imposed in the interests of the safety of the population as a whole to restrict the operations of armed criminals.[21]

In light of the MOD's statement, the curfew had not been imposed under Special Powers Regulation 19, therefore it can be argued that the curfew was, indeed, unlawful.

Internment

The outbreak of the Conflict in Northern Ireland in the late 1960s quickly led to consequences in relation to imprisonment. On 9 August 1971, internment without trial was introduced, dominating the landscape for the next four years (Amnesty International 1971/1972; Brady et al. 1975; Compton Report 1971; Faul and Murray 1974a, 1974b; Kennally and Preston 1971; McGuffin 1973, 1974; Spjut 1986). During this period, a total of 1,981 people were interned: 1,874 Nationalists and

---

[20] It was not until February 1973, that the first Loyalists were arrested. Even by mid-1974, there were only an estimated 60 Loyalists interned, compared with 600 Republicans (Coogan 1995, pp. 155–156). The end of internment or 'detention without trial' was announced by Westminster in December 1975.

[21] 803 H.C. Debs, col. 329 (6 July 1970).

107 Loyalists (Bowcott 2010). In a written answer to Parliament in May 1977, the Secretary of State for Northern Ireland reported that a total of 2,257 people had been interned between the introduction of internment on 9 August 1971 and its ending on 31 December 1975. Hogan and Walker (1989, p. 94) put the total at 2,169 (Table 1).

The female internees were held at the only women's prison in the North of Ireland: Armagh Prison. Women were not interned until late December 1972/early January 1973 (Bernard 1989, p. 87). It was in 1973 when Liz McKee, a 19-year-old woman from Belfast, became the first woman to be interned under the Special Powers Act, followed by a young woman who was barely 18 at the time (Aretxaga 1997; Brady et al. 2011). In the period of internment from 1971 to 1975, a total of 33 women were interned in Armagh Prison from 1973 to 1975 (Brady et al. 2011, p. 32). Many of the women were teenagers, some were mothers with young children and a grandmother, Madge McConville, was arrested (Northern Ireland Civil Rights Association 1973). For the most part, the men were brought to a disused military airfield called Long Kesh[22] in which they were held in Nissan huts.[23]

The number of sentenced prisoners committed each year rose by 50 % during the 1960s, except in the case of a small number of female committals, which declined substantially (Rolston and Tomlinson 1986). In the 1970s, however, committals of sentenced prisoners, including

Table 1 Number of prisoners interned, 1971–1975 (see Hogan and Walker 1989, p. 94)

Number of internees	
Suspected Republicans	2,060
Suspected Loyalists	109
Total	**2,169**

Source: HC Deb 16 May 1977, Vol. 932 c37w

---

[22] Footnote 23.

[23] The site of Long Kesh/Maze prison comprises over 300 standing buildings on a 360 acre site (including both prison and army base) outside the city of Lisburn, approximately 10 miles from Belfast. As an historic site it has a short history. Unused since vacated by the RAF shortly after World War II, the site was renamed the Long Kesh Detention Centre and the preexisting Nissan huts were utilised to cope with the overflow of prisoners from Crumlin Road Jail, Belfast.

young offenders, levelled off somewhat at between 2,000 and 2,200 per year, with 1977 proving a peak year and, by the end of the decade, the numbers were declining. By 1980, 58 women, 1,132 men and 613 young offenders received custodial sentences, the lowest figures for more than a decade. Since 1969, the female prison population in the "Ordinary Decent Criminals" (ODC)[24] category remained a constant 9–10 at any one time. The vast majority of women prisoners had been charged with 'terrorist type' offences, although they considered themselves to be political prisoners and did not recognise the court. A woman recounts her experiences of the Diplock Court:

> In May 1977, I went for trial. Didn't recognise the court. Refused to recognise the court. Didn't have any representation and therefore was sentenced to 12 years.

Another states:

> You did not recognise the court because it was a British Institution, and that was like pleading guilty. The judge had carte blanche there.

The prison system in Northern Ireland was placed under severe strain with the introduction of internment in 1971. The total number of prisoners in custody increased from a daily average of about 600 in 1969 to 3,000 by 1979 and, given the seriousness of paramilitary-related offences, long-term prisoners comprised up to two thirds of the prison population (McEvoy 2001, p. 16; see Gormally et al. 1993). The size of the lifer population grew from 13 in 1969, to 181 in 1976 and 377 in 1980, to 421 in 1983 (Rolston and Tomlinson 1986, p. 165). After 1980, trends changed dramatically. Between 1980 and 1986, custodial receptions jumped from 1,800 to over 3,700. By 1988, the rate of imprisonment in Northern Ireland was higher than any member state of the Council of Europe at 125 per 100,000 of the population. In 1986, the average length of a long-term sentence was over 10 years (Pickering 2002). Thus, within the space of six years, the numbers receiving custodial sentences

---

[24] Ordinary Decent Criminals are prisoners convicted of non-scheduled offences.

more than doubled. Receptions of untried prisoners from 1981, however, remained fairly stable at around the 2,000 mark.

The prison estate in Northern Ireland consisted of five establishments, each with a historically distinct and unique role in containing political prisoners, including *HMS Maidstone* (the prison ship). Imprisonment was widely used as a way of combating political violence during the four decades of the Conflict. Although no exact figures are available, it is estimated that 15,000 Republicans and between 5,000 and 10,000 Loyalists were imprisoned during the Conflict (Shirlow and McEvoy 2008). Jamieson and Grounds (2002, 2008) estimate that between 13,400 and 38,192 individuals served time in prison as a result of politically motivated activities during the Conflict.[25]

The Impact of the Conflict on the Prisons

'Prisons symbolise, mirror and shape the communities and countries in which they exist' (Buntman 2009, p. 401).

One of the most striking aspects of penal policy and the approach used to suppress political protest in Northern Ireland was the way that specific prison regimes and policy were purposely adapted to deal with political protest (for a detailed analysis, see McEvoy 2001; Shirlow and McEvoy 2008). This section will address the key policy directives implemented to deal with political protest.

The government's reaction to political protest was the introduction of internment on 9 August 1972 and the commissioning of the Diplock Report (1972), which spelt out the arrangements for imprisoning offenders. The offences for which activists were tried were known as 'scheduled offences', and trials took place in jury-less courts in front of a judge sitting alone.

In effect, the legal arrangements represented the government's recognition that those being imprisoned were politically motivated activists. When internment was introduced, those who were detained were not

---

[25] Political prisoner groups argue that to obtain a true reflection of the extent of the effects of imprisonment one needs to multiply the number of prisoners by at least three to take account of the collateral consequences of their incarceration on family and friends (see Coiste na n-Iarchimí 2008).

treated like ordinary convicted criminals (McGuffin 1973). The right to be treated as a political prisoner was extended in June 1972 to those who had been convicted in the courts and who claimed to have been politically motivated. As politically motivated prisoners, they had *de facto* prisoner of war status. They were held in self-organised segregated compounds/wings away from 'ordinary' prisoners and prisoners of opposing paramilitary factions. They were also granted the same rights and privileges regarding visits, letters and parcels, and were able to wear their own clothes, just as un-convicted prisoners on remand. They did not carry out prison work and, in addition, they maintained their military structures with compulsory daily drilling, complete with officers in command (OCs), who dealt directly with the prison. Contact with prison staff was therefore minimal (Adams 1990, 1996; D'Arcy 1981; Murray 1998), thus, completing the picture of political motivation (Republican Press Centre 1977).

Crawford (1982) points out that the government abdicated responsibility for the allocation of politically motivated prisoners. It was up to the paramilitary organisations to accept the prisoner into their compound: 'Once found guilty of a scheduled offence, the prisoner was offered to the compounds. Whichever accepted him got him' (Crawford 1982, p. 156). The total number of prisoners in custody increased from a daily 'average of about 600 in 1968 and 1969 compared to the period in August 9, 1971 to February 14, 1972, when 2447 people were detained, with 934 of them later being released' (Spjut 1986, pp. 7–8). Owing to the increase in the conviction of politically motivated prisoners, the prisons were unable to cope with the numbers and internees were held at other prisons such as Crumlin Road Gaol, at Armagh, Long Kesh/the Maze and Magilligan, and 'for a time aboard the Maidstone prison ship moored in Belfast Lough, simply because the space was not available within the existing prison system' (Adams 1990, p. 12). Internment placed the prison system under severe strain and, in response to this policy, the level of violence in prison and beyond increased to an unprecedented scale, which has not been matched either before or since (Fay et al. 1999).

The then Secretary of State for Northern Ireland, Merlyn Rees,[26] established the Gardiner Commission in 1975 to review the powers needed to

---

[26] Merlyn Rees was the Home Secretary of State from 1976 to 1979 in James Callaghan's Labour administration.

deal with 'terrorism' and 'subversion', while preserving, 'to the maximum extent practicable', civil liberties and human rights (Gardiner 1975, para. 6). Gardiner recognised the unsustainability of internment as a long-term policy, the ultimate effect being to 'fan a widespread sense of grievance and injustice' and, thus, the report recommended the end of its use, noting however that this 'grave decision' could only be made by the government (rec. 37). Gardiner also recommended (rec. 31) the removal of special category status at 'the earliest practicable opportunity' as the resulting 'prisoner-of-war' mentality; coupled with 'social approval' in communities and the 'hope of an amnesty', had the effect of lending 'tacit support to violence and dishonesty' (para. 19).[27] The Gardiner Report of 1975 recommended the release of the internees and the removal of political status from those convicted before the courts, introducing a new policy of criminalisation. The report concluded that internment had 'brought the law into contempt' (Gardiner 1975, pp. 38–43). Following Gardiner, internment was abandoned, with the last 46 internees being released in December 1975. During the period of internment, a total of 1,981 people were interned, 1,874 of whom were Catholic/Nationalist and 107 Protestant/Loyalist (Bowcott 2010; CAIN). Hogan and Walker (1989) dispute this figure and state that a 'total, 2,060 suspected Republicans were detained, compared to 109 suspected Loyalists'. A further indictment that internment was ineffective and counter-productive was in a statement made by William Whitelaw (Spjut 1986), former Secretary of State for Northern Ireland, who admitted that: 'If you say that I put some in who shouldn't have been in, yes I would think that is certainly right ... I have the greatest doubts looking back whether internment was ever right' (Spjut 1986, p. 729). The Army issued a statement criticising the policy of internment:

'Both the introduction of internment and the use of deep interrogation techniques had a major impact on popular opinion across Ireland, in Europe and the US. Put simply, on balance and with the benefit of hindsight, it was a major mistake' (Operation Banner, para. 220).

Internment had the opposite effect it intended in Nationalist and Republican areas, by strengthening the resolve and galvanising support for the IRA. Farrell notes (1976, p. 284), that 'IRA membership soared ...

---

[27] See Gardiner (1975).

northern Catholics now felt the Northern Ireland state was irreformable. Their objective was not to reform it but to destroy it … By any standards, internment had been a disaster'.

Moreover, internment was condemned internationally by the European Court of Human Rights, which recognised that the internees had been subjected to inhuman and degrading treatment (Gillespie 2006). Wishing to dispel the idea that the violence was political in nature, the British government introduced a strategy of criminalisation, for those convicted of offences committed after 1 March 1976, including those convicted in the jury-less Diplock Courts. Margaret Thatcher[28] reiterated this when she said: 'There is no such thing as political murder, political bombing or political violence. There is only criminal murder, criminal bombing and criminal violence. We will not compromise on this. There will be no political status' (*The Times*, 6 March 1981). Internment was ended by the Secretary of State, Merlyn Rees, in 1975. It was phased out in Armagh Prison in April 'and in the Cages[29] of Long Kesh in December of the same year, when the remainder of the internees were released' (Ryder 2001, p. 152).

From that point on, prisoners would be required to wear a prison uniform, do prison work, integrate with ordinary prisoners (McKeown 2001) and be held in cellular confinement in the new H-Blocks.[30] In 1975, to reflect this policy, the prison was renamed HMP Maze (or 'the Maze') and the new cells were built in the shape of the character H.[31]

---

[28] Margaret Thatcher was the Prime Minister for the UK between 1979 and 1990.

[29] See Footnotes 16 and 23.

[30] HMP Maze is referred to the H-Blocks due to the distinctive shape of the buildings. It was built on the prison site from 1975 and began housing prisoners from 1976. This new prison was based on eight replicated single-storey H-Blocks, built over three phases across the site from 1975 to 1978 at a cost of £32 million. The layout of the prison 'surrounding the H-Blocks, was a compound containing Nissan huts' (English 2003, p. 189). In the 1970s, Republican prisoners referred to these as the 'cages'. They were 'huts surrounded by barbed wire' (see Adams 1990, p. 10). In these were held existing prisoners with special category status. The cellular part of Long Kesh/the Maze housed prisoners convicted of post-1 March 1976 offences (those without special category status). It is known as the Maze, the Blocks, the camp (prisoner terminology) or the Maze Cellular (official prison terminology).

[31] The H-Blocks were single-storey and there were eight of them. Each block consisted of four wings, each of which contained twenty-five cells, a dining room, toilet area, exercise yard and hobbies room; the central linking section held classrooms, the prison officers' room, treatment room and stores.

The changes had the impact of establishing the Conflict as a problem of law and order[32] and not a war (Hillyard 1987; Walsh 1988). Reforms were introduced to standardise the Northern Irish prison system with that of the rest of the UK. As a result of the Gardiner Report (1975), government policy shifted: prisoners were to be treated as regular criminals, rather than politically motivated offenders. This was resisted strongly by both Loyalist and Republican prisoners (Corcoran 2006, 2006b; McEvoy 2000a, b, 2001; McKeown 2001; Moen 2000). It was the latter who set the pace in terms of resistance (Corcoran 2007). The women at Armagh Prison kidnapped Governor Cunningham, escaped, went on hunger strike (Sinn Féin n.d.) and took part in the no wash protest (some of these events are detailed in the forthcoming chapters). The protesting male politically motivated prisoners went on the no wash protest refused to wear the prison uniform and were clothed solely in towels and blankets (This became known as the 'blanket protest'[33] and they became known as the 'blanket men' (Coogan 1987; Faul and Murray 1979; O'Rawe 2005).

On 4 September 1976, Kieran Nugent, the first Republican prisoner to be sentenced under the new arrangement, initiated the blanket protest whereby Republican prisoners refused to wear the prison uniform, or do prison work, and thus each had only a blanket to cover himself (Beresford 1987; Campbell et al. 1994). Within two years, the men extended their protest and went on the no wash protest smearing excreta on the walls of their cells. The prisoners' claim for political recognition was framed into what became known as 'the five demands':

1. The right to wear their own clothes;
2. Not to do prison work;

---

[32] This move by the newly elected Labour government, in the wake of the Gardiner Report (1975), was mostly in response to a growing international concern over the increasing militarisation of the struggle.

[33] The blanket protest began on 4 September 1976 when Kieran Nugent refused to conform to the new penal policy of criminalisation and demanded to be treated as a politically motivated prisoner. In other words he was denied special category status under this new regime. He refused to wear the prison uniform and when asked for his clothes size for a uniform, he reportedly replied, 'They will have to nail a prison uniform on my back first' (Republican Fact File 1991). Nugent was placed in a cell without clothes, covering himself with the blanket. Thus, began what became known as the 'blanket protest'.

3. To have free association;
4. Access to education and recreation activities;
5. To have lost remission restored.

In resisting the criminalisation policy, prisoners were deemed by the prison authorities to be in breach of prison discipline and, in addition to the violence the prisoners endured on a daily basis, they lost the entitlement to the 50% remission scheme operating in Northern Ireland at the time. It also meant that, for each week of the protest, they lost one week of remission, were given three days' cellular confinement and, in addition, privileges were withdrawn; that is, evening association, visits, letters or parcels in excess of the statutory minimum. The prison authorities' response to the hardening of the political protest was 'further punishment and stricter enforcement of the prison regulations ... when prisoners refused to comply with even the simplest of orders, warders beat prisoners; when prisoners tried to defend themselves against warders, or assault them, warders administered savage retaliation' (O'Malley 1990, p. 21), which is indicative of a situation reaching crisis point.

On 27 October 1980, seven prisoners at Long Kesh/the Maze went on hunger strike; they were joined 30 days later by three Republican women prisoners at Armagh. On 18 December 1980 (D'Arcy 1981; McCafferty 1981), the first hunger strike ended. The situation in Armagh remained stable until February 1980 when, in the course of a cell search, the women were beaten, locked in their cells and were not permitted to use the toilets on the way to their statutory hour of exercise (Brady et al. 2011; Darragh 2011). In response, the women adopted the same tactics that had been used in Long Kesh/the Maze in 1978, that of refusing to wash or use the toilets and of living in cells covered with excreta and menstrual blood. Though, unlike the men, their right to an hour's exercise each day and to wear their own clothes was still upheld[34] (Faul 1980). From 1969 to 1976, over 236 women politically motivated prisoners, some of whom were sentenced and others interned, had served time at Armagh jail.

---

[34] After 1972, women at Armagh Prison were able to wear their own clothes when they won the fight for political status.

The spiralling escalation of violence in prison and conflict on the streets meant that, by September 1980, there were 1,400 prisoners at Long Kesh/the Maze. Of these 370—half of whom were Republican and half of whom were Loyalist— had special status. Of the others, 700 were Republican and 300 Loyalist, and approximately 450 were 'on the blanket' (Northern Ireland Prison Service 1980). Bobby Sands, (Republican Officer in Command) and leader of the second hunger strike, issued the following statement:

> We are still able to declare that the criminalisation policy which we have resisted and suffered, has failed.
>
> If a British Government experienced such a long and persistent resistance to domestic policy in England, then that policy would almost certainly be changed … We have asserted that we are political prisoners and everything about our country, our arrests, interrogations, trials and prison conditions, show that we are politically motivated. (Irish Republican Information Service, p. 17; see also the Bobby Sands Trust)

The second hunger strike began on 1 March 1980, the fifth anniversary of the end of political status, concluding on 3 October 1981, 217 days after it had begun. It had resulted in the deaths of ten prisoners— Bobby Sands,[35] Francis Hughes, Raymond McCreesh, Patsy O'Hara, Joe McDonnell, Martin Hurson, Kevin Lynch, Kieran Doherty,[36] Tom McElwee and Micky Devine (Beresford 1987; Campbell et al. 1994; Collins 1986; Feldman 1991; O'Hearn 2006; Robinson 1981; Sands 1981, 1998, 2001; Yuill 2007). As a result, there was a massive international response to the deaths of the hunger strikers, which served to embarrass the British government and showed the world that 'the Republican movement was indeed a political and popular force' (O'Hearn 2006, p. 376:).

Three days after the second hunger strike had ended, the government granted concessions to one of the five demands—the right to wear their

---

[35] Two of those who died on hunger strike, Bobby Sands and Kieran Doherty were elected—Bobby Sands as MP for Fermanagh-South Tyrone in the North of Ireland and Kieran Doherty was elected Teachta Dála (TD) in the Republic of Ireland for Cavan-Monaghan. Paddy Agnew one of the hunger strikers was elected as TD to represent the constituency of Co. Louth.

[36] Kieran Doherty was elected TD in the Republic of Ireland for Cavan-Monaghan.

own clothes at all times (McKeown 2001). Over time, only one of the 'five demands' remained outstanding: the right not to do prison work. On Sunday, 25 September 1983, 38 male members of the Provisional IRA broke out of Long Kesh/the Maze Prison[37] (see Kelly 2013; Republican Press Centre 1977). Subsequently, the politically motivated prisoners were no longer allowed to work and thus the prison workshops were closed, effectively granting all of the 'five demands' but without any formal recognition of political status from the government. Eventually, political status was returned in all but name and the organisation of each of the H-Blocks came under the control of each military group. Republican prisoners, in particular, demonstrated what was possible in this relatively 'liberated zone'. They organised self-education inspired by socialist ideas and the writings of Paulo Freire (see Friere 1972) and created an Irish-speaking wing in one of the blocks (Mac Ionnrachtaigh 2009, 2013; McKeown 1998, 2001).

As Hillyard notes (1987, pp. 269–279), Gardiner argued that the recognition of political prisoners through the introduction of 'special category status' was a 'serious mistake'. It led to the longest collective struggle over the imprisonment of political prisoners in the history of Britain and Ireland. In phasing out special category status in response to the Gardiner Committee, all those convicted would be held as ordinary criminals and denied the special privileges that had been granted since the early 1970s. Penal policy during this period was ad hoc and piecemeal, and the consequences of internment, removal of special category status and the government's refusal to grant the five demands led to a series of events and grassroots activism that the British government could not have envisaged. The level of opposition to the British government intensified rather than weakened the resolve of Republican prisoners and resulted in penal policies such as internment being recognised as a flawed policy to control paramilitary activities.

---

[37] In 1983, 38 Irish Republican Army (IRA) prisoners escaped from Long Kesh/the Maze Prison, regarded as the most secure prison in Western Europe. In response to the escape, Sir James Hennessey remarked in a television interview: 'I would refer to the Maze Prison at the time as rather like Colditz during the War, an impregnable fortress … for the prisoners to have got control of their block, the H7 block from which 38 escaped, in a matter of twenty minutes was absolutely staggering. For anyone to achieve that, it must be regarded as a matter for congratulation' (Interview, 'Unlocking the Maze, Counterpoint', Ulster Television Broadcast, 22 September 1993).

The failure of these policies led to a shift in penal policy towards a more managed response to the Conflict in relation to paramilitaries in the North of Ireland. This change is reflected in the reduction of the prison population. During the height of the Conflict, the prison population exponentially rose from approximately 600 prisoners in 1969 to 3,000 by 1979 and, at any given time during this period, paramilitary prisoners comprised between 'a half and two thirds of the entire prison population in North of Ireland' (McIvor 2001, p. 16). It would also be remiss not to note the role of the Emergency Provisions Act, jury-less Diplock trials and brutal interrogation techniques (used to force a confession) in contributing to this rise. But, by the late 1990s, there was a political turn in the direction of penal policy, such as the release of paramilitary prisoners under the Good Friday Agreement 1998.[38] The question that begs to be asked is whether prison policies and the prison regimes such as internment and criminalisation comprised a systematic planned approach, or were a reactive response to a situation that was unique to Northern Ireland. Research has shown that the British government and its responses during the Conflict were not managed or strategically planned but, rather, reflected a prison system in crisis.

The Impact of Ulsterisation, Criminalisation and Normalisation of the Prison Estate

In response to politically motivated prisoners' strategies of resistance and the growing intensity of the Conflict, the British government changed its policy in relation to politically motivated prisoners. McEvoy (2001) identifies three strategic models of prisoner management: reactive containment from 1969 to 1975; criminalisation from 1976 to 1981; followed by managerialist strategies, which continue to dominate, informed by a broader policy of Ulsterisation[39] (see Gormally et al. 1994). This

---

[38] Under the terms of the Good Friday Agreement (also known as the Belfast Agreement) in 1998, the British and Irish governments, together with the range of pro-agreement parties, agreed to release most of the prisoners by the year 2000. Under the terms of the Agreement, 452 prisoners qualified for release.

[39] Ulsterisation was a strategy adopted by the British government to manage the Conflict in Northern Ireland.

move reflects a broader strategy of the time, 'ulsterisation, criminalisation and normalisation' (Coogan 1980, p. 55). Despite the British government's insistence that it would not cave in to terrorism, it was clear that criminalisation had failed. In the years following the hunger strikes there was a shift in penal policy. McEvoy (2001) has termed this form of penal policy as 'managerialism', which is characterised by a more pragmatic response to the day-to-day issues, coupled with a refusal to give official recognition to the political motivation of prisoners.

Reactive Confinement 1969–1975

In August 1969, British troops were deployed on the streets of Derry and Belfast (Gillespie 2008) in response to civil unrest; they maintained a visible presence in Northern Ireland for a further 38 years (Bernard 1989). The withdrawal of the British Army from Northern Ireland in 2007 was a significant stage in the peace process.

From Reactive Containment, Criminalisation and Normalisation: 1974–1980

By the mid-1970s, British troops had been involved in the Conflict in Northern Ireland for six years. The Gardiner Committee recommended the ending of internment in favour of a policy of criminalisation. To reflect this policy, Long Kesh was renamed HMP Maze.

The ending of internment and the increased use of Diplock Courts reinforced the belief that the state colluded with criminal justice personnel. As part of this process of Ulsterisation, there was a reduction in the visibility of the Army, in turn giving security primacy to the RUC and the locally recruited Army, the Ulster Defence Regiment (UDR).[40] Simultaneously,

---

[40] The Royal Ulster Constabulary (RUC) was the police force of the Northern Ireland State from its formation until 2001, when it was renamed the Police Service of Northern Ireland, under the Patten reform proposals guided by the 1998 Good Friday Agreement. The Ulster Defence Regiment (UDR) was formed after the disbandment of the 'B' Specials and mainly recruited from the Loyalist and Unionist community.

this set of practices and policies was an attempt to reframe terrorist violence as a *law and order* problem rather than one of *political conflict* (Gormally et al. 1993, pp. 56–57; Hillyard 1987; Walsh 1988), thus portraying the Conflict as 'Catholic and Protestant warring tribes with Britain as the neutral broker' (McKeown 1998, p. 17). This policy reflected the British government's policy of normalisation. Normalisation necessitated the primacy of the RUC in order to represent the situation in Northern Ireland and to undermine the political legitimacy of the crimes performed against the state (Pickering 2002). In order to normalise the prison system, special category status was removed at 'the earliest practicable opportunity (Gardiner 1975, p. 10) and for regimes to revert to 'ordinary prison discipline and order' (Corcoran 2006a, p. 15). The use of emergency powers was further extended, enabling the arrest of suspicious persons, rather than persons suspected of criminal acts (McEvoy et al. 2007). Many were held at Castlereagh, Town Hall Street Barracks, for up to seven days, then charged and imprisoned either at Armagh Prison or Crumlin Road Gaol, and then brought in front of a Diplock Court before being sentenced (Taylor 1980).

One woman recalls that:

Violence, intimidation and sexual violence was a common tactic used by the interrogators on the young women.

Another Volunteer states:

One of the times I was arrested. I was brought up in the Springfield Road Barracks and they were moving me, I was up the stairs, and they were bringing me down to another interview room downstairs and one of the soldiers, he was standing at the top of the stairs, put his foot out. I fell down the stairs. They did things like that. They'd pushed you against the wall and when I had time at Castlereagh they'd came and hit you (shows me) here at the back of the head.

Umm … I never got any sleep or anything at all. They would constantly come in. I remember they would just bang your head on the table.

It was the first time they'd held a female for so long and they were actually saying they were going to actually intern me in August '72.

Another recalls the journey to the interrogation centre:

A lot of verbal abuse. One of the occasions where I was restrained in the back of the Saracens, it was the Green Jackets,[41] I got a terrible time with the Green Jackets. They were singing 'Bye Bye Miss American Pie' and banging their feet and banging their rifles on the bottom of the Saracen, and they were saying that they were going to bring me up to the Shankill Road[42] and throw me out and they'd already had people waiting in the Shankill to pick me up. They were driving about and all this singing and then they just suddenly pulled up, opened the doors and threw me out. I actually fell out onto the ground, and I thought you know *this is it*. You just … it's hard even to think now, yes.

(Gets tearful)

Another woman recounts her experience:

And they were very, very degrading. You know they called me all sorts of names—slut and you know this type of talk you know and it was all grown men.

I mean I never had a female interrogator.

They were just, just trying to *degrade* you. They tried to put *fear* into me by threatening me. And you didn't know if they were going to carry out the threats because I had heard and read about other people being tortured you know … in different interrogation centres.

AW: Can you explain what the interrogation centre was like, what it looked like?

Well, it was mostly a wee small room and I think that was intentional you know that you're so close with your interrogators and you know very grim and grey walls. The food was atrocious and you're often afraid—you've heard they might be spiking your food.

Well, they could have spat into it or anything. Because I mean they made it known, very well known that *you're only Fenian scum and dirt*.

Another woman explains that:

---

[41] The term Green Jackets denoted soldiers from the British Army.
[42] The Shankill Road runs through a predominantly Loyalist-working class area known as the Shankill in Belfast, Northern Ireland.

It was in a dungeon in Town Hall Street. After I was initially arrested, I was held for about 5 days in March '73, and was told I was being interned, so I was moved from Castlereagh to Town Hall Street, and Town Hall Street is just like a very dark dungeon.

So, I was put into this block where the cells were in the dungeon. I was the only female, and all these were all Loyalists, and there was one particular one, he was just opposite my cell and the cell doors were just solid but at the bottom of them about that size a gap. There's wee grids you kind of look out through at the bottom on the floor, and I'll never forget this character, because he kept shouting his name. Winston Churchill right. He was shouting things that—what he was going to do to me were just unbelievable—sexual things—were horrific, cutting my limbs off and all this here. All the rest of them in the other cells were all you know cat calling and then the screw [prison officer] came down, and he started laughing and he said, 'you're not so tough now', and all this shit.

I was young and I was just sitting on this dirty mattress that was a bit of old board or something on the floor. I was sitting there and then he turned the key and opened my cell door and, 'see how tough you are now', and he walked away.

Well, I was in fear, oh my God, I was so.

Women's uncertainty about the nature of violence they were to experience, and their inability to predict what is supposed to be typical (and thus not threatening), or what is aberrant (and thus threatening) male behaviour opens up an ever-present spectre of fear that makes women uneasy about their safety. This fear reflects a recognition of their vulnerability *as women* to men's behaviour and, thus, to the possibility of the impunity of male violence.

This fear stems from their powerless and precarious position: being vulnerable to men's threatening, sexually harassing or physical behaviour and unable to predict when the threatening, sexually harassing or physical behaviour will turn to violence.

Vulnerability takes on additional meaning; for women, it is, above all, the 'ever-present potential of sexual violation' (Stanko 1985, p. 12; see Hird 2002). As Catherine MacKinnon correctly recognises, 'vulnerability means the appearance/reality of sexual access (MacKinnon 1982, p. 530).

One of the female Volunteers who had just turned 17 recalls:

> I was put into then a boiler suit but it wasn't a boiler suit as in the men you know the legs, it was like a dress which gaped at everything; I had no underwear on.
>
> I knew there was a *psychological war* going on between me and them. 17 is a vulnerable age to be where you know you're not covered and all the modesty stuff and then they [the police/interrogators] played on that, so when they began to interview you, they would get close up to you.
>
> It was two men, because they changed shift every few hours, but most of them are men. They would have tried to make me feel uncomfortable. Trying to expose me being naked and playing on my sexual vulnerability.
>
> It was more *psychological* and more *playing on* my *sexual vulnerability* and there was the *sexual element to it* [the interrogation] in the sense you know—the heavy breathing all over you. I'm gaping here [shows me her leg, groin area and upper torso] which you can expose in certain ways, it was just a *mind game.*

The quotes reveal that the potential for sexual violation makes women's sexuality the 'material reality of women's lives, not just a psychological, attitudinal, or ideological one' (MacKinnon, 1982:532). Kelly (1987) found that in all women's lives, violence, its fear, its threat and its reality, is ever-present, whether related to intimacy in the private sphere or danger in the public sphere. This reality rings clear in account after account of women who experienced sexual and/or physical assault on the streets by the Army, RUC, in prison by officers and while held in detention by the British Army.

> Well, I was first arrested in March '74 and I was brought to Town Hall Street, and it was more verbal. I did get a slap across the back of the head but nothing compared to what some women got. It was more *psychological torture* more than *physical torture.*

These feelings of vulnerability and the potential of sexual violence and violation were reiterated in the voices of the women who had been strip searched and whose cells had been raided (McGuire 1982). Stanko (1990) argues that the reality of physical and/or sexual vulnerability is part of women's experience of *being in* the world which takes on an illusion of normality (Stanko 1985, p. 9). Moreover, theorist Susan Markus argues, 'the horror of rape is not that it steals something away from us but that it makes us into things to be taken' (Marcus 1992, p. 389). Sexual violence is often theorised as an assault on what it means to be a woman, yet also inherent to what a woman should expect: she is at once reduced to her body and always rapeable.

> They broke my nose and three of my ribs, and I was there for about five days before they charged me. Yes, so I think, I'll tell you what I found worse; it was the *filthy pornographic talk*. I mean the [hittings], I could take. It's just you have a soldier and an RUC man in the room and they are talking to you in a completely pornographic way: "Would you like a bit of dick. We're going to rape you. We're going to strip you. Nobody fucking knows you're here. I can put you up that wall and I'm going to have you from the front. He's going to have you from the back and we'll call somebody else and have his dick in your mouth', and that went on morning, noon and night. Complete filth and it's an element that's never spoken about.

For all of the female ex-combatants in the study it was not the direct physical violence that was the hardest aspect of brutality by the RUC and British Army but the potential and threat of and manipulation of their sexual vulnerability.

> I wasn't really physically assaulted, it was more emotional. I would call it *emotional torture*. But because I was aware of their tactics maybe I coped with it a bit better. The good cop, bad cop. Banging on the table. Calling you this and that "you're an Irish whore and you're going to be found in the Shankill on a slab and we're not letting you out of here". And it went on and on and on, and for the whole time that I was in. (Emphasis in original)

The threat of being left in a Loyalist area was used routinely playing on women's sexual vulnerability 'to be beaten, raped or killed'.

They also threatened to bring me up to Sandy Row, which is a Protestant area, which would be known as a UVF[43] stronghold. They threatened to bring me and throw me out.

AW: For what purpose?

I think from their point so I could be beaten, raped or killed.

Aspects of women's bodies were used to degrade them and reinforce the sense of powerlessness.

They didn't physically touch me at that time. I had my period and I had no fresh sanitary towels and they wouldn't give me any.
They were very aggressive and saying that they were going to come at night and rape me and all this.

The testimonials below highlight the level of sexual violence employed by the state forces.

They use a lot of *sexual intimidation* and as a 20 year old growing up in West Belfast; you didn't have much experience of any of that. So it was scary. It could be scary, but because I had the training and I knew to expect it, and I said "they're doing this to *try and break you*". *But it is disgusting* how grown men—men in their 40s and 50s, could talk to a young girl using sexual language like that—what they were going to do. No matter what they thought about you—to talk to a young girl, the ages of their daughters. But you *expected no less from the Special Branch.* (Emphasis in original)

Violence should be understood as any action or structure that diminishes another human being and in accepting this definition; the basic structures of our society are often violent in concept. As Pinthus (1982, p. 2) observes:

---

[43] UVF: Ulster Volunteer Force.

Violence might also be seen as that which violates or causes violation. It can take varying forms including physical, sexual, emotional, verbal, cognitive, visual and representational forms. Violence may also comprise the creation of the conditions of violence, potential violence, threat and/or neglect. Sometimes the mere presence of someone is violating and thus violent. Violence can be dramatic or subtle, occasional or continuous. (Cited in Ramazanoglŭ 1989, p. 64)

We must recognise that violence is built into many of our institutions, such as prisons. They are competitive, hierarchical, non-democratic and, at times, unjust.

A woman recounts her experience:

I mean they'd deliberately shoved you around. They would push you on your breasts, and stuff, but not, I mean your full blown sexual assault. I felt *abused* but verbally. I mean, I was physically hit, you know, and they don't mind if they shove your breasts or call you a fenian whore. I was big-chested then and was very thin but with very big breasts then and you know they'd make comments about your breast size and all the rest of it. I mean they would grab you by the breasts when they were hitting you but it was more verbal. They would grab your boobs or the bra strap.

Well, for me it was the bra. The prison officers done the same thing, it was very handy just to grab you there in-between your breasts and pull you about your breasts and move you about like that. In prison their favourite thing was to put you in a crucifix position face down, and then they grab you with the bra strap. The bra strap would snap and your breasts would be … fall out you know. I just thought fuck this is weird.

I might sound casual about it all but I *wasn't a bit* casual. I found it very disturbing but over the years, you do get *used to it*. You know the tactics and it was quite shocking for me at the time. But as I say, I expected to be hit. I expected to be physical assaulted. I was more shocked at the language. My brother would say I wouldn't give a shit what they said to me, you know as long as they didn't beat me, but I would be prepared to be hit but maybe it's just a female thing. I mean there's only so much to you can do to a man but to a woman and I mean the imagination of those guys was limitless. (Emphasis in original)

While it is accepted that organisations are centrally concerned with power, domination and control (Morgan 1995), it may seem strange at first to conflate organisations and violence. And yet, many concepts in organisational analysis, such as 'power', 'domination', 'control', even 'authority', can be used as euphemisms for violence. This is most obviously so in analysing organisations where there is legitimised use of violence, as in the police force, the military, in prisons, in detention centres and in other state custodial organisations (Scraton et al. 1991). In prison, in interrogation centres, 'violence' becomes both an element in the achievement of goals, and an element in the routine performance of work.

> They forced me to stand up and they were shouting into my face, and you know, it was very, *frightening* for a young girl. It was really threatening and the language they used was of sexual nature. I was a Catholic girl and we just didn't talk about those things. *Disgusting*. (Emphasis in original)

Violent regimes became institutionalised, even though violence was not part of official organisational aims or practices. In such organisations—for example, prisons—violence may be used as a form of control by managers, staff or others in authority (De-Pretis 2000, 2001).

> So the three fellas I was with were locked up in the other wing but I was locked up in the wing with Loyalists, and they would lay down and look under the cell door and they started to shout abuse—sexual abuse at you, and we had to walk up to the toilet in Town Hall Street and they were all lying on the floor looking up your skirt. I just had that sort of feeling that anything could happen.

In the case of the prison, the level of violence against women during the Conflict in Northern Ireland was tolerated and normalised as part of the organisational behaviour of prison officers, the RUC and the British Army.

AW: Were there cases where women were...?

> I know there was a girl that was sexually assaulted. They boasted about it—the Army and the Police boasted about it, and I was in prison with her, but she would never talk about what happened. It's a *very hard thing* you know, a *very difficult thing*. Because this girl's quite a genteel girl. I reckon that was the reason they done it, because I was cheeky, when they talk about it I would 'Oh fuck off', or 'Ah you won't'. Right, so, yes, I know it

happened. But it is not spoken about. I know that she would rather do an extra two years in jail than admit what happened to her. I think she felt sullied, I think she felt that. (Emphasis in original)

The women's testimonies reveal the level, nature and silence surrounding sexual violence and sexual harassment that were legitimated in the practices of the British soldiers and the RUC. Aretxaga (1997, p. 132), in her study, highlights the impunity with which the RUC and the British Army operated on the streets and in detention centres. The possibility of a successful legal suit against the RUC or the British Army for sexual harassment is virtually precluded by the judiciary in Northern Ireland, which has in some cases acted on behalf of the police rather than as an independent administrator of justice (see examples of state collusion— that is, Bloody Sunday, the Ballymurphy Massacre and the Pat Finucane inquiry).

The female Catholic body becomes a site in which gendered norms operated *within*, *on* and *were* subverted and used to heighten feelings of sexual vulnerability and, in some cases, led to actual sexual violence. Foucault argues that: 'sexuality is an especially dense transfer point for relations of power. Sexuality is not the most intractable element in power relations, but rather one of those endowed with the greatest instrumentality: useful for the greatest number of manoeuvres and capable of serving as a point of support, as a linchpin, for the most varied strategies' (1978, p. 103). The women's experience of sexualised violence by agents of the state is further compounded by their age, religious beliefs, modesty and embarrassment about all things bodily.

You have to remember, we were very Catholic, very modest if you like very religious. I mean I'd never saw him [my husband] naked. You know that type of thing. He never saw me naked. I was always covered with pyjamas and things and he was the same. We were 20, but we never, I mean I was still a virgin and so was he when we got married.

The women's bodies become a tool *of* and *for* torture. A space in which violence was deployed in a way that was clearly gendered differentiated from their male comrades.

It is estimated that 80% of people who were arrested, interrogated and convicted in this period were based on 'confessions' extracted by force, torture and sexual intimidation (Hillyard 1987, p. 291; Walsh 1988, p. 95). As Bowyer Bell (1993, p. 429) argues, during 1974 there were signs of the beginning of an 'unarticulated strategy … a typical British response; no theory, only practice, unarticulated values, personal experience and self-interest shaped by an Irish exposure'. The lack of due process leading to criminal convictions and the use of Diplock Courts led to international condemnation. Those individuals who came into contact with this system 'considered [themselves] as political in the courtroom but criminal for the purposes of punishment' (Tomlinson 1980, p. 193).

References

Adams, G. (1986). *The politics of Irish freedom*. Dingle: Brandon.

Adams, G. (1990). *Cage eleven*. Dingle: Brandon.

Adams, G. (1996). *Before the dawn*. Dingle: Brandon.

Amnesty International. (1971/1972). *Report of an enquiry into allegations of ill-treatment in Northern Ireland*. London: Amnesty International.

Amnesty International. (1994). *Political killings in Northern Ireland*. London: Amnesty International.

Aretxaga, B. (1997). *Shattering the silence: Women, nationalism and political subjectivity in Northern Ireland*. Princeton, NJ: Princeton University Press.

Ashe, F. (2006). The McCartney sisters' search for justice: Gender and political protest in Northern Ireland. *Politics, 26*(3).

Ashe, F. (2008). Gendering ethno-nationalism in Northern Ireland. In C. Coulter (Ed.), *Northern Ireland after the troubles*. Manchester: Manchester University Press.

Barzilay, D. (1977). *The British Army in Ulster* (Vols. 1, 2). Belfast: Century Books.

Beresford, D. (1987). *Ten men dead: The story of the 1981 Irish hunger strike*. London: Grafton.

Bernard, M. (1989). *Daughter of Derry: The story of Brigid Sheils Makowski*. London: Pluto.

Bowcott, O. (2010, October 11). MOD took softer line on loyalist paramilitaries, secret files reveal. *Guardian*.

Bowyer Bell, J. (1991). *The gun and Irish politics*. New Brunswick, NJ: Transaction Publishers.

Bowyer Bell, J. (1993). *The Irish troubles: A generation of violence 1967-1992*. Dublin: Gill and Martin.

Boyle, K., Hadden, T., & Hillyard, P. (1980/1975). *Law and state: The case of Northern Ireland*. London: Roberson.

Brady, B., Faul, D., & Murray, R. (1975). *Internment 1971-1975*. Document.

Brady, E., Patterson, E., McKinney, K., Hamill, R., & Jackson, P. (2011). *The footsteps of Anne: Stories of republican women ex-prisoners*. Belfast: Shanway Press.

Buntman, F. (2009). Prison and democracy: Lessons learned and not learned, from 1989 to 2009. *International Journal of Politics, Culture and Society, 22*.

Burton, J. (1990). *Conflict, resolution and prevention*. New York: St. Martin's.

Campbell, B., McKeown, L., & O'Hagan, F. (1994). *Nor meekly serve my time: The H-Block struggle, 1976-1981*. Belfast: Beyond the Pale.

Campell, C., & Connolly, I. (2003, September). A model for the 'War Against Terrorism?', Military intervention in Northern Ireland and the 1970 falls curfew. *Journal of Law and Society, 30*(3).

Challis, J. (1999). *The Northern Ireland prison system 1920-1990: A history*. Belfast: Northern Ireland Prison Service.

Coiste na n-Iarchimí. (2008). *Building the future in Ireland*. Building the Future in Ireland: Belfast.

Collins, T. (1986). *The Irish hunger strike*. Dublin: White Island Book.

Corcoran, M. (2006). *Out of order: The political imprisonment of women in Northern Ireland, 1972-1998*. Cullompton: Willan.

Corcoran, M. (2006a). *Out of order: The political imprisonment of women in Northern Ireland, 1972–1998*. Cullompton: Willan Press.

Corcoran, M. (2006b). Talking about resistance: Women political prisoners and the dynamics of prison conflict, Northern Ireland. In A. Barton, K. Corteen, D. Scott, & D. Whyte (Eds.), *Expanding the criminological imagination: Critical readings in criminology*. Devon: Willan.

Corcoran, M. (2007). Normalisation and its discontents: Constructing the 'irreconcilable' female political prisoner in Northern Ireland. *British Journal of Criminology, 47*.

Compton Report. (1971). *Report of the enquiry into allegations against the security forces of physical brutality in Northern Ireland arising out of events in the 9th August 1971 Cmnd: 4823*. London: HMSO.

Coogan, T. P. (1980). *On the blanket: The H-Block story*. Dublin: Ward River Press.

Coogan, T. P. (1987). *Disillusioned decades: Ireland 1966-87*. Dublin: Gill and Macmillan.

Coogan, T. P. (1995). *The troubles: Ireland's ordeal, 1969-95, and the search for peace.* UK: Hutchinson.

Coogan, T. P. (2000). *The IRA.* New York. Harper Collins.

Cormack, R., & Osborne, R. (1991). *Discrimination and public policy in Northern Ireland.* Oxford: Clarendon.

Crawford, C. (1982). The compound system: An alternative penal strategy. *Howard Journal of Criminal Justice, 21*(1–3), 155–158.

Darragh, S. (2011). *'John's Lennon dead' – Stories of protest, hunger strikes and resistance.* Belfast: Beyond the Pale.

D'Arcy, M. (1981). *Tell them everything. A Sojourn in the prison of her majesty Queen Elizabeth II at Ard Macha (Armagh).* London: Pluto.

De-Pretis, M. (2000). *To take arms in the armed patriarchy.* Unpublished paper presented at the Women and Law conference on Strategic Thinking for the Millennium, University of Westminster, London.

De-Pretis, M. (2001). *Women, politics and political violence in Northern Ireland: A study in historical feminist criminology.* Unpublished PhD thesis, University of Bristol.

Devlin, B. (1971). *Barricades or ballot boxes.* Leicester: Leicester University Press.

Dewar, M. (1996). *The British Army in Northern Ireland* (2nd ed.). London: Weidenfeld Military.

Diplock Report. (1972). *Report of the Commission to Consider Legal Procedures to Deal with Terrorist Activities in Northern Ireland, Chairman Lord Diplock.* London: HMSO.

Ditch, J., & Morrissey, M. (1992). Northern Ireland: Review and prospects for social policy. *Social Policy and Administration, 21*, 1–18.

Edgerton, L. (1986). Public protest, domestic acquiescence: Women in Northern Ireland. In R. Ridd & H. Callaway (Eds.), *Caught up in conflict: Women's responses to political strife.* London: Macmillan.

English, R. (2003). *Armed struggle: The history of the IRA.* Oxford: Oxford University Press.

Farrell, M. (1976). *The orange state.* London: Pluto.

Farrell, M. (1980). *Northern Ireland: The orange state.* London: Pluto.

Faul, D. (1980). *Black February Armagh Prison: Beating women in prison, pamphlet.* Armagh: The Authors.

Faul, D., & Murray, R. (1974a). *Long Kesh, the inequity of internment, August 9th 1971 – August 9th 1974.* Dungannon: Dungannon, c/o St Patrick's Academy and Authors.

Faul, D., & Murray, R. (1974b). *The flames of Long Kesh, 15-16 October 1974: The murder of Hugh Gerard Convey, internee*. Dungannon: Dungannon, c/o St Patrick's Academy and Authors.

Faul, D., & Murray, R. (1979). *H Blocks: British jail for Irish political prisoners*. Dungannon: Authors.

Fay, M. T., Morrissey, M., & Smyth, M. (1999). *Northern Ireland's troubles: The human costs*. London: Pluto.

Feldman, A. (1991). *Formations of violence: The narrative of the body and political terror in Northern Ireland*. Chicago: University of Chicago Press.

Foucault, M. (1978). *The history of sexuality* (Vol. 1). New York: Pantheon.

Freire, P. (1972). *Pedagogy of the oppressed*. Harmondsworth: Penguin Books.

Gardiner, L. (1975). *Report of a Committee to Consider in the Context of Civil Liberties and Human Rights, Measures to Deal with Terrorism in Northern Ireland*, Cmnd. 5847.

Gearty, C. (1991). *Terror*. London: Faber and Faber.

Gearty, C., & Tomkins, A. (Eds.). (1996). *Understanding human rights*. London: Mansell.

Gillespie, G. (2008). *Years of darkness: The troubles remembered*. Dublin: Gill and Macmillan.

Goodwin, J. (2006, June). A theory of categorical terrorism. *84*(4).

Gormally, B., McEvoy, K., & Wall, D. (1993). Criminal justice in a divided society: Northern Ireland prisons. In M. Tonry (Ed.), *Crime and justice: A review of research* (Vol. 17). Chicago: University of Chicago Press.

Gormally, B., McEvoy, K., & Wall, D. (1994). Politics and prison management: The Northern Ireland experience. *Prison Service Journal*.

Hamill, D. (1985). *Pig in the middle: Army in Northern Ireland, 1969-84*. London: Methuen.

Hayes, B., & McAllister, I. (2001). Sowing dragon's teeth: Public support for political violence and Para-militarism in Northern Ireland. *Political Studies, 49*, 9.

Hillyard, P. (1987). The normalisation of special powers from Northern Ireland to Britain. In P. Scraton (Ed.), *Law, order and the authoritarian state*. Milton Keynes: Open University Press.

Hillyard, P., Pantazis, C., Tombs, S., & Gordon, D. (2005). *Beyond criminology: Taking harm seriously*. Canada: Fernwood.

Hird, M. (2002). *Engendering violence: Heterosexual interpersonal violence from childhood to adulthood*. London: Ashgate.

Hogan, G., & Walker, C. (1989). *Political violence and the law in Ireland*. Manchester: Manchester University Press.

Irish News. (1970, July 6). 3,000 Strong army of women help to feed the lower falls.

Jackson, J., & Doran, S. (1995). *Judge without jury: Diplock trials in the adversary system*. Oxford: Oxford University Press.

Jamieson, R., & Grounds, A. (2002). *No sense of an ending: The effects of long term imprisonment amongst republican prisoners and their families*. Monaghan: Ex-Prisoners Assistance Committee.

Jamieson, R., & Grounds, A. (2008). *Facing the future: Ageing and politically-motivated former prisoners in Northern Ireland and the border region*. Monaghan: EXPAC/Border Action.

Jamieson, R., & McEvoy, K. (2005). State crime by proxy and juridical othering. *British Journal of Criminology, 45*(4), 504–527.

Kelly, G. (2013). *The escape: The inside story of the 1983 escape from Long Kesh prison*. Belfast: M & G publications.

Kelly, L. (1987). The continuum of male violence. In J. Hanmer & M. Maynard (Eds.), *Women, violence and social control*. London: MacMillan.

Kennally, D., & Preston, E. (1971). *Belfast, August 1971: A case to be answered*. London: Independent Labour Party.

Lee, J. (1989). *Ireland 1912-1985: Politics and society*. Cambridge: Cambridge University Press.

Mac Ionnrachtaigh, F. (2009). *Language, resistance and revival: Republican prisoners and the Irish language in the North of Ireland*. Unpublished PhD thesis, Queen's University, Belfast.

Mac Ionnrachtaigh, F. (2013). *Language, resistance and revival: Republican prisoners and the Irish language in the North of Ireland*. London: Pluto.

McCafferty, N. (1981). *The Armagh women*. Dublin: Co-op Books.

MacKinnon, A. C. (1982). Feminism, marxism, method, and the state: An agenda for theory. *Signs, 7*(3), Feminist Theory (Spring).

Marcus, S. (1992). Fighting bodies, fighting words: A theory and politics of rape prevention. In J. Butler & J. Scott (Eds.), *Feminists theorize the political*. New York: Routledge.

McEvoy, K. (2000a). Law, struggle and political transformation in Northern Ireland. *Journal of Law and Society, 27*, 542–571.

McEvoy, K. (2000b). *Law, struggle and political transformation in Northern Ireland*. Oxford: Blackwell.

McEvoy, K. (2001). *Paramilitary imprisonment in Northern Ireland: Resistance, management, and release*. Oxford: Oxford University Press.

McEvoy, K., McConnachie, K., & Jamieson, R. (2007). Political imprisonment and the 'War on Terror'. In Y. Jewkes (Ed.), *Handbook of the prison*. Cullompton: Willan.

McGarry, J., & O'Leary, B. (1993). *The Northern Ireland conflict: Consociational engagements.* Oxford: Oxford University Press.

McGuffin, J. (1973). *Internment.* Trelee: Anvil Books.

McGuffin, J. (1974). *The guineapigs.* Hammondsworth: Penguin.

McGuire, M. (1982). *Cambridge Studies in Criminology: Vol. XLIX. Burglary in a dwelling.* London: Heineman.

McKearney, T. (2011). *The provisional IRA: From insurrection to parliament.* London: Pluto Press.

McKeown, L. (1998). *Unrepentant Fenian bastards: The social construction of an Irish Republican Prisoner Community.* PhD thesis, Faculty of Arts, Queen's University Belfast.

McKeown, L. (2001). *Out of time: Irish republican prisoners Long Kesh 1972-2000.* Belfast: Beyond the Pale.

McKittrick, D., Kelters, S., Feeney, B. and Thornton, C. (1999) *Lost Lives: The Stories of the Men, Women and Children who Died as a Result of the Northern Ireland Troubles.* Edinburgh: Mainstream.

Moen, D. (2000). *The criminalisation of political prisoners in Northern Ireland.* Unpublished paper presented at the Annual conference of the British Society of Criminology, Liverpool, 13–16 July.

Morgan, V. (1995). Women and the conflict in Northern Ireland. In A. O'Day (Ed.), *Terrorism's laboratory: The case of Northern Ireland.* Aldershot: Dartmouth.

Murray, R. (1998). *Hard time: Armagh Gaol 1971-1986.* Cork: Mercier Press.

Northern Ireland Civil Rights Association. (1973, May 22). *Information sheet on women internees.* Pamphlet, Belfast.

Northern Ireland Prison Service. (1980). *Report on the Administration of the Prison Service for 1980 (Cmnd 800).* Belfast: HMSO.

Ó Fearghail, S. (1970). *Law (?) and order: The Belfast 'Curfew' of 3–5 July 1970.* http://cedarlounge.wordpress.com/2010/07/03/left-archive-law-and-orders-the-belfast-curfew-of-3-5-july-1970-central-citizens-defence-committee/. Accessed 3 July 2014.

O'Hearn, D. (2006). *Booby Sands: Nothing but an unfinished song.* London: Pluto.

O'Keefe, T. (2013). *Feminist identity development and activism in revolutionary movements.* London: Palgrave Press.

O'Malley, P. (1990). *Biting at the grave: The Irish hunger strikes and the politics of despair.* Belfast: Blackstaff.

O'Rawe, R. (2005). *Blanketmen: An untold story of the H-Block hunger strike.* Dublin: New Island.

Pickering, S.J. (2002). *Women, policing and resistance in Northern Ireland.* Belfast: Beyond the Pale.

Pinthus, E. (1982). Peace education. In *Quaker peace and service* (pp. 2–10). London: Friends House.

Purdie, B. (1990). *Politics in the street: The origins of the civil rights movement in Northern Ireland.* Belfast: Blackstaff.

Ramazanoglŭ, C. (1989). *Feminism and the contradictions of oppression.* London: Routledge.

Republican Fact File. (1991). *Republican prisoners and the prison struggle in Ireland.* Sinn Féin.

Republican Press Centre. (1977). *Prison struggle: The story of continuing resistance behind the wire.* Belfast: Republican Press Centre.

Robinson, P. (1981). *Self-inflicted an exposure of the H-Blocks issue.* Belfast: Democratic Unionist Party (Out of Print).

Rolston, B., & Tomlinson, M. (1986). Long term imprisonment in Northern Ireland: Psychological or political survival? In B. Rolston & M. Tomlinson (Eds.), *The expansion of European prison systems: Working papers in European Criminology.* European Group for the Study of Deviance and Social Control: Belfast.

Ruane, J., & Todd, J. (1996). *The dynamics of conflict in Northern Ireland: Power, conflict and emancipation.* Cambridge: Cambridge University Press.

Ryder, C. (2001). Inside the maze: The untold story of the Northern Ireland prison service. London: Methuen Publishing.

Sands, B. (1981). *The diary of Bobby Sands: The first seventeen days of Bobby Sands' H-Block hunger strike to the death.* Dublin: Sinn Féin Publicity Department.

Sands, B. (1998). *Writings from prison.* Ireland. London: The Mercier Press Ltd.

Sands, B. (2001). *One day in my life.* Ireland. London: The Mercier Press Ltd.

Schafer, S. (1974). *The political criminal: The problem of morality and crime.* New York: Free Press.

Scraton, P., Sim, J., & Sidmore, P. (1991). *Prisons under protest.* Milton Keynes: Open University Press.

Shirlow, P., Graham, B., McEvoy, K., Purvis, D., & O'hAdhmaill, F. (2005). *Politically motivated former prisoner groups: Community activism and conflict transformation..* Belfast: Northern Ireland Community Relations Council and Northern Ireland Human Rights Commission.

Shirlow, P., & McEvoy, K. (2008). *Beyond the wire: Former prisoners and conflict transformation in Northern Ireland.* London: Pluto.

Spjut, R. (1986). Internment and detention without trial in Northern Ireland 1971-1975. *Modern Law Review, 49*.

Stanko, E. (1985). *Intimate intrusions women's experience of male violence.* London: Routledge.

Stanko, E. (1990). *Everyday violence.* London: Pandora Press.

The Sunday Times Insight Team [STIT]. (1972, April 23). Insight on bloody Sunday: The decision to put civilians at risk. *Sunday Times*, pp. 15–18.

Taylor, P. (1980). *Beating the terrorists? Interrogation in Omagh, Gough and Castlereagh.* London: Penguin.

Taylor, P. (2001). *Brits: The war against the IRA.* London: Bloomsbury.

Tomlinson, M. (1980). Reforming repression. In L. O'Dowd, B. Rolston, & M. Tomlinson (Eds.), *Northern Ireland: Between civil rights and civil war.* Belfast: CSE books.

Walsh, D. P. J. (1983). *The use and abuse of emergency legislation.* London: Cobden.

Walsh, D. (1988). The Royal Ulster Constabulary: A law unto themselves? In M. Tomlinson, T. Varley, & C. McCullagh (Eds.), *Whose law and order?* Dublin: Sociological Association of Ireland.

White, L. (2015). *Transitional justice and legacies of state violence: Talking about torture on Northern Ireland.* London: Routledge.

Yuill, C. (2007). The body as weapon: Bobby Sands and the republican hunger strikes. *Sociological Research Online, 12*(2).

4

Mná sa Streachailt: The Role of the Accidental Activist*

There was a total feeling of *injustice* and *we were going to do something about it.*

Although, much has been written about the recent political struggles in Northern Ireland, the experiences of women combatants have too often been silenced and under-explored (Aretxaga 1997; McWilliams 1995). The aim of this book is to address these lacunae and question why women should be so marginalised when they played such a pivotal role in the Conflict and in the transition to peace. The experiences of women combatants demonstrate that their relative invisibility (and, indeed, the lower numbers of women taking up arms as compared with the numbers of men) is a result of ideological constructions of womanhood and manhood in society, rather than a reflection of considered decisions based on objective difficulties in incorporating women in combat roles. In addition, in the last ten years leading women activists in Northern

---

Mná sa Streachailt is Gaelic for Women in Struggle.
*McWilliams (1995, p. 21) describes 'accidental activism', as 'women organising as women' to create social change in Northern Ireland. Women become politicised through their direct action.

© The Editor(s) (if applicable) and The Author(s) 2016
A. Wahidin, *Ex-Combatants, Gender and Peace in Northern Ireland,*
DOI 10.1057/978-1-137-36330-5_4

Ireland have died leaving little of the written material which has, in other struggles, so often been of use to the next generation of activists.[1] It is difficult to determine the reason for this gap in the literature; partly, it is due to the fact that these women were so completely engaged in pragmatic politics that they had little time for writing reflectively about their activities (Haug 1989).

A general theme running through the experiences of the women combatants is the paradox of an activism which defies stereotypical notions of women and breaks the confines of the domestic caring roles conventionally viewed as the 'private' (as distinct from the 'political') sphere. Yet, at the same time, this paradox is rooted largely in the experience of defending that sphere from attack, as the British military presence turned Republican homes and communities into political and military battlegrounds, and therefore had effects partially specific to them in their roles and subjectivities *as women*. The concept of the 'accidental activist' in this context refers to the way that women organised *as women* out of the direct necessity to defend their communities, their political convictions emerging from these immediate experiences, rather than necessarily by pre-existing ideologies.

This chapter, then, outlines the experiences forming the context for women's direct activism from the period beginning in 1969, generally known as 'the Troubles'. However, in the light of the historic role of women's organisations in Irish independence struggles (see Chap. 5), the distinction between 'accidental' activism and that which is motivated by a pre-existing political commitment should not be overstated. Neither should we overlook the prior role of that struggle in shaping historically-specific ethno-nationalist versions of gender ideology and gendered identities which, in turn, define the spaces for women's resistance. The latter theme will also be developed over the course of this chapter.

From the beginning of the Conflict in 1969, women began to organise themselves in order to provide support structures within their communities. As the Conflict continued, women increasingly began to take on

---

[1] Very little material is available on the lives of Cathy Harkin and Madge Davidson who died in 1984 and 1991, respectively. Both were leading activists in the Civil Rights Movement and were influential in the development of the Women's Movement in Northern Ireland.

more public and politicised roles within and beyond their own communities, as will be discussed later in this book.

Context

Women's direct activism came to the fore with the re-introduction of internment in August 1971. On 9 August 1971, 342 men were arrested in dawn swoops. This move was directed against the Catholic population and caused great alienation. Moreover, it failed as an attempt to crush the Republican movement as most of those interned were not actively involved in the IRA. While so many men were interned or 'on the run', women became the mainstay of their communities. They were the ones visiting family members, partners and friends in Long Kesh/the Maze while rearing the children, keeping the home and community together. One of the female ex-combatant states:

> The women were rearing the children while they [the men] were in jail, and they [the women] were multi-tasking all over the place.

In the predominantly Nationalist[2] communities in West Belfast, the women, out of necessity, invented an alarm signal to alert members of the community that the British Army was patrolling particular areas. 'Women in the ghettos' defended their communities by 'rattling dustbin lids to alert the inhabitants' (Farrell 1980, pp. 282–283). From 1971 to 1972, British soldiers swamped Catholic areas, escalating counter-insurgency measures against the IRA, which led to over 36,000 house searches; the figure doubling by 1973 (Coogan 2000). Newsinger (1995) records that 250,000 house searches took place in a five-year period where virtually every Catholic working-class home, was raided routinely. From 1988 to 1991, there were 13,692 recorded searches by the RUC. While compensation for damage during the house raids existed through the Northern Ireland Office (NIO), no information is available regarding the number

---

[2] Definitions of Nationalist and Republican are contested. 'Nationalist' refers to a supporter of Irish Nationalism, generally though not exclusively from the Catholic community. 'Republican' refers to supporters of Irish Nationalism and those aligned to a Republican party.

of claims made. To date, there are still no published figures as to the amount of illicit material or how many illegal items were found during searches; neither are there any records of how many people were arrested or charged (Dickson 1993, p. 37). However, some figures provided by the NIO established that, in the early 1990s, the rate of successful searches was in the range of 5–10% (Helsinki Watch 1991). Although there are no comprehensive records on the intensity or number of house searches, it is clear from the literature that the effects were devastating.

House raids have historically been a central part of security force measures used to subjugate, harass and intimidate women and their communities. The procedures used by the security forces have raised substantial human rights questions (Amnesty International 1991, 1978; Helsinki Watch 1991). Dawn raids were commonly used to arrest and intimidate people, and took place between the hours of 10:00 am and 6:00 pm when people were most vulnerable (see Fairweather et al. 1984). Women who have been through these dawn raids detail their experiences:

> So you had *all* this harassment going on in the background, and then you were watching this *all* on the street. They [the British Soldiers] would come and kick your door in. I mean my brother was interned also, he was just taken out. You know they would come at three o'clock in the morning, four o'clock and you're in a deep sleep and these people [the British Soldiers] would just kick your door in. Come in and throw people out of bed. So you were constantly witnessing all this. Experiencing it. You *do* develop a hate for these people that are coming into your home, or these people that you see beating people up in the street for no reason whatsoever. So you are biased against them because of what you are witnessing. *You're seeing it. You're experiencing it* and it's not as if you're listening to second-hand information. *You're actually living it* ... People were *living* through this *every day.* You know it's just *horrible.* It was awful. (Author's emphasis)

Before discussing women's increased politicisation in resisting the attacks of the security forces on the private feminised domain of the home, it is worth considering in detail the impact of house raids on women living in predominately working-class Nationalist/Republican areas. The effects of the house raids became a specific ground for struggle and resistance (Ridd and Callaway 1986). Not only was the impact of the raids gender-specific in violating the private sphere of the home, but the subjective impact of British military actions on Catholic women as such was immense. On a daily basis, women were living with the threat of violence, harassment, injustice and fear for their children, family and friends.

> Well, I think when I'd seen what had happened initially after internment. They [the British Army] were just constantly stopping people. Stopping fellas. Strip searching them. Searching them. Just being physically brutal to them. Beating them with their batons that they had or hitting and throwing them in the back of Saracens, and this was constantly going on *every* single day. You went *out* and *this* was *happening*. You know you're thinking 'this is wrong'. (Emphasis in original)

This has been described as an 'armed patriarchy' (Edgerton 1986, p. 76)[3] in which intimidation and fear had become a part of daily living (Edgerton 1986; McWilliams 1995). House raids had the effect of mobilising the women into direct action. The house raids disrupted the boundaries between the public and the private, where the Conflict invaded the personal space of the home. Their immediate space was under siege and their identity as mothers, as nurturers and protectors of the family and the community was constantly being threatened. The above highlights the role of traditional gendered discourses embedded in ethno-nationalist feminine identities as 'protectors of the family', in motivating and legitimising Republican and Nationalist women's involvement in political protests when the safety or welfare of the family was being threatened (Ashe 2007/2009; Yuval-Davis 1989).

The house raids not only exposed the coercive nature of the state, but the collusion of security forces and the use of emergency legislation[4] by

---

[3] Sources that use this term include Edgerton (1986) and Evason (1991). McWilliams (1995, p. 34) states that the term was first coined by Cathy Harkin when she worked at Women's Aid in Derry City between 1977 and 1981. Harkin stated, 'both Orange and Green nationalism retained their ultra conservative view that women were both the property of, and inferior to men' (cited in Harkin and Kilmurray 2002, p. 386).

[4] Emergency legislation in Northern Ireland differs from ordinary legislation in as much as it is usually introduced for a limited period to address political violence. However, it has become a

members of the state for the legitimate destruction of homes and to harass and intimidate family members. Moreover, it left the women no place to remove themselves from the day-to-day political, economic and social realities of the Conflict (Devlin 1971; Dowler 1998; Sales 1997). The private space of the home became another site of conflict and struggle. In the reclaiming of space, the security forces became the catalyst for change whereby assaulting the identity of woman in terms of domesticity, motherhood, sexuality and femininity defined women's political consciousness and moved them into organised political action.

> Internment and the widespread raids of people's homes blurred the boundaries between household and communal space and at certain moments practically erased them … The disproportionate and arbitrary nature of the searches, which sometimes included sealing off whole streets, asserted their character as collective punishments … The military enactment of state power in a space culturally defined as feminine created a gendered colonial dichotomy. By forcefully entering the household, the army was not only invading women's physical space but also violating their psychological and affective space. (Aretxaga 1997, p. 69)

In response to the effects of the Conflict entering the female territory of the home, women from these working-class, predominantly Nationalist/Republican areas patrolled the streets on a rotating basis, taking turns to follow the soldiers everywhere they went.

A woman recalls:

> The first time I noticed the whistles and the bin lids was with the advent of internment, because it was a way of warning them [IRA Volunteers] that they [the British Army] were coming to intern people. Maybe, it was before that but that's the first time I remember seeing women banging bin lids to warn people.

---

feature of government attempts to quell violence in Northern Ireland in much the same way as other forms of emergency legislation have been part of a much longer line of exceptional measures directed against Irish people dating from the early nineteenth century (Hillyard 1993).

The women soon became known as 'hen patrols' or the 'bin lid brigades', forming communities of resistance. This is a good example of grassroots collective activism and had previously been employed by women in the 1950s living in public housing estates in Northern Ireland, who used the noise of their bin lids to warn neighbours of the visiting housing officials who would come unannounced to inspect their houses. This method was appropriated in the 1970s. The women organised a night-watch and sent out signals to women who were at home to bang the lids of rubbish bins on the pavement to warn the community of the British Army's entry into their neighbourhood.

Another woman states:

> Once you heard the bin lids going and you knew what area they were coming from, you sort of got to know the different sounds. So we used to hear them in Turf Lodge[5] and we'd say 'they're raiding Turf Lodge, they'll be here next'. So anybody who was staying in Ballymurphy moved out to a different area. So they [the IRA] *depended* on the women, big time.

From the early to mid-1970s, the women would announce the impending raid of the British Army in this way. Thus, whenever the British Army came into an area, women, children and young people were mobilised, taking to the streets, banging bin lids, shouting, chanting and blowing their whistles to warn people in the area that the British Army was approaching, which served to frighten and embarrass the young male soldiers. In this way, the women took up the very tools and symbols of their feminine roles to subvert the gendered power dynamic created by the soldiers invading their homes, instead asserting their control and ownership of the space.

By operationalising an effective warning system to protect their streets and communities, women demonstrated strength and unity against the broader structure of (military) gendered power which was simultaneously elided with the power relation between an Army of occupation and the Republican community as an occupied people. By moving from the pri-

---

[5] Turf Lodge is a predominantly Nationalist and Republican area which joins with the Falls Road in West Belfast.

vate space of the home to the public space of the streets, women began to occupy and transform gendered space (De-Pretis 2000)—a powerful illustration of situating Lefebvre's assertion that 'to change life.. we must first change space' (1991, p. 190). Women changed life—they subverted the rules governing gender and sexual relations. As Fanon concludes in his seminal book, 'she literally forged a new place for herself by her sheer strength' (1967/1970, p. 109).

Community Organisation

There were many reasons that prompted women into collective action. This poignant account of one young woman's political awakening is typical:

> I was 17. All I had ever thought was that I wanted to go to university but that night I kept thinking *somebody, somebody's going to come along.* You know the police will have to come along and arrest these soldiers and *stop them shooting. Stop them* shooting innocent people.
>
> There were 10 shots fired. I stood there, and people lay wounded for hours and no one could help them. That night passed, I mean it's very hard to know that your uncle and your friends and your friend's mother were lying wounded and you can't get near them. No one could get near them. They were lying there for hours, six, seven, eight hours. It was dark before their bodies were brought into the Army barracks.
>
> I was *filled with rage.* I kept waiting on some higher thought: the law. How, I thought the law would have to; someone's going to have to be arrested for these murders. Someone … but they weren't. Then the newspapers went, 'ELEVEN PEOPLE SHOT DEAD IN A GUN BATTLE', you know this was a mother with 10 kids. My Uncle Joe had 10 kids. A wee boy of 10. A priest giving people the last rites and yet the papers were full of this GUN BATTLE.
>
> I was there. I saw it. Then something in my head went fuck 'em. You know, they're [the British government] are supposed to be *making* the laws and they're [the British government] are *breaking laws.* Well, they are your fucking laws and I went and joined the Republican Movement.

I didn't come from a Republican family—a Socialist family maybe. But when I saw the indiscriminate shooting by the British Army—it just fucking made me mad and I *went and I joined and I wasn't on my own.* A lot of young people like me at that age went over and we joined the Republican Movement. So just seeing that, just witnessing the massacre. That's why I joined the Republican Movement. It was a reactionary thing for me but I don't regret it because six months later they [the British Army] done it again, with Bloody Sunday.[6] You know the same soldiers and the same regiment were involved. (Emphasis in original)

The above narrative demonstrates that it was a deep-seated sense of injustice and loss of belief in the law to deliver justice that forced women to mobilise and come to the defence of their community, family and friends.

One of the women recalls an incident that occurred when she was aged 11:

I remember the doors getting kicked in. I remember on one occasion I was home from school sick. I think I was about 11 years old, and the British Army raided our house looking for my brother, and he wasn't there. So they arrested my father and put him in the back of the Saracen and took him away, and left me in the house on my own. So you know all that and so it wasn't an upbringing of Republicanism.

I was shaped; I was *shaped* by the society. I mean what happened was *visited upon me and my community* which made me a Republican. (Emphasis in original)

Some of the women were born into a strong Republican family and others became involved because of their experience of oppression and suffering at the hands of the state: by experiences of displacement,

---

[6] On 30 January 1972 in the Bogside area of Derry, Northern Ireland, British soldiers shot 26 unarmed civilians during a protest march against internment. As a result, 14 people died: 13 males were killed outright, while the death of another man four-and-a-half months later was attributed to his injuries. Many of the victims were shot while fleeing from the soldiers and some were shot while trying to help the wounded. Two protesters were also injured when they were run down by British Army vehicles. The march had been organised by the Northern Ireland Civil Rights Association and the soldiers involved were mostly members of the 1st Battalion, Parachute Regiment, also known as '1st Para'.

educational disruption, curfews and poverty. The dawn raids, the harassment of young boys and girls and men forced the women into action because of the prevalent:

> Feeling of *injustice* and that we *were going to do something about it*. (Author's emphasis)

Another recalls:

> We came out in protest and I mean for me bin lidding was part of Republicanism. It alerted the community that houses were being raided. We immediately ran for our bin lids and whistles and surrounded the British Army and that to me was all *part of the struggle—that was Republicanism. That was resistance. That was fighting back.* I actively became a Republican in the sense of becoming a member of the IRA properly, when I was not much more than 16. (Emphasis in original)

Resistance to the state forces took many forms but, at the onset of internment, what became known as the 'hen patrols' became an effective form of organised direct action by women. These women can be described as 'accidental activists' or organic activists in the sense that they were involved in social change by resisting the conditions imposed by the military (Cohen 1993). Their activism was born out of the immediate experience of social injustice, rather than as a consequence of a pre-existing belief (Hackett 2004; Hyatt 1991). According to this notion, women who previously did not see themselves as in any way political became advocates and agents for social change (Williams 1995). The point here is that engaging in political action, brought about by responding to conflict, transformed women so that even those who did not previously see themselves as political and/or feminist, but who found themselves fighting for a cause, discovered how rewarding and important their contributions were (Paige 2008). Furthermore, where women are alienated or excluded from the formal political system, they become empowered and empower others by their activism. In many accounts, a shared theme was the need '*to do something*'.

A couple of women got together and said 'we have to do something. We'll take on a patrol', because the soldiers were coming in and arresting everyone around them. They were arresting pensioners and young people. They said we'll do a rota and we'll go out from, say, 12 o'clock at night to 4 am. These are women I'd probably think they were maybe in their forties and fifties. But yes, they were older, a lot older. So they went from 11pm to 4am or 11pm to 3am and then from 5pm to 11pm.

The women, they set up a system and it was like a 24 hour system but it was mostly to cover the night. And there would have been maybe 14 of them. We had a rota, say you do two hours then they come and let you go home, and the women used to go up to the top of Divis[7] flats, say three of them, and they had their whistles and their bin lids.

The women not involved in the night watch had an equivalent role to play:

So the women that weren't doing the patrol thing, they'd go out with their bin lids. So there was a whole racket. It was all over the place. So they had that system. It wasn't just sort of 'oh, we'll do it tonight and we'll not do it tomorrow night'. This went on for months.

The Hen Patrols[8]

Women in groups directly confronted the British Army patrols by showing communal solidarity. In this way, the women alerted the community—and active Republicans in particular—to the presence of the British Army, thus thwarting and de-stabilising military control in and over the community. As one woman describes:

---

[7] Divis Flats is a high rise block of flats named after the Divis Mountain in Belfast. It was a flash point during the Conflict.

[8] The women who participated in bin lidding were also labelled the 'petticoat brigade'; the name was also given to the women who formed the Ladies Land League to continue the campaign of Charles Stewart Parnell.

Every area got involved. It was *through necessity.* It really was. So when the soldiers came out the women followed them and then they were blowing whistles and then they took the bin lids out. (Author's emphasis)

Another woman details the impact of this type of resistance:

The women banged bin lids and whistled because of internment, because they [the British Army] were coming doing dawn raids and pulling people out of bed, and then that process continued. Any time the Army came on the streets of these estates the women would get out and rattle their bins and blow their whistles. So the IRA, the movement was warned when there were Brits about. So if they were carrying out operations or moving gear or anything, they knew where the Brits were because the women always gave them warning.

The women in the houses came out, if they saw something happening they *all* ran out and got round the soldiers. So the soldiers would have got a wee bit panicky because crowds of women came out and were lambasting and shouting at them. So nine times out of ten they walked the length of the fella and they [the soldiers] would walk away. Sometimes they didn't. Sometimes we just trailed a fella and that would just *throw* him.

AW: What did the troops do when they had a group of women following them?

I think they were afraid of the women! I really do think that some of them were really afraid. Some of them were very young soldiers and some were really nasty. But you knew some of the young ones didn't want to be here. They were embarrassed about it. Even when they were raiding houses some people would tell you that some soldiers apologised. While the others raided badly and destroyed everything, the other ones were saying 'I'm really sorry'. (Emphasis in original)

The hen patrols drew on their humour, solidarity and identification with similar areas to frighten the military and develop strategies to cope with the intimidation and violation of the public and private space. Through this act of resistance, there was a degree of delight derived from disempowering the soldiers. The humorous nickname 'duck patrols'

undermined the intimidating impact of military discipline by representing it as comical.

There are a number of interpretations as to where the names 'hen' and
'duck' patrols came from but the most common account was:

> I think it was because they all walked in a wee line. They [the British sol-
> diers] walked one behind each other. You just called them the duck patrol.

For others, the name 'ducks' developed because it was common for the
British soldiers to blacken out their faces when raiding or patrolling the
Nationalist/Republican areas.

As one woman states:

> When the British Army used to be in here and they would be patrolling at
> night, they would have blackened out their faces. Sometimes you wouldn't
> even see them. You could have stumbled over them and we used to call
> them "duck patrols". Then when the women came out with the bin lids
> they were called the "hen patrols".

The use of humorous nicknames such as 'duck patrols', quack-quacking
as the soldiers entered communities and singing 'Old MacDonald Had
A Farm' was a way of managing and, to a certain extent, subverting
what was otherwise a threatening situation. In the literature, it has been
argued that the use of humour or metaphoric assertions 'makes man-
ageable objects of the self and of others and facilitates the performance'
(Fernandez 1986, p. 6). The hen patrols, without a uniform, camouflage
or guns (they had only bin lids and whistles) were the antithesis of the
image of the highly structured British military. The women demystified
and counteracted the symbolic power of the British Army as they challenged practically the effects of state authoritarianism (Aretxaga 1997).

The gendered character of this metaphoric performance must not be
underestimated because it is the key to its subversive character. Hens are
known as 'naturally' chased creatures, and the derogatory term 'hen-pecked'
is used of a man who allows his supposed 'masculine' status and authority
to be compromised by a woman, who is thereby deemed to have transgressed her supposed 'feminine nature' as pliant and ineffectual. The term

'duck' is used colloquially to mean 'love' or 'dear' and, thus, can be deemed as patronising/infantilising, thereby challenging the power of the Army's intrusion. The humour evoked by the image of hens chasing male fowl psychologically transformed a threatening situation into a less fearful one and thereby brought the interaction between the soldiers and community members under a certain degree of control. This gender transformation created a space wherein action occurred and through which submission produced by fear was effectively counteracted (Kaufman and Williams 2010).

> As for politics … space, like identity, is contingent, differentiated, and relational, and … it thus makes little sense to conceive of any space as stabilised, fixed, and therefore outside of the possibility of counter hegemony. In this view, all space-identity formations are imbued with oppositional potential. And thus a practical task for politics is to activate this potential through denaturalisation, exposure, and contestation so as to achieve new appropriations and articulations of space and identity. (Jones and Moss 1995, p. 256)

Women observed that the British soldiers were unnerved by the destabilising impact of these encounters, and capitalised on a gendered assumption that the soldiers would be reluctant to beat them, hit them with rifle butts, sexually abuse them or shoot the women who were involved in some form of direct action. But, over time, this belief was challenged, with the death of Katie Thompson in 1971 (known by her friends as Kitty); the first woman to be shot dead while rattling a bin lid.

Women were propelled to the forefront of a struggle in which they could be shot, sexually harassed, sexually assaulted, brutalised, tortured and arrested. Women's resistance to the invasion of Nationalist, working-class areas by the British Army was not only spontaneous, but was also a non-hierarchal form of collective action which was shaped by, but also reconfigured and weaponised, women's traditional roles and identities. British soldiers responded with increasing violence against Republican women, underlining the erosion of gendered distinctions between support and combat roles. For the women represented in this book, they considered armed struggle as members of the Republican paramilitary as the only possible response to the daily struggle against militarised violence.

What the voices of the women and the men reveal is that women's resistance was not drawn from a separate quest for equality but, rather, from a symbiotic relationship to class, Nationalism, Republicanism, community and family, and thus transformed their roles within the family and community. Edgerton describes the position of women generally in Northern Ireland as one in which they are socialised into a strong maternal role directed to 'keeping the family together', 'making ends meet' and 'serving political campaigns largely determined by men' (1986, p. 61). Moreover, the patriarchal control of women is assisted by the more general political situation. Edgerton (1986, p. 43) comments: 'power gained outside the home may be deployed within it, adding an extra dimension to all of the means men normally have for oppressing women and engendering fear'. However, the political conflict has also acted to open spaces for women's resistance to traditional gender identities (Shirlow and Dowler 2010). Women's participation in the Conflict disturbed relationships of power between men and women within nationalism by, for example, challenging practices such as domestic violence and the political marginalisation of women's issues in nationalist cultures (Aretxaga 1997; Cockburn 1998; Coulter 1993; Dowler 1998; McWilliams 1995).

The role played by these female activists resonates with Gramsci's concept of the 'organic intellectual', who gives 'symbolic expression to the collective identity of the groups [s/he] represents', using their own political awareness to 'elaborate, political, social and cultural fields (Jones 2006, p. 84 cited in Mac Ionnrachtaigh 2013, p. 192; see also, Gramsci 1971). For example, women's participation in struggles for housing, prisoners' rights and civil rights in the Nationalist community politicised women and allowed them to develop skills that they later employed to challenge sexism and structures of gendered power in their own communities (Aretxaga 1997; McWilliams 1995). Similarly, in Latin America it was 'through direct confrontation with military regimes that women became aware of their own interests not only as members of working class sectors of society, but also as women' (Fisher 1993, p. 2). Their challenges have not been based predominantly on the desire to create an alternative destiny for women but, often, in resistance against the impossibility in these conflict situations of being a woman (Rowbotham 1992). As discussed elsewhere in this book, in Northern Ireland, women's membership in their national and ethnic collectivities is of a double nature (Yuval-Davis 1989, 1991, 1996). The devastation of the protracted Conflict has put massive pressure on women 'to maintain the community on the outside, the prisoners on the inside' (Barry 1998, p. 318) while confronting, on a daily basis, poverty, threat and violence. In addition, they were caught up in a gendered nexus in which women were affected by national and ethnic processes, in which there are always specific rules and regulations which relate to women as women.

Chapter 5 will outline the historical background to women's involvement in the Provisional Irish Republican Army (IRA) by focusing on the history of the women's Nationalist organisation Cumann na mBan[9] and its eventual absorption into the IRA. Subsequent chapters will show how these ordinary women in extraordinary circumstances created pathways to change by challenging traditional constructions of femininity and masculinity.

References

Amnesty International. (1978). *Report of an Amnesty International Mission to Northern Ireland (28 Nov–06 Dec. 1977)*. London: Amnesty International (Out of Print).

Amnesty International. (1991). *United Kingdom-Human Rights Concerns*. London: Amnesty International.

Aretxaga, B. (1997). *Shattering the silence: Women, nationalism and political subjectivity in Northern Ireland*. Princeton, NJ: Princeton University Press.

Ashe, F. (2007/2009). From paramilitaries to peacemakers: The gender dynamics of community-based restorative justice in Northern Ireland. *British Journal of Politics and International Relations, 11*(2), 298–314.

Barry, U. (1998). Women in Ireland. *Women Studies International Forum, 11*(4), 298–314.

Cockburn, C. (1998). *The space between us: Negotiating gender and national identities in conflict*. London: Zed Books.

---

[9] Cumann na mBan (women's association/organisation).

Cohen, C. (1993). War, wimps and women: Talking gender and thinking war. In M. Cooke & A. Wollacott (Eds.), *Gender war talk* (pp. 227–246). Princeton University Press, NJ.

Coogan, T. P. (2000). *The IRA*. London: Harper Collins.

Coulter, C. (1993). *The hidden tradition: Feminism, women and nationalism in Ireland*. Cork: Cork University Press.

De-Pretis, M. (2000). *To take arms in the armed patriarchy*. Unpublished paper presented at the Women and Law conference on Strategic Thinking for the Millennium, University of Westminster, London.

Devlin, B. (1971). *Barricades or ballot boxes*. Leicester: Leicester University Press.

Dickson, B. (Ed.). (1993). *The C.A.J handbook-civil liberties in Northern Ireland* (2nd ed.). Belfast: Committee on the Administration of Justice.

Dowler, L. (1998). And they think I'm just a nice old lady: Women and war in Belfast Northern Ireland. *Gender, Place and Culture, 5*(2), 159–176.

Edgerton, L. (1986). Public protest, domestic acquiescence: Women in Northern Ireland. In R. Ridd & H. Callaway (Eds.), *Caught up in conflict: Women's responses to political strife*. London: Macmillan.

Evason, E. (1991). *Against the grain: The contemporary women's movement in Northern Ireland*. Dublin: Attic Press.

Fairweather, E., McDonough, R., & McFaydean, M. (1984). *Only the rivers run free: Northern Ireland, the women's war*. London: Pluto.

Fanon, F. (1967/1970). *Black skin, white masks*. London: Pluto.

Farrell, M. (1980). *Northern Ireland: The orange state*. London: Pluto.

Fernandez, J. (1986). *Persuasions and performances: Of the beast in everybody and metaphors of everyman in persuasions and performance. The play of tropes in culture*. Bloomington: Indiana University Press.

Fisher, J. (1993). *Out of the shadows: Women, resistance and politics in South America*. London: Latin American Bureau.

Gramsci, A. (1971). *Selections from the prison notebooks*. New York: International Publishers.

Hackett, C. (2004). Narratives of political activism from women in West Belfast. In L. Ryan & M. Ward (Eds.), *Irish women and nationalism: Soldiers, new women and wicked hags*. Kildare: Irish Academic Press.

Harkin, C., & Kilmurray, A. (1985). Working with Women in Derry. In M. Abbott & H. Frazer (Ed.). Women In Community Work. Belfast: Farset Press.

Haug, F. (1989). *Lessons from the women's movement in Europe. Feminist Review*, 31, 109–128. Feminist.

Hillyard, P. (1993). *Suspect community*. London: Pluto.

Helsinki Watch. (1991). *Human rights in Northern Ireland*. New York: Human Rights Watch.

Hyatt, B. S. (1991). *Accidental activists: Women and politics on a council estate*. Amherst: Department of Anthropology, University of Massachusetts, Vol 4.

Jones, S. (2006). *Antonio Gramsci*. London: Taylor & Francis.

Jones, J. P., & Moss, P. (1995). Democracy, identity, space, environment and planning. *Society and Space, 13*(3).

Kaufman, J. P., & Williams, P. (2010). *Women and war: Gender identity and activism in times of conflict*. Sterling, VA: Kumarian Press.

Lefebvre, H. (1991). *The production of space*. London: Wiley-Blackwell.

Mac Ionnrachtaigh, F. (2013). *Language, resistance and revival: Republican prisoners and the Irish language in the North of Ireland*. London: Pluto.

McWilliams, M. (1995). Struggling for peace and justice: Reflections on women's activism in Northern Ireland. *Journal of Women's History, 6/7*(4/Winter/Spring), 13–39.

Newsinger, J. (1995). British Security Policy in Northern Ireland. *Race and Class, 37*(1), 83–94.

Paige, W. E. (2008). *From freedom fighters to terrorists: Women and political violence*. London: Ashgate.

Ridd, R., & Callaway, H. (Eds.). (1986). *Caught up in conflict: Women's responses to political strife*. Basingstoke: Macmillan Education in assoc. with the Oxford University women's Studies Committee.

Rowbotham, S. (1992). *Hidden from history: 300 Years of women's oppression and the fight against it*. London: Pluto.

Sales, R. (1997). *Women divided: Gender religion and politics in Northern Ireland*. London: Routledge.

Shirlow, P., & Dowler, L. (2010). 'Wee Women No More': Female partners of republican political prisoners in Belfast. *Environment and Planning, 42*, 384–399.

Yuval-Davis, N. (1989). National reproduction and the 'demographic race' in Israel. In N. Yuval-Davis & F. Anthias (Eds.), *Women nation state* (pp. 92–109). London: Macmillan.

Yuval-Davis, N. (1991). The citizens hip debate: Women ethnic processes and the state. *Feminist Review, 39*, 58–68.

Yuval-Davis, N. (1996). Women and the biological reproduction of 'the nation'. *Women Studies International Forum, 19*(1/2), 17–24.

5

From Footnote Soldiers to Front-Line Soldiers

Wars are mostly carried out by men, and it's very much a male-dominated environment. I suppose society doesn't particularly expect women to be involved on the frontline. It's expected that men will do that, not women. (Female Volunteer)

This chapter seeks to document the role of Cumann na mBan (Women's Association/Organisation), its subsequent demise, and the reasons behind the greater involvement of women in the Provisional Irish Republican Army[1] (PIRA) which, in turn, led to Cumann na mBan being absorbed into the PIRA. It will then chart the growing involvement of women and the challenges women faced in demanding the right to be treated as equals in the PIRA. It will be argued that, throughout the twentieth century, women played crucial roles operationally, behind the

---

[1] The Provisional Irish Republican Army has been referred to as Óglaigh na hÉireann (Gaelic for 'Irish Volunteers'), 'the Provos', the 'RA', 'IRA' (most commonly), 'Provies', 'Pinheads', 'Pinnies'. (These last two names are not meant to be derogatory: 'Pinheads' refers to the use of pins with which the traditional Easter Lilies have been attached to clothing to commemorate the original IRA's uprising in 1916; this contrasts with the sticky gum seen to be used by the Official IRA, hence their nickname 'stickies' or 'sticks'.

© The Editor(s) (if applicable) and The Author(s) 2016
A. Wahidin, *Ex-Combatants, Gender and Peace in Northern Ireland*,
DOI 10.1057/978-1-137-36330-5_5

scenes and on the front line. The second part of this chapter will focus on how women joined the Provisional IRA and the growing tensions between those women who demanded equality of status and women who 'were content to perform whatever services were demanded from them' (Ward 1995, p. 250).

The Soldiers of Cumann na mBan[2]

The inaugural public meeting of Cumann na mBan was held on 2 April 1914 in Wynne's Hotel in Dublin during a period of great political turmoil. The meeting was chaired by Agnes O'Farrelly,[3] who clearly outlined the role women were to play in the Nationalist movement, which was to 'put Ireland first, by helping to arm the men' (Ward 1995, p. 93).

She went on to state:

> Each rifle we put in their hands will represent to us a bolt fastened behind the door of some Irish home to keep out the hostile stranger. Each cartridge will be a watchdog to fight for the sanctity of the hearth. (*The Irish Volunteer*, 18 April 1914)

In this assertion, O'Farrelly strikingly encapsulates the shaping of ideals of womanhood by conditions of resistance to occupation and, indeed, the way the ideal of women as protectors of 'hearth and home' is invoked in articulating the ethno-nationalist identities which inspire and sustain militarised resistance. The contradictory effects on the position of women are clear, as they are simultaneously radicalised (and to a degree militarised) to the Nationalist cause while thereby being confirmed in their gendered roles both as practical supporters and as symbolic icons of the cultural identity inspiring the (male) fighters. In some ways, this parallels—ironically—to the development of bourgeois ideals of femi-

---

[2] The title is taken from the song: '*The soldiers of Cumann na mBan*'. '*All honour to Óglaigh na hÉireann, all praise to the men of our race … Their loyal and true hearted comrades the soldiers of Cumann na mBan*'.

[3] Agnes O'Farrelly, Professor of Irish at University College Dublin (UCD). She was also the first female Irish-language novelist and a founding member of Cumann na mBan.

ninity in Imperialist Britain, and the way that gendered discourses have been mobilised by the British government in the service of 'patriotism' (in particular, in the First World War and, later, notoriously, the German Nazi regime). The conditions of Republican activism opened up spaces for women to contest these gendered constraints, ultimately contributing to wider changes in women's social and political status. However, the history of Cumann na mBan clearly demonstrates that there is nothing new about Nationalist women insisting on the right to bear arms on the same terms as men, perhaps suggesting that the gendered ideological basis for women's involvement was sometimes contradicted by the practice (and practicalities) of the military campaign.

The constitution of the Cumann na mBan reiterated the parameters of the supporting role women were expected to play. This came under the following three headings.

1. **Military**: First Aid classes, signaling, drill, scouting, cleaning and the unloading of rifles when practicable;
2. **Educational**: Irish language and the history classes, conduct of public affairs;
3. **Social and Commercial**: Formation of Dáil Eireann, Loan Clubs, running of Aeridheachta, Céilidthe, Displays, Concerts, or sales to develop a Gaelic social life and to make their branch financially solid (Conlon 1969, p. 305).

Although the inaugural meeting was small due to the lack of publicity and its starting at 4:00 pm, the *Irish Times* estimated that: 'there were about 100 ladies present' (*Irish Times*, 3 April 1914) and, by 1920, it was estimated to have in excess of 3000 members (Ward 1995, p. 156). It was a female-only auxiliary to the Irish Volunteer Army, carrying out support work for the Irish Volunteers. Cumann na mBan absorbed Inghinidhe na hÉireann (Daughters of Erin), which was the first all-women's group, founded in the 1900s. The most famous member of Inghinidhe na hÉireann was Maud Gonne and, although the latter had a militant commitment to the struggle for Irish freedom from British rule, their aim was to address the exclusion of Nationalist women from all existing Nationalist organisations of that time. They remained a separate branch of the Irish

Republican Brotherhood until merging with Cumann na mBan at the time of the latter's formation in 1914.

A Convention of the Cumann na mBan was held in Dublin on 31 October 1915. Among other matters dealt with was the adoption of a green uniform with a slouch cap. It was outlined in the record of the Convention that: 'A uniform was adopted and it was resolved that the use of the uniform be optional, but that none other be adopted by the branches. It consists of a coat and skirt of Volunteer tweed and hat of same, four pockets in coat, skirt at least seven inches off the ground, tweed or leather belt, haversack with first aid outfit. A grey or green felt hat and a haversack are recommended where a uniform is not possible. Members of Cumann na mBan are in honour bound to give preference when purchasing to goods of Irish manufacture' (Conlon 1969, p. 16). In the early years, many members made their own uniforms from 'Volunteer' tweed. When Cumann na mBan first paraded in uniform, they were pelted with mud and stones by the wives of British soldiers and were given 'the undignified name of grasshoppers' (Chumhaill 1933).

Cumann na mBan was divided between members who were inspired by the British suffragette movement and believed that they could combine the struggle for Irish freedom with women's rights in terms of both social and economic power, and other founding members such as Louise Gavan Duffy, who believed that women's social and economic rights took second place to the struggle for independence. The suffragist-Nationalist position contributed to Cumann na mBan's refusal to accept the Anglo-Irish Treaty: their desire was not just for the creation of the Republic, but also for the freedom and equality promised to Irish women in the Proclamation at the 1916 Easter Rising, which asserted 'religious and civil liberty, equal rights and equal opportunities to all [Ireland's] citizens', and a commitment to universal suffrage (not fully achieved in the UK until 1928).

During the War of Independence (1919–1921), Cumann na mBan branches became affiliated to units of the IRA and became 'an army of women' (Conlon 1969, p.15) and, by 1921, the organisation had established over 800 branches (Conlon 1969, p. 16). In 1920, the Government of Ireland Act was passed; this partitioned Ireland and cemented the split in the IRA between those in favour and those opposed to partition. Following the Anglo-Irish Treaty of 1921, which ended the Irish War of Independence by setting up the Irish Free State as a self-governing dominion within the British Empire, the vast majority of Cumann na mBan remained with the anti-treaty Volunteers during the resultant Civil War of 1922–1923. The new 'Free State' defeated the anti-Treaty forces and, in the aftermath of the Civil War, 11,000 Republican men and women remained interned and the Dáil continued to enforce repressive legislation to quash the efforts of the IRA and of the Cumann na mBan. Membership declined and so did the availability of armoury as members were imprisoned for their involvement.

In October 1922, the Catholic Church had excommunicated Cumann na mBan members and all other militant Republicans (Brady et al. 2011, p. xii). Many imprisoned women and men had trouble gaining the rights of Holy Communion during their prison terms since the Catholic Church condemned anti-treaty forces. The only way Republican prisoners were allowed to take Communion was by accepting the priest condemning the activities of the 'irregulars'. In opposition, the women stood up to Church figures and challenged the Church's attempt to coerce women into surrendering their political beliefs by withholding their sacred rites. In a letter written by Mary MacSwiney to Archbishop Edward Bryne of Dublin, she stated this was: 'unjust, irreligious, I can no more deny the justice of the cause of Joan of Arc. The Bishops got her burned as a heretic to please England but the Church has now declared her one of God's saints' (Walsh 1990, pp. 80). Margaret Buckley likewise challenged a priest who refused to hear her confession: 'I told him I would likely be going on hunger strike, that I hoped I would die on it rather than give in, and now I placed all my sins on him' (Buckley 1938, p. 30).

These challenges to the Church officials show that although the women were very religious, they despised the Church's attempts to control their behaviour by refusing them Communion and confession. In general, the women felt that the Church abused its power by refusing them their most basic religious rights.

In terms of military involvement, approximately 90 women had participated in the Easter Rising 1916, including 60 Cumann na mBan members (Eager 2008).They were largely deployed in medical aid, procuring rations, as dispatch couriers, in scouting or intelligence operations or transferring arms; but some also engaged in direct combat roles including sniper attacks, armed raids and bombings. The 1916 rebel Frank Henderson nevertheless recalled the role Cumann na mBan women played in the Dublin rising in terms of the medical and culinary help that they offered the men. He states that 'they [the women] cooked our food and served it to us' (Henderson and Hopkinson 1998, pp. 58–61).

By 1922, apparently little had changed: 'the Cumann na mBan … are providing comforts for the prisoners as their resources allow' (IRA Report, 2 October 1922). The IRA's Tom Barry praised the women's organisation as being invaluable to the IRA in the War of Independence but, in doing so, he set out their decidedly auxiliary role. The Cumann na mBan:

> were groups of women and girls from the town and countryside, sisters, relatives or friends of the Volunteers, enrolled in their own organisation, for the sole purpose of helping the Irish Republican Army. They were indispensable to the army, nursing the wounded and sick, carrying dispatches, scouting acting as intelligence agents, arranging billets, raising funds, knitting, washing, cooking for the active service men and burying our dead. (Barry 1995, pp. 208–209)

The IRA Commandant Brennan also noted the role the Cumann na mBan played in both the War of Independence, which preceded the formation of the Irish Free State, and in the resultant Civil War, observing that 'the IRA flying columns would have collapsed without Cumann na mBan' (Ward 1989, p. 260).

The roles of Cumann na mBan women extended to holding political office in the self-proclaimed Irish Republic, with Countess Markievicz being elected to the First Dáil in the 1918 General Elections, joined in the 1921 Irish Elections by fellow Cumann na mBan members Mary MacSwiney, Ada English and Kathleen Clarke. Following partition, the problem of the Six Counties[4] attracted the attention of many of the more political Cumann women. Veteran member Márie Comerford[5] stated in an interview in the 1970s:

---

[4] The Six Counties of Northern Ireland are: Antrim, Armagh, Down, Fermanagh, Derry and Tyrone.

[5] Márie Comerford was an Irish Republican who worked as a journalist at De Valera's newspaper the Irish Press and witnessed the creation of the First Dáil.

People refer to the emancipation of Ireland as though Freedom has already been won. But if a man is handcuffed or tied by the foot to another man or to something else, is he a free man? Can Ireland be held to be free while a portion of her territory is held? The partitioned area includes Armagh, the ecclesiastical capital of Ireland. It includes the crowning place of the O'Neills, the kings of Ireland, and it includes areas inhabited by the people with the most ancient Gaelic traditions. And they're all abused, treated as inferiors. They have been deprived of houses and of votes. They've been gerrymandered and every crime in the calendar of civil rights has been committed against them ... Partition has made it impossible for the nation to develop, impossible to have democracy and impossible to have anything in the country but civil war. This evil has been persistent for many years. It came to the surface in 1968 and 1969 with the demand for civil rights, and the consequent attack on the nationalist population has meant that men have again had to take up arms to defend their people. It is a defensive war and—I love to hear this repeated as often as possible—it is generally admitted that the guerrilla cannot be defeated. So obviously, I would like to see Britain withdraw her troops and partition end. (Griffith and O'Grady 1999, pp. 357–358)

The following section will examine women's involvement in the IRA.

Breaking with the Old: My Coat Is Swinging in the Door[6]

'By the late 1960s as the tensions and conflicts in Northern Ireland heightened, many women had already become disillusioned with their subsidary role (Alison 2004) and the strict parameters set by Cumann na mBan. They sought to play a more 'pro-active role' by joining Óglaigh na h-Éireann (Irish Volunteers), which at the beginning provided the main source of membership for the IRA's active service units (ASU's). By joining or being co-opted into the IRA they were far more likely to engage in front-line activities (Talbot, 2004) than their Cumann na mBan comrades. Women's involvement in the IRA was prominent in the

---

[6] Personal communication with Eibhlín Glenholmes.

Table 2 Gender density across time; percentage within recruitment phase

Recruitment	Phase				
		1969–1976	1977–1980	1981–1989	1990–1998
Gender	Female (%)	5.1	2.9	6.3	3.4
	Male (%)	94.9	97.1	93.7	96.6

Source: Gill and Horgan (2013), p. 443.

early 1970s, with women accounting for 1 in 20 Volunteers recruited in the period 1969-1976 (Gill and Horgan, 2013: 443; see Table 2). From as early as 1970–1972, women were joining the Irish Republican Army and, from 1973, the number of women internees grew.[7] During 1969–1970, the IRA had split from the Original IRA[8] into two separate organisations: the Provisional IRA and the Official[9] IRA (English 2003). The Provisional IRA is the organisation generally referred to as the Irish Republican Army. The Official IRA had a strong socialist ideology and was the first of the two organisations to give its female members opportunities as combatants. The Officials disbanded Cumann na mBan and the women were accepted into the Officials. Ex-members of the Official IRA have stated that women were trained in all its activities. The Provisionals initially maintained Cumann na mBan as a separate organisation.

In 1975, another split occurred in the Officials which led to the formation of a new organisation, the Irish National Liberation Army (INLA). Many women Volunteers who joined INLA were women who had belonged neither to the Officials nor to the Provisionals, but saw INLA and its political wing, the Irish Republican Socialist Party (IRSP), as an alternative to the other organisations. This new rival to the Provisional IRA never really attracted women Volunteers.

---

[7] Northern Ireland Civil Rights Association (1973). No women were interned until 1973. Liz McKee was the first woman to be interned in January 1973.

[8] The Original IRA was born from the 1916 Easter Rebellion in Dublin.

[9] The 'Provisional IRA', became the largest Republican armed grouping. The Irish National Liberation Army (INLA) was formed as a faction group from the Officials but has declared a ceasefire. The Continuity IRA and the Real IRA emerged in the wake of the 1994 Real IRA ceasefire. Éirígí is the Socialist Republican Party.

As a separate organisation, Cumann na mBan had its own women's leadership, structure and rules. Although they and the IRA were fighting a common cause, tensions arose from being a separate organisation that nevertheless shared some common activities. Even though women were seconded into the IRA—which meant that they were on active service—they were denied the status of full members and thus regarded as inferior. However, with the restructuring of the IRA women could also be accepted into the organisation on 'an equal basis with men … [although] it is unlikely that many have attained high military ranking' (Ward 1989, pp. 258–259).

After the 1969 split in the Irish Republican Movement, Cumann na mBan became the women's auxiliary section of the IRA, and the women were: 'to act as auxiliaries for the old Irish Volunteers' (Ward 1995, p. 120). According to Moloney (2003, p. 55), their role in the early merger acted as the:

> IRA equivalent to being stuck in the kitchen and the bedroom; they carried messages and smuggled weapons and explosives and they nursed wounded IRA Volunteers. They could be useful for gathering intelligence and carrying weapons, but they did little, if any, actual fighting.

The Armagh Prison reception records suggest this statement is questionable, and that women were, in reality, involved in quite serious operations from the start (for example, as the makers of bombs, and even detonating them).

Although Cumann na mBan was part of the same structure, they largely provided the support networks to IRA activities: membership of Cumann na mBan did not necessarily mean full membership of the IRA. The Cumann na mBan were defined as an auxiliary organisation with a partially separate but subordinate command structure but, at the same time, an organisation in which Cumann na mBan members were ipso facto members of the PIRA. Thus, in the initial stages of the merger, the women had a separate status and, as Corcoran notes, their role: 'was subordinated within the Republican structure' (2006a, p. 6; see Brady et al. 2011 and also Buckley and Loughran 1984). This point was made by several of the women in the study, as this testimonial demonstrates:

> Although the Cumann na mBan were affiliated to the IRA, they had a different manifesto. A different structure. The women were responsible for certain activities but they were there to help the IRA men to carry weapons.

The women's roles varied and included gathering intelligence, scouting and providing warnings to IRA members of the presence of the British Army (Sales 1997). Another woman recalls one of her roles as a Volunteer:

> You might have been standing doing nothing, just looking out. I would call out, '*dick at the corner*', which meant British soldiers coming along if our lads were going to do an operation or something of that nature. Just warn them that the Brits were close.

The activities of the female Volunteers included acting as decoys and posing as part of a couple (Bloom 2011). Another woman states:

> If there was an operation going on they might have got us to get into a kissing position and be the decoy, if you like.

The women acted as 'honey-pot traps', luring British soldiers to apartments, into cars or down alleyways where they were assassinated (Dillon 1999, p. 211 passim; see also *Sunday World*, 6 September 1981). One Volunteer was labelled by the *Belfast Telegraph* as the IRA's Mata Hari (*Belfast Telegraph* 2009).

The same woman goes on to say:

> We were weapon carriers. We would have brought weapons to houses, take them away, and I just *wasn't* very happy with that. I felt [the Cumann na mBam] was very restrictive. Very conservative, as was the IRA to a degree but not as closed as Cumann na mBan.

Another woman illustrates the secondary status that women played within the movement:

Cumann na mBan women would have been part of the structure. Yes, they would have been but not an *equivalent*. What I mean by that is the IRA would have *used* us. We would be *used*—standing at the corner with a Volunteer.

As this woman's testimonial illustrates, the secondary role led to frustration:

We were very *annoyed* by the role of Cumann na mBan. I mean … there was a feeling that we were *not seen as equals*, but half the time we did *do stuff* but it wasn't official.

I mean, you'd be with a really young fella and God love him he'd be so nervous that he couldn't actually fire the weapon. So, I know a few girls who'd done the shooting and all that. *But we did resent this.* You know, and there was a *strong feeling on the ground that this wasn't fucking going to go on any longer.* So the women did object and Cumann na mBan was disbanded and the women were incorporated into the Army.

Another woman disillusioned by the gender stereotypes and traditional mind-set of Cumann na mBan gave her reasons for leaving and for joining the Army:

You got to *do more* in the Army. In Cumann na mBan, you got to go on camps and you *learnt* how to use weapons and different things, but with the Army it was the *real thing*. You were in there doing the *real thing*. Doing what they [the men] were doing. You got *to do* more. You learnt more and you got *more respect*.

I just went into the Army. I went into 'A' Company and I never bothered with Cumann na mBan. Just stayed doing what I was doing—we were known as the sleepers.[10]

The various divisions also began to show in Cumann na mBan, with some women joining the Official IRA and many others becoming members of the IRA (De-Pretis 2000). Disillusionment and disaffection arose

---

[10] A sleeper cell comprises of sleeper Volunteers because they lie dormant until the cell receives orders to act.

because of conflict between the leadership of Cumann na mBan and the IRA. For example, in emergency situations, Cumann na mBan members were expected to get clearance from the leadership before going on any form of active service and, at times, this was not possible. This would mean women were being disciplined, which was one of the reasons why they left to join the IRA; others 'found Cumann na mBan to be very traditional'.

> I found Cumann na mBan to be very *traditional*. This is going to sound awful. I found Cumann na mBan to be in some ways very *oppressive* to women. I mean, they seemed to be happy to go along with women's *secondary* status. I found we were too accountable. In contrast the IRA Volunteers just seemed to be able to operate, obviously within the remit of the IRA but ... I'll give you one example that might explain it better. I had a friend who was in the Cumann na mBan, who fell pregnant at 17 and she was dismissed straight away. The fella that she married later was an IRA Volunteer and he remained in the movement. (Emphasis in original)

The organisation reinforced traditional gender roles and symbolically highlighted gender differences which the women fought to erase by taking on the role as soldiers. In all the women's testimonials, they illustrate the secondary status of the organisation and also the double standards that surrounded women's sexuality.

Other women who were operating under the two organisations found themselves court-martialled for operating outside the confines of prescribed typifications of femininity and sexuality, as stipulated by Cumman na mBan.

> I had no concept that there were two different Movements. That there was the IRA, and Cumman na mBan. I ended up in Cumman na mBan. In hindsight, I wish I had have been in the IRA because I found Cumann na mBan to be a hindrance in that the Cumann na mBan always wanted to know what you were *doing*, and I was working in the IRA, in a structure where nobody was to know what you were doing. So I used to get a lot of trouble for not reporting them.
>
> What happened at that time, was that a lot of girls left Cumman na mBan and moved into the ranks of IRA.

Within the Cumman na mBan there was resistance by members against keeping its identity and function separate to that of the IRA. Tension in terms of structure, activities and the demand made by the women to be integrated into the IRA as full members was beginning to highlight the need for Cumman na mBan to be absorbed into the IRA. The IRA leadership was facing growing pressure from the women themselves, sympathetic men in the movement, and a realisation for the need to have 'some military trained women' (Ward 1989, p. 259). The demands of war meant that women were needed. The statement below summarises the feeling of many women:

> It suited my life better to be an IRA Volunteer than it did to be in Cumann na mBan because *I* could influence the road that *I took*. (Emphasis in original)

Although the women were operating outside of the traditional gender roles as active Volunteers, they also faced innumerable sexist attitudes from some of their male comrades who believed that women 'should play a more subordinate role and not become full combatants':

> The Army was *for* the men, so that was really funny too because you found yourself going with the guy—they fired the weapon and then you were handed this weapon to take away. You were handed the weapon. You weren't allowed to actually *do* the firing of the weapon even though you were a better shot than the man.
> So you were taking the weapon away after the shooting or you were used to carry a bomb because you were a girl. You [would be] dressed nice and you could get into places that maybe a young fella wouldn't have got in. You know you're nicely dressed and you could get a bomb into the city centre.

Another perceives the role of women as helpers, helping to fight the war the men were fighting:

> We women were *helpers* to the IRA. To *help* them fight the war that *they were fighting*. To get the Brits out of Ireland.

> I think we *were* seen as *helpers* but in a lot of cases they [the IRA] did need women—like being in a car and going across the border. It didn't look right two men driving across the border. But if it was a man and woman there, you know, you're a couple. The Brits wouldn't be as suspicious. So you had a better chance with a woman there, *so we were needed*. We definitely were *needed*. (Emphasis in original)

The above testimonial demonstrates how constructions of hetero-normative masculinity opened up possibilities for women to move through spaces with ease 'that maybe a young fella wouldn't have got in'. Within the spatialities of struggle, women moved through spaces in an unthreatening, silent way, (un)noticed and almost invisible to the gaze of British state forces. Many women resented the subsidiary and conventional gender role they were expected to play.

The above woman further adds:

> If I was either going to go to prison or die in the struggle then I wanted it to be in the IRA because you could quite easily, even as a Cumann na mBan person, be shifting a weapon from A to B down your trousers. You're going to do 10 years if you got caught. So I just didn't want to be moving the weapon from A to B. What I wanted to do was to *use* the weapon and then move it to B, *on my own* and be a *very proactive Volunteer*.
>
> So that's the only thing that I didn't like about the Cumann na mBan and that's why I wanted to move into the IRA structure. My careers officer at school said to me, I should join the British Army, meaning the WREN,[11] and I obviously followed his instructions. I joined the Army -the IRA!' (We laugh). (Emphasis in original)

Another states:

> Cumann na mBan, was mainly a women's structure, and I decided to join the Army. I did so because I think that there was both a perception that the women in Cumann na mBan were being *used to assist those people who were*

---

[11] WREN: The Women's Royal Naval Service (officially known as the Wrens) was the women's branch of the United Kingdom's Royal Navy. First formed in 1917 for the First World War, it was disbanded in 1919, then revived in 1939 at the beginning of the Second World War, remaining active until it was integrated into the Royal Navy in 1993.

fighting as opposed to being able to fight themselves, and I decided that *I wanted to actively become involved* and therefore *I didn't join Cumann na mBan, I joined the IRA.* (Emphasis in original)

As all the testimonials illustrate, the women resented the idea, and were frustrated by the constraints of gender-role expectations and the traditional attitudes held by those women that remained in Cumann na mBan (Bloom 2011; Bloom et al. 2012). The paradox of the gender constructions espoused at the time is that the women could carry and hold the gun but not point and shoot.

These views were shared by the women in the study and are echoed in Brady et al. (2011, p. 20), who states that the contradictory gender role expectations oscillated between 'a combination of respect for women and the commonly held belief that women were faint-hearted species'; but, at the same time, the IRA utilised heteronormative perceptions and societal norms regarding women's femininity, domesticity and sexuality to its advantage. The reluctance on the part of the state security forces to search women—in particular, women with babies (because of the negative publicity attached to this)—was one of the key factors enabling women to play a central role in transporting, moving, hiding and storing weapons and explosives because they were less likely to be stopped and searched than their male comrades.

The above are examples of how gendered constructions were utilised by the IRA. A senior male Volunteer states:

Depending what was required to be done, there were activities which were specific and really only ever carried out by women.

That was gender based *but it was tactical and it was smart.* (Emphasis in original)

AW: Why?

You only differentiated for specific operations, and I'm not homophobic but you wouldn't have sent two males to a location or I wouldn't have gone with a male to a location. It would always have been better with a woman, and I don't mean that in sexist terms. It's just we were able to go and do whatever we'd to do easier with a woman.

There were times when women had to be specifically a woman. It was just whatever had to be done. It wasn't gender-based. It was whoever was available. But by the laws of whatever the hell it is in society, there were always proportionately far more men in the IRA than women and that probably would be reflected internationally. (Author's emphasis)

The next section will examine the role of female Volunteers in the IRA and how the operation of gender was negotiated by the movement.

Fighting Two Battles: No Longer Footnote Soldiers

The increasing number of women involved in the IRA was resisted by some men but was driven by a number of factors: changing gender attitudes, pressure from the women, recognition by the leadership for the need to have some military-trained women as more young men were interned or died in combat, and there was a strategic need to have more fighters. This, and the fact that IRA male officers were providing women with military training, led to women becoming integrated into the IRA, particularly from the mid-1970s onwards (Buckley and Loughran 1984; Morgan 1995). The women fought to be treated as equals and to have an equal political identity as front-line soldiers. This had the effect of culturally desexualising them as women by reasserting that gender and their position as women could be rejected as a differentiating factor in political militancy. They were after all, '*IRA Volunteers and at war*'. But although the women fought to be treated as the *same* and as *equals*, in practice their gender continued to differentiate them.

> Once, I told them I'm as good a woman as you are a man, they didn't like it and I said what is it that you can do that I can't?

For some, they felt that the training and inclusion in certain activities was restricted on the sole basis of their gender. One woman recounts how she was excluded and was made to feel her gender and, in turn, her difference.

> No, they didn't treat us as they would their male counterparts. But when I joined the IRA, the training camps we went to would have been the same as the men. But no, we were never treated as equal, never.

AW: Can you give me an example?

> I would be in a call house sometimes as the only woman and *sometimes* I was completely left out of conversations—ordinary conversation. They [male Volunteers] maybe would have brought me into the conversation. I always felt it was this attitude '*she's only a woman*'. No matter what you had done. What you had been involved in, and it didn't matter who the man was, it was always there.
>
> I don't ever remember meeting one and thinking to myself, 'you're entirely different from anyone that I have met before. And it didn't matter … apparently X broke the mould. My own father was an out and out feminist and I wasn't used to being treated like a second class citizen by men, because I wasn't treated like that in my own home'. (Emphasis in original)

Another female Volunteer touches on the theme of cultural 'conservatism' within the movement which idealises women but, at the same time, denigrates and denies them status as comrades:

> 'The sexism was rampant. I know of incidents where remarks were made to women which were very derogatory and I remember one incident, a girl coming to my home crying over something that had been said to her. There were men who were great, but in general there was still that attitude, that very conservative male Irish thing that the men did the fighting'.

AW: Where did that come from?

> I just think that was a very Irish thing. Although women are celebrated all throughout the struggle. I think there was always this feeling that we were secondary. Women played their part, obviously. It was a very *necessary* part. Men, for the most part, wouldn't have been shipping guns from house to

house. I *never* remember ever in my life ever sitting in a house anywhere with men and just feeling as an *equal* or being talked to the *same way as other men in the room* would have been spoken to. *We had to fight very hard to be seen as equals.* (Emphasis in original)

Although women's involvement became more prominent over time, on reflection:

There were *never* that many women giving out orders anyway, not that I ever remember. I would say in certain operations some women would have held higher ranks than men that were involved. But that would be *very, very* rare. *Women were never treated as equals, and they're not now.* (Emphasis in original)

Others, though, felt that they *were* treated as equals:

AW: And did your male comrades treat you with the same respect as they did their fellow comrades?

Absolutely, yes—probably more so. Still to this day there is a lot of respect from the men because I carried out my tasks.

Another woman asserts the collective identity:

We were IRA Volunteers and we were at war. So there was *a lot* of camaraderie, there was *a lot of looking out for each other.* (Emphasis in original)

Another woman states:

I never found any doors closed because I was a woman. Anything, that I wanted to learn or do *I did.* I was treated as an *equal.* (Emphasis in original)

Resistance to women's involvement was generally felt to come from the 'old school, who found it difficult'. These were men who were 'tremendously conservative, and if the male ideal was the Republican martyr then the female ideal was the devoted Republican wife and mother' (Aretxaga 1997, p. 151). Since, however, the IRA leadership recognised the need to have militarily trained women (Ward 1989, p. 258), the 'old school' had 'out of necessity' to adjust:

> The young fellas were absolutely fine about it. It was the *old school* that would have found difficult, but the *old school were going*. There were a few older ones that were fine, but you know, it was out of *necessity*.
>
> If I'm not treated equally as a man, I'm *not* doing it. So they [the men] had to *make* the adjustments and also the young fellas the same age as myself had *no* bother about it. (Emphasis in original)

Other women would:

> Not take crap from men.

A senior female ex-combatant describes how she had to earn the respect of male comrades before being treated as an equal.

AW: Did you ever get any?

> Seriously, in my time, no. Any people I worked with, especially in the cells,[12] treated me with respect. At the early start of the Conflict they were 'do this and do that'. [I'd say] 'Well, would you do it?' So you learn. You would maybe come across men who would push their luck, 'I don't think so. Hello. Can you do it?' So they would soon realise that 'she's no mug. She knows her stuff'. I knew what I was doing. (Emphasis in original)

Two key male members of the IRA, Seán McStiofáin[13] (1975, p. 217) and Bik MacFarlene, had broken with previous Republican views on women's roles on the basis that British military strategists had 'failed to appreciate' the contribution of women in other colonial struggles 'because they came from societies in which women's contributions are usually underrated'. From the early 1970s:

> A selected number of suitable women were taken into the IRA and trained … on the basis of full equality with men … Some of the best shots I ever

---

[12] Cells are groupings of agents working within a sub-group of a larger structure.

[13] Seán McStiofáin was the Provisional IRA's Chief of Staff, a position he held from 1969 to 1972.

knew were women. So were the smartest intelligence officers in Belfast …
[I]n support roles, the Women's Action Committees were very effective
organisers of demonstrations, early warning networks, and alarms. (ibid.,
p. 218)

Shannon states that 'from [the early 1970s] women were admitted [to
the IRA] on the basis of full equality with men, as in the Israeli, Chinese,
and other armed forces' (1989, p. 12). The effect of the incorporation of
women into all aspects of the IRA conveys the message that women 'are
(symbolically) equal members of the collectivity, and that all members of
the collectivity are symbolically incorporated into the military' (Yuval-
Davis 1997, p. 98).

In the early years of the Conflict, conservative Catholic ideology still
persisted amongst some of the older male Republican Volunteers, and
older women Volunteers seem more likely to have experienced sexism
than those in later years (Ryan and Ward 2004). Although some women
in the study acknowledged sexism in the movement, others rationalised/
neutralised this behaviour and a few agreed with Seán MacStiofáin's claim
that they were, indeed, treated the same as men.

An anonymous female Volunteer told Fairweather et al. (1984, p. 241):

I am very conscious of being a woman Volunteer. Within the Army you
have to assert your position to be treated equally. You are constantly fighting this battle for equal status, and it's a very persistent one at that, particularly with the newer members.

It still shocks me that I have two battles to fight—one against the Brits
and secondly with the men of my own organisation.

As the women became highly trained in the use of modern weapons,
making explosives and moving weaponry to areas that needed protection,
and rarely breaking under interrogation, in their fight for equal treatment
they had to battle against sexism and discrimination. Unlike their male
comrades, the women had to prove their ability (Alison 2009). As the
voices of the women demonstrate, they were there because men had
allowed (or even co-opted) them to be, not because they were entitled to
be there. Ward writes:

While women were undoubtedly valuable and valiant fighters within the Nationalist movement, one important qualification needs to be kept in mind ... the high points of women's participation were also moments of exceptional political crisis, when women were either drawn into the movement because of the temporary (enforced), absence of men, or they were encouraged to participate because a strong, united front was needed and because women, when the military struggle began, were also needed for essential back-up service. (1982, p. 2; see Cockburn 2001, p. 21)

The above statement is echoed by the women Volunteers in the study:

I did at times, and I hate to say it, but sort of the traditional male resented our young women. But at the same time too when they saw the outcome and it worked: they [the men] couldn't do anything else but accept that *we were in the IRA*. (Emphasis in original)

Later she states:

There were sexist norms from some of the men. The [IRA] wasn't a universal place where you found that equality shone through. It was different to the world in which we live in now. There were attitudes that reflected society which found expression within the structures that we operated in. There were challenges that you had to put to your male comrades. Sometimes you had to *fight the fight*. You had to *demand your right to a place* and you weren't some kind of an *addendum* or an *add-on*. But that said, there were other male comrades who treated you absolutely equally. (Emphasis in original)

Up to 1977 and before the reorganisation of IRA, the women in the movement were given greater responsibility for playing a variety of roles from being a member of IRA's General Headquarters[14]; Army Council, officers, officers in command and battalion officers, to name a few. After the restructure was made within IRA, there was a reduction of women taking front-line roles and fewer women were recruited. The 'Staff Report' documents the organisational changes by stating:

---

[14] The General Head Quarters consisted of 5–60 individuals tasked with 'overall maintenance and conduct of IRA activities as directed by Army Council policies' (Horgan and Taylor 1997, p. 9).

Cumann na mBan [PIRA's female unit], we propose, should be dissolved with the best being incorporated in IRA cells structure and the rest going into Civil and Military administration. (cited in Coogan 2000, pp. 465–467)

Conclusion

There is a long illustrious history of women's involvement in Irish Republicanism beginning with Inghinidhe na hÉireann,[15] Cumann na gCailíní,[16] and Cumann na mBan which facilitated the involvement of generations of women by allowing women access to important political debates at all levels of the struggle. However, the aim of this book is to address the absence of a comprehensive understanding of women combatants which includes knowledge of their motivations, roles and experiences.

Women transgressed and destabilised traditional boundaries of femininity by entering the public sphere of warfare. This process challenges patriarchal relationships in the move to be recognised as equals in opposition to British rule and in terms of transformational citizenship (Alison 2004; Benjamin 1998; Kiluva-Ndunda 2004). Na gCailíní and Cumann na mBan acted as 'a feeder for the IRA, first-level indoctrination units, and for some, especially in the Republic, simply a scouting opportunity' (Bowyer Bell 1997, p. 163). The women provided significant military assistance to the Irish Volunteers/IRA and many hundreds of women throughout the country played active and essential roles in the guerrilla war (ibid.). Cumann na mBan, as an organisation, made the IRA aware of the various roles woman could play and the importance of their involvement in the struggle.

What this chapter demonstrates is that the figure of the female combatant remains riven with tension and ambivalence, and is often uneasily accepted. The political violence such women participated in was seen as more shocking and less acceptable than comparable violence commit-

---

[15] Inghinidhe na hÉireann (Daughters of Ireland) was a radical Irish Nationalist women's organisation led by Maud Gonne from 1900 to 1914.

[16] Cumann na gCailíní, is the junior wing of Cumann na mBan.

ted by men, indicating an underlying discomfort with such a challenge to gendered expectations (or established ideas of societal security) (Ryan and Ward 2004). Women's involvement in the IRA and their expanding role in the Conflict challenged men's attitudes towards women as combatants, forcing recognition of the important role that women could, and did, play in resisting British colonial power (Clayton 1998). Moreover, this resistance to women's involvement is indicative of male comrades' masculinity being threatened.

Giving women greater freedom and responsibility in military operations inevitably changed the nature of the struggle itself. Without a doubt, these women took enormous risks for the Republican cause. Hundreds were arrested and imprisoned (Buckley 1938; McCoole 1997). Thousands had their homes raided and searched, and some had their children taken away and placed in care. Many were interrogated, intimidated, threatened (Clarke 1991; Clarke and Litton 1991; McDonnell 1972) and imprisoned. The women participated in the same hunger strikes (*An Phoblacht/Republican News* 1980) and no-wash protests as their male PIRA comrades (Smyth 1987). In addition, large numbers of women were shot at. Many were injured and several were killed (Conlon 1969)—including Sinn Féin vice-president and leading Cumann na mBan member Máire Drumm, who was shot dead by Loyalists in 1976. There is also growing evidence to suggest that sexual violence was used as a weapon of war, by the RUC, the British Army and prison officers.

The presence, and obvious importance of such large numbers of women raised several complex issues for the male-dominated Republican army (Ryan 1999). The role of the female combatant in the Republican movement, historically and symbolically, has at times been ambiguous and contradictory, and the military roles women have played have continued to be perceived as unconventional or exceptional, reflecting a temporary aberration in a time of national crisis. The above discussion shows how the fight for gender equality could never fully be won in the context of a broader cultural/societal organisation of gender which, amongst other things, dictated a gender-specific deployment of the IRA personnel; for example, weaponising gender expectations by the deployment of women's bodies as sexual decoys, or using the iconography and symbolism of motherhood to facilitate the carrying of weapons (Backett-Milburn and McKie 2001).

As the voices of the women demonstrate, some female combatants felt excluded by some male members who experienced 'women's involvement in the movement as a challenge to their masculinity' (Alison 2004; Ward 1989, pp. 258–259). Yet others felt that the common cause they were fighting for and the shared camaraderie gave them access to equal status as combatants. Women combatants in their accounts of struggle illustrate that, as women, they were caught *between* and *in* intersecting systems of oppression, and that acts of resistance had intended and unintended—but nevertheless far-reaching—consequences.

Despite their involvement, many women post–conflict were re-marginalised and returned to traditional roles (Hagan 2006). As Wilford (1998, p. 35) notes, 'fighting alongside men to achieve independence does not provide a guarantee of women's inclusion as equal citizens', and 'even where women have been active as warriors ... they invariably are left holding the wrong end of the citizen stick'. Moreover, their re-marginalisation illustrates that their involvement was, to a great extent, a temporary exception answering the demands of a period of crisis, rather than it leading to sweeping societal change in gender roles. Alison argues that, while women's involvement in ethno-national armed conflict 'can be tolerated (and is often necessary) in times of crisis, it is less acceptable in a post-conflict, 'normal society' context—indicating, again, the ambiguous and uneasy nature of the role of the female combatant (Alison 2004, p. 457). As the women became more politicised and highly trained in combat, they also became confident in viewing themselves as equals: as soldiers fighting to protect the community against the British government's oppressive legislation. In turn, these women began to address the socio-political inequalities in society at various levels of the political spectrum. This experience helped to politicise women and moved some women from the domestic sphere to the public arena of ethno-nationalist politics.

'The great irony is that the war of the last 15 years has made women stronger, more independent, braver, and more determined. The war has politicised people; these years have inspired the debate between feminism and nationalism, have made women question the institutions that generations before them had taken for granted—marriage, the church, birth control, the law'. (Fairweather et al. 1984, p. vii)

Although female combatants' involvement was recognised as necessary, some women experienced paternalistic behaviour and sexism within the IRA. The concluding quote from a male ex-combatant clearly demonstrates the multi-layered role that women as a whole played during the Conflict, in a spectrum of activities which are not only rooted in, but also reconfigure and disturb the boundaries of expected female roles:

> In fact our whole struggle was held together by women and that was from whether it would be my grannies, my aunts, who all went to the prisons, fed the Volunteers, hid the weapons, sometimes carried the weapons, and delivered the bombs. But they wouldn't class themselves as Volunteers. It was the women who *held* the struggle together and not the men. So for men it was the women who from the very start held the movement together and men are kind of secondary. (Emphasis in original)

Chapter 6 will examine the role of Armagh Prison as a site of political struggle and how the prison structure reflected the broader strategic and ideological elements of the Conflict. The following section charts the key moments of prison resistance and how gendered bodies were used both by the political prisoners and by the state to place femininity in dissent (see Carlen 1983).

References

Alison, M. (2004). Women as agents of political violence: Gendering security. *Security Dialogue, 35*(4), 447–463.

Alison, M. (2009). *Women and political violence-female combatants in ethnonational conflicts.* London: Routledge.

An Phoblacht/Republican News. (1980, November 22). *Armagh prisoners, decision final. Women Join the Hunger Strike.* www.Anphoblacht.Com/Contents/13890.

Aretxaga, B. (1997). *Shattering the silence: Women, nationalism and political subjectivity in Northern Ireland.* Princeton, NJ: Princeton University Press.

Backett-Milburn, K., & McKie, L. (Eds.). (2001). *Constructing Gendered Bodies.* London: Palgrave Press.

Barry, T. (1995). *Guerrilla days in Ireland.* Boulder, CO: Roberts Rinehart.

Belfast Telegraph. (2009, December 18). Dissidents plan honey traps in bid to kill troops.

Benjamin, J. (1998). *The bonds of love: Psychoanalysis, feminism and the problem of domination.* New York: Pantheon.

Bloom, M. (2011). *Bombshell: The many faces of women terrorists.* Toronto: Penguin.

Bloom, M., Gill, P., & Horgan, J. (2012, January). Tiocfaidh ár Mná: Women in the provisional Irish Republican Army. *Journal of Behavioral Sciences of Terrorism and Political Aggression, 4*(1), 60-67.

Bowyer Bell, J. (1997). *The secret army: The IRA.* New Jersey: Transaction.

Brady, E., Patterson, E., McKinney, K., Hamill, R., & Jackson, P. (2011). *The footsteps of Anne: Stories of republican women ex-prisoners.* Belfast: Shanway Press.

Buckley, M. (1938). *The jangle of the keys.* Dublin: James Duffy.

Buckley, S., & Loughran, P. (1984). Women and the troubles 1969-1980. In Y. Alexander & A. O'Da (Eds.), *Terrorism in Ireland.* London: Croom Helm.

Carlen, P. (1983). *Women's imprisonment: A study in social control.* Routledge and Kegan Paul.

Chumhaill, N. E. (1933, April 8 and 19). The history of Cumann na mBan. *An Phoblacht.*

Clarke, K. (1991). *Revolutionary woman.* Dublin: O'Brien Press.

Clarke, K., & Litton, H. (1991). *Kathleen Clarke revolutionary woman.* Dublin: O'Brien Press.

Clayton, P. (1998). Religion, ethnicity and colonialism as explanations of the Northern Ireland conflict. In D. Miller (Ed.), *Rethinking Northern Ireland: Culture, ideology and colonialism.* London: Longman.

Cockburn, C. (2001). The gendered dynamic of armed conflict and political violence. In C. Moser & F. Clark (Eds.), *Victims, perpetrators or actors? Gender, armed conflict and political violence.* London: Zed Books.

Conlon, L. (1969). *Cumann na mBan and the women of Ireland 1913-1925.* Kilkenny: Kilkenny People.

Coogan, T. P. (2000). *The IRA.* London: Harper Collins.

Corcoran, M. (2006a). *Out of order: The political imprisonment of women in Northern Ireland, 1972-1998.* Cullompton: Willan.

De-Pretis, M. (2000). *To take arms in the armed patriarchy.* Unpublished paper presented at the Women and Law conference on Strategic Thinking for the Millennium, University of Westminster, London.

Dillon, M. (1999). *The dirty war: Covert strategies and tactics in political conflicts.* London: Routledge.

Eager, W. P. (2008). *From freedom fighters to terrorists: Women and political violence.* Hampshire: Ashgate.

English, R. (2003). *Armed struggle: The history of the IRA.* UK: Oxford University Press.

Fairweather, E., McDonough, R., & McFadyean, M. (1984). *Only the rivers run free: Northern Ireland, the women's war.* London: Pluto.

Gill, P., & Horgan, J. (2013). Who were the volunteers? The shifting sociological and operational profile of 1240 provisional Irish Republican Army members. *Terrorism and Political Violence, 25*(3), 435–456.

Griffith, K., & O'Grady, T. (Eds.). (1999). *Curious journey: An oral history of Ireland unfinished revolution.* Boulder, CO: Robert Reinhart.

Hagan, L. (2006). Missing voices: Women and the three 'Ps': Politics, Prejudice and Paternalism. *Canadian Journal of Irish Studies, 32*(1): 12-22, Women's Irish-Canadian Connections.

Henderson, F., & Hopkinson, M. (1998). *Frank Henderson's Easter Rising: Recollections of a Dublin Volunteer* (pp. 58–61). Cork: Cork University Press.

Horgan, J., & Taylor, M. (1997). The provisional Irish Republican Army: Command and functional structure. *Terrorism and Political Violence, 9*(3), 1–32.

Kiluva-Ndunda, M. (2004). *Women's agency and educational policy.* New York: SUNY Press.

McCoole, S. (Ed.). (1997). *Guns and chiffon, women revolutionaries and Kilmainham Gaol, 1916-1923.* Dublin: Government of Ireland, Stationary Office Books.

McDonnell, K. (1972). *There is a bridge at Bandon: A personal account of the Irish war of independence.* Cork: Mercier Press.

McStiofáin, S. (1975). *Revolutionary in Ireland.* London: Scribner.

Moloney, E. (2003). *A secret history of the IRA.* New York: Norton.

Morgan, V. (1995). Women and the conflict in Northern Ireland. In A. O'Day (Ed.), *Terrorism's laboratory: The case of Northern Ireland.* Aldershot: Dartmouth.

Northern Ireland Civil Rights Association. (1973, May 22). *Information sheet on women internees.* Pamphlet, Belfast.

Ryan, L. (1999, July). 'Furies' and 'Die-hards': Women and Irish republicanism in the early twentieth century. *Gender and History, 11*(2), 256–275.

Ryan, L., & Ward, M. (Eds) (2004). *Irish women and nationalism: Soldiers, new women and wicked hags.* Dublin: Irish Academic Press.

Sales, R. (1997). *Women divided: Gender religion and politics in Northern Ireland.* London: Routledge.

Shannon, E. (1989). *I am of Ireland: Women of the North speak out.* London: Little, Brown Book Group.

Smyth, J. (1987). Unintentional mobilisation: The effects of the 1980-1981 hunger strikes in Ireland. *Political Communication and Persuasion, 4,* 179–190.

Talbot, L. (2004). Female combatants, paramilitary prisoners and the development of feminism in the republican movement. In M. Ward & L. Ryan (Eds.), *Irish women and nationalism: Soldiers, new women and wicked hags.* Dublin: Irish Academic Press.

Walsh, O. (1990). Testimony from imprisoned women. In D. Fritzpatrick (Ed.), *Revolution Ireland.* Dublin: Trinity History Workshop (pp. 1917–1923).

Ward, M. (1982). "Suffrage First - Above All Else!": The Irish suffrage movement. *Feminist Review 10,* 21–36.

Ward, M. (1995). *Unmanageable revolutionaries: Women and Irish nationalism.* London: Pluto Press.

Wilford, R. (1998). Women, ethnicity and nationalism: Surveying the ground. In R. Wilford & R. L. Miller (Eds.), *Women, ethnicity and nationalism: The politics of transition.* London: Routledge.

Yuval-Davis, N. (1997). *Gender and Nation.* London: Sage.

6

Sites of Confinement: The Stories of Armagh and Maghaberry Prison

This chapter establishes the context for the changing contours of women's experiences of imprisonment, outlining the history and layout of Armagh Prison and the way that conditions there developed as British government policy towards politically motivated prisoners went through a series of changes, and as the population of political prisoners rose during the period known as the Conflict. It examines the women's initial reactions to imprisonment and their early struggle for political status, establishing their resistance to the prison regime as a continuation of the wider political struggle of which events behind the prison walls were to become a key component.

Armagh Gaol was opened in 1780, being extended during the mid-nineteenth century and remained open until 1986, when the women were transferred to Maghaberry Prison. It is a listed Victorian building with an impressive frontage in the heart of the ecumenical city of Armagh. It was the sole prison for women in the North of Ireland[1] but, at one point, it also housed young men between the ages of 17–20 years,

---

[1] The Six Counties of Northern Ireland are Antrim, Armagh, Down, Fermanagh, Derry and Tyrone.

© The Editor(s) (if applicable) and The Author(s) 2016
A. Wahidin, *Ex-Combatants, Gender and Peace in Northern Ireland,*
DOI 10.1057/978-1-137-36330-5_6

known as 'Borstal Boys' because they had been transferred from the open Borstal at Millisle, County Down, due to their disruptive behaviour. Depending on good behaviour they were returned to Millisle after three to six months. When Monsignor Murray became the Catholic chaplain to Armagh Prison in 1967, there were some 40 Borstal Boys (personal communication). As well as women internees and convicted political prisoners, the prison also held the young girls and women known as ODCs (Ordinary Decent Criminals; that is, prisoners convicted of non-scheduled offences). Young Republican women under the age of 17 were held at St Joseph's Training School, Middleton, Armagh.

The prison was staffed by male and female officers. Generally speaking, the men were in charge of the Borstal Boys and the women were in charge of the women prisoners (Murray 1998, p. 7). In August 1972, 132 men—who were the overspill of the men from Crumlin Road Gaol—went to Armagh Prison (Brady et al. 2011, p. 10), before being transferred to the new Maze Prison near Belfast (previously Long Kesh Detention Centre). The influx of new prisoners and the overspill from Crumlin Road Gaol led to Armagh Prison being 'faced with acute problems of accommodation, staffing, education, training and discipline' (Northern Ireland Prison Service 1977, p. 5).

Síla Darragh (author and former politically motivated prisoner) recalls the layout of Armagh Prison:

> Inside the gaol two long wings for its females inmates radiated from a 'circle' which contained the administration section, kitchen and hospital. Separate from the main buildings is the old infirmary but it was known to us as the 'Annex' and housed a number of male prisoners who worked in the kitchen and did minor repair work in the gaol.
>
> 'A' wing has a prison laundry in the basement, then a ground floor and one upper tier.
>
> 'B' wing has a ground floor and two upper tiers and housed its own secret in its basement. Outside 'B' wing, on the opposite side from what was the exercise yard, there are stairs leading down to the basement cells close to the corner at the back of the wing where it joins the circle on the outside. Still visible in the corner is the remains of what was a wooden platform about nine feet above ground level. This is where the gallows stood and the basement cells, accessible only from the outside and down a

narrow flight of stone steps, are where the condemned prisoner spent their last days. Close to the infirmary, or the 'Annex', lies the graveyard where prisoners were laid to rest in a bed of lime. (2012, p. 20)

The Borstal was situated on the ground floor of 'B' wing (that is, B1) until 1975, while female remand prisoners, female ODCs and female Ulster Defence Association prisoners occupied the ground floor of 'A' wing (A1). Republican women were housed on A2, B2, B3 and then on B1 when the Borstal Boys were transferred in 1975. Only convicted prisoners occupied the first storeys of 'A' and 'B' wings, while internees were housed on the upper levels.

These wings held 140 cells in all. In 1976, a new cell block was built known as 'C' wing; this was a two-storey building with 30 cells (Murray 1998), on the far side of 'B' wing's exercise yard (known as the old breaker's yard). The building was completed in 1977, built in the same style as the H-Blocks and was intended to house prisoners convicted of political offences (after 1 March 1976, when political status was removed).

In 1977 the women with political status were moved to 'C' wing and the ordinary sentenced prisoners and those of us on protest were moved to 'B' wing. (Darragh 2012, p. 49)

The conditions in Armagh Prison were austere. The cells were 8 feet by 10 feet in area, with an arched window high above as the only source of natural light. The cell contained a metal bed, plastic chair, small table, chamber pot (known by the women as a 'po'), a small locker and a bible. Prisoners often found themselves doubled up in single cells with only a slop bucket for waste, so they had to throw the contents of their chamber pots in a sluice. Corcoran (2006, p. 21) states: 'The needs of male prisoners prevailed over those of women in the allocation of resources and facilities. The exercise yard was a 'small muddy patch of ground' and its use by women brought 'verbal abuse and obscenities [from the] soldiers patrolling the perimeters' (ibid.). Recreation facilities consisted of one 'small room' (ibid., p. 22) used by all women. The need to segregate male and female prisoners, and the need to separate the categories of women prisoners, led to the ad hoc sub-division of the already congested wings' (ibid., p. 23).

The Impact of Prison Policy: From Reactive Containment to Criminalisation [2]

At this point, a brief excursion into the development of British government policy towards Republican political prisoners will help to provide a context for exploring the experiences of the Armagh women, changes in the size and composition of the prison population during the period from the late 1960s onward, and the extension of the militarised Republican campaign through the prisoners' struggles for political status.

- The policy of internment (imprisonment without trial), which had been used a number of times during Northern Ireland's history, was reintroduced on Monday 9 August 1971 in the context of 'Operation Demetrius', a British Army operation resulting in the arrest and imprisonment of 342 people suspected (in many cases, wrongly) of involvement with the IRA. Internment continued in use until 5 December 1975.

Convicted paramilitary prisoners (that is, those dealt with through the courts) were treated as ordinary criminals until July 1972, when special category status (SCS) was granted by William Whitelaw, the British government's Secretary of State for Northern Ireland, to all prisoners convicted of politically motivated offences.

---

[2] Criminalisation was a strategy employed by the British government in Northern Ireland between 1976 and 1981, which sought to de-politicise those involved in paramilitary activities. This policy implemented the removal of special category status (*de facto*, prisoner of war status). Violence in prison against the political prisoners intensified during this period. The government's stated intention was to portray the Conflict as a law and order or security problem, rather than a political problem.

- Special category (or 'political') status was *de facto* prisoner of war (POW) status, providing them with some of the privileges of POWs. SCS prisoners did not have to wear prison uniforms or do prison work, were housed within their paramilitary factions and allowed to self-organise within their paramilitary command structure, and were allowed extra visits and food parcels.
- The Northern Ireland (Emergency Provisions) Act 1973 established the Diplock Courts, in which terrorist offences were tried by a judge without a jury. The number of cases heard in Diplock Courts reached a peak of 329 per year in the mid-1980s. With the Northern Ireland peace process, that figure fell to 60 per year in the mid-2000s, and the Courts were effectively abolished in 2007.

The Diplock Courts were so-called because they emerged from recommendations in a 1972 report to Parliament by Lord Diplock, which marked the beginning of the new policy of 'criminalisation' whereby the state removed legal distinctions between political violence and normal crime, with political prisoners treated as common criminals.

- On 1 March 1976, the new Labour Secretary of State for Northern Ireland, Merlyn Rees, announced the phasing out of SCS. Anyone convicted of a scheduled offence after March 1976 would be treated as an ordinary criminal and would have to wear a prison uniform (in the case of male prisoners), do prison work and (again, in the case of male prisoners) serve their sentence in the new Maze Prison, in what became known as the H-Blocks (see Wahidin et al. 2012).

The criminalisation policy backfired seriously on the British government, placing prison conditions squarely at the centre of the Republican struggle and resulting in a new IRA policy which saw the killing of 19 prison officers between 1976 and 1981. The 'blanket protest', begun in September 1976 by new H-Block prisoners refusing to wear the prison uniform, escalated by April 1978 into the five-year 'dirty protest' in which prisoners refused to leave their cells to 'slop out' and, instead, smeared their excrement on the cell walls.

In February 1980, over 30 prisoners in Armagh Prison joined the no wash protest following a series of disputes with the prison governor, including allegations they had been ill-treated by male prison officers. They did not conduct a blanket protest, as women prisoners in Northern Ireland already had the right to wear their own clothes, but the protest did include smearing excrement and menstrual blood on the cell walls. The no wash protest ended in March 1981, with the commencement of the H-Block hunger strike which resulted in the deaths of 10 men, and the subsequent relaxation of prison policy, including the right of male prisoners to wear their own clothes.

Prior to 1970, Armagh never housed more than a dozen or so women at a time, serving sentences for a range of offences including drunkenness, assault, theft, fraud, forgery, prostitution and murder. After 1969, the majority of women prisoners were charged with 'terrorist type' offences, and considered themselves to be politically motivated prisoners. The official definition of terrorism given in Section 31 of the Northern Ireland (Emergency Provisions) Act 1973 is 'the use of violence for political ends' (Taylor 1980, p. 37).

The First Hunger Strike and Removal of the Uniform

Prior to 1972, the women wore prison clothes but, following their involvement in the hunger strike in 1972, the women won the right to wear their own clothes (see Murray, 1988:10). In the interview and several informal conversations with Monsignor Murray, he recalls the uniform the women had to wear:

> Well they [the women] wore a polka dot blouse, a heavy serge skirt, heavy stockings and bulky kind of shoes. I need to look at the book—remand prisoners had a blue blouse and sentenced prisoners had a green blouse with white dots. So they wore prison clothes and the borstal boys wore prison clothes as well.

One of the first women to enter the gates of Armagh Prison recalls:

I went into Armagh and I had to wear this prison uniform which was horrendous. The women had to wear a uniform and it had been in place circa since 1840. That's how old the style was. I went on hunger strike, in 1972, because I didn't want to wear this prison uniform.

The hunger strike coincided with the hunger strike with the men at Crumlin Road Gaol.

As one woman states:

That happened at the end of '71. It was me, X, Y and Z that was four. X and Y went on the hunger strike and then Z and then me. We were on it for political status.

AW: You went on before the men then?

No, the men were already on it when they got word to us and we went on it, and we were fighting for political status. I think Y was on it for 17 days.

AW: And what was that like?

It was pretty tough, but at that time you didn't have political status. It was hard but it was for something we were fighting for. At the end of 17 days, I remember the Governor sending for us to tell us that we had political status. They brought me in my guitar and they brought me in my jeans and my sneakers and it was like 'oh it was worth it, it was worth it!' We got the uniform and fired it out onto the wing, 'we don't have to wear that no more!' because after your sentence you had to wear it every day, you didn't have *nothing* else. Then Eileen Hickey[3] came in. (Emphasis in original)

The women were then allowed to wear their own clothes and the gains the politically motivated prisoners achieved benefited all the other women in the prison as the women's stories below reveal.

One of the first political women prisoners to be imprisoned in 1972 recalls:

---

[3] Eileen Hickey was the first Officer in Command at Armagh prison and served in this role for the period between 1973 and 1977.

Well, we were the first women in Armagh. There was myself, Susan, Bridie, Margaret, four of us went on the hunger strike, and Billy McKee, went on [hunger strike] in the Crumlin jail. Fortunately, it didn't last *too* long, three or four weeks, and William Whitelaw was the Secretary of State. He gave us our demands, so we didn't have to wear the uniform after that and we were allowed a visit every week: before it was one a month. We were allowed free association. We were allowed the right to education, because every-thing before that was a *privilege which could be taken away* from you, and what I was particularly pleased about was that it was also extended to the ordinary prisoner.

You know the ordinary prisoner also got the same rights as we did [the political prisoners], but it was never talked about. In fact very few people know that there was a women's hunger strike in '71, which set in stone the special category status that Merlyn Rees took away in '76 which in turn led to the whole Bobby Sands hunger strike. Us women and the men in Crumlin prison got special category status with that hunger strike and in '76 they removed it and forced the uniform back on people. With the con-sequence that it ended up in a big hunger strike and 10 men dying. (Emphasis in original)

Initial Reactions to Armagh Prison

On arrival, women prisoners would be met by a prison officer who was constantly on duty in the circle to lock and unlock doors and gates. The prison and the regime were austere.

The initial reaction of this woman is typical:

Very draconian. It's an old Victorian prison. I found it very oppressive, cold and damp.

Another states:

Well, I was 18, yes. It was a very daunting building. It's an old Victorian building, very dull, damp and drab and they just took you into the recep-tion area. You're told to have a bath and hand over your clothes, and to be honest you just did it then. You didn't know what to expect, but I suppose after the barracks[4] it was, for a lot of people getting to Armagh it was a relief.

This feeling of relief was echoed throughout the women's testimonials. Although fearful as to what to expect the women were relieved to have survived the interrogation centres and to be meeting fellow comrades and friends.

AW: Because?

You *weren't getting tortured anymore*. You weren't getting harassed.

AW: When you talk about being tortured, what do you mean?

Well, most people went there—to the barracks. We were interrogated constantly. You didn't get any time for sleep. No food. The lights were turned on and off constantly. The noise. The shouting, so at that age, it was just frightening. It was physically and mentally torturous and you also didn't know what was coming next.
[Pause]
What was worse was the fear of the unknown.

AW: Do you remember what your initial reaction to Armagh was?

My initial reaction was that *I'm here and I'm alive*. There were that many killed at the time. My reaction was *I'm here and I'm alive and I'm going to study. That was it.* I was *so* glad to see the other women. (Emphasis in original)

During the early 1970s, the prison officers refused to call the women by their first name, which gave the prison officers an excuse to humiliate the women in their charge.

They wouldn't call you by your name. It was surname or number. Of course we refused to answer anything, so then that was an excuse to lock you up or search you or stop you and strip you. Yes, I mean strip searches were very common and they brought them back in again once they took away political status.

---

[4] One of the Interrogation Centres in Belfast.

On arrival, the women entered the circle, were told to have a bath and then they were taken to their designated wings and then to their cells.

> They brought me up to 'A2' wing. Downstairs was 'A1' and upstairs was 'A2', and I went up there, and at that time I would have been the 13th person brought up on that particular day. There were 12 other girls there and they asked did I need anything and how did things go, and then I was brought into talk to Mairéad Farrell[5]. and X, who were at that time the OC [Officer in Command] and the Adjutant of the wing. You always had a debriefing when you go inside. So I got the debriefing. It was basically telling them what happened from when you were arrested until you got there. It was absolutely horrifying. Bars on the windows and when I looked at the chamber pot I thought 'oh god, I can't use that. The first night horrified me, by the following day it was a matter of fitting in and getting on with life.

Seeing their cells for the first time with the 'po' placed in the corner frequently evoked horror:

> We did all our own cleaning of our own wings, our own cells, polished the floors. Your cell would have two beds in it, a wee locker, a plastic 'po', I hated that with a passion! I'm very prudish about things like that.

But for others it gave the women for the first time a bed and space that they didn't have to share.

> It was a great joke in our family that when I got arrested when I was 17, and they put me in a prison cell. It was the first time in my life I'd ever had a bed of my own. I was the only woman who went to prison where the standard of living went up...! (laughs)

Another woman echoes the above sentiments, demonstrating the humour the women shared with each other and their families:

---

[5] Mairéad Farrell was the IRA Officer in Command in Armagh Prison from December 1979–1986.

Put it this way, most of us came from massive big families with maybe four to a bed in our own homes. All of a sudden you sort of looked on Armagh well, this is an opportunity to turn this into a self-contained bedroom for yourself and you didn't have to share a bed with three other sisters. The humour kept us going.

We also said we'd like to decorate our own cells, and we did. We took over the prison. The screws [the prison officers] totally gave up because we only took orders from Eileen Hickey and her leadership was strong. Plus the fact, the craic[6] was good. I mean our imagination soared; there was always something every week.

Other women took the space and rewrote the blank walls by 'mak[ing] the cells their own' (Adams 1992).

I had my cell lovely. I think just as I came in the girls started to realise well we're going to be here for a long time so we're going to change this cell and send over to female screws [prison officers], 'could you send us over paint'. Well, normal colours was maybe pale yellow or green or blue, but we wanted pinks and lilacs and deep purple, and every couple of months paint was sent over to us.

AW: Different colours?

Different colours and we were allowed to hang curtains as long as the screws [prison officers] could see the bars and we started getting in nice bedspreads and a wee rug, and some of the girls would have took it a wee bit further and some of them [my comrades] had lino down, some of them had the real deal wooden floors. They'd have scrubbed the floors, polished them up, waxed them, shined them, and after doing that they didn't want you walking on them. So you sort of came to their door and they had an old blanket cut up with two pads.

AW: (Laughing)

And then when I went into see one particular girl, you shimmied up and you sat down on her bed and she made you a cup of tea. You had your

---

[6] Craic: Irish word for fun/enjoyment.

conversation and you shimmied back down because you didn't want any footprints on her floor.

Charting the Rise of the Armagh Prison Population

The women internees, I was the sixth to go there. There was Liz, Tish, Margaret, Ann, Moira and then me. They were the first six.

There were 24 political prisoners when I went in. By the time I was sentenced there were maybe 50/60 girls, and by the next year you had 100 girls, and they opened another wing. Very basic—two toilets, two baths. I can't remember a shower, a couple of sinks and you just got on with it.

The effects of the resurgence of political Conflict in Northern Ireland and the use of internment without trial is illustrated in Murray's revelation that 'the number of women political prisoners increased from two in 1971 to more than 100 from 1972–1976' (cited in Brady et al. 2011, p. 10). Of the 32 women politically motivated prisoners sent to Armagh in 1972, 18 were aged under 25 when sentenced and the other 14 were aged under 20. All were from strong Republican areas of Northern Ireland; 14 were sentenced to between ten years and life (WAI 1980, p. 2). Drawing on his own personal records for the period from the 1970s to 1980s, Monsignor Murray, showed that some '400 women political prisoners were jailed at various times in the 1970s and 1980s for political offences (ibid.). As the political situation deteriorated by 1975, Armagh Prison held up to 120 Republican women; over 60 internees and the rest were sentenced prisoners. The last internee left Armagh in mid-1975, leaving behind between 60 to 70 prisoners.[7] Most of the women political

---

[7] The sharp division in the great numbers of men interned in 1972 compared with what may seem to be a small number of women is actually somewhat misleading. During the height of the Anglo-Irish war in 1920–1921, although there were 4,000 men interned throughout the whole of Ireland, according to Challis, 'The Government felt it unnecessary to intern women, as they felt it was sufficient to curb terrorist activity [sic] by the internment of males' (1999). The proportionately small area and population of the Six Counties (as opposed to all 32 in 1920–1921) must be taken into account.

prisoners were young women in their teenage years but one internee was in her 60s.

In 1976, the British government's new Secretary of State for Northern Ireland, Roy Mason, introduced the criminalisation policy: all prisoners who were sentenced after 1 March 1976 were denied political status and held in separate wings from their comrades who already had it (the last woman with political status was released in 1984). For the women, as with the men, the loss of status also meant reduced exercise, limited food parcels and little time for handicrafts. Political papers and film shows were stopped.

HMP Maghaberry: Mourne House and 'Normalisation'

Armagh Prison closed in 1986 and the women were transferred to Mourne House, the women's unit in the newly-built high-security Maghaberry[8] Prison complex. Mourne House was managed as if it were another unit of the male jail, which held 'politically' motivated and 'ordinary' prisoners, and could accommodate 59 women over four wings. This move reflected the 'normalisation' policy in which Mourne House, at the cost of £32 million pounds (House of Commons Debate 1986, p. 551), with an additional £5 million spent on security measures. This investment created a 'secure and high standard accommodation' in a 'modern, state-of-the-art' prison (NIPS, 1988:1) based on 'an integrated regime' (see Moore and Scraton 2013:89). Although, the prison was modern and the conditions were far better than in Armagh, the prison itself was symbolic in reflecting the prison policy of normalisation.

Although 'there was no apparent general sense of crisis' (Rolston and Tomlinson 1988, p. 167), tensions were mounting. The Republican women were, in practice, treated differently to the men in terms of visits, education and medical care. The gender difference was highlighted in March 1992, when prison officers violently conducted a mass strip search on all of the 21 political women and 13 of the 14 ordinary prisoners (see Chaps 8 and 9).

---

[8] HM Prison Maghaberry opened on 18 March, six years later and 11 years after the Murray Commission was set up to draw out the recommendations by the Gardiner Report.

The following two quotes describe the women's successful demands for equality of treatment in the provision of vocational training, disrupting preconceptions as to what counts as 'women's' and 'men's' work:

> Well, at the beginning it was different—at the beginning you had three visits a week while on remand until you were sentenced and then it went down to one visit, but part of what we were campaigning for was for the better conditions—to have equality of treatment with the men. The men in Maghaberry had what was called vocational training [V.T.] and they had workshops where they were being trained for vocational type work, so we wanted that. Their attitude [the Northern Ireland Prison Service] was that it's not women's work. It's men's work. All those vocational training workshops aren't for you: painting and decorating; woodwork; mechanics; the kind of work that men do but women don't do.
>
> We said we want to have these workshops, so eventually they gave us V.T., and it was a huge success. But it took a few years before they [the Northern Ireland Prison Service] let us have that and it started with a small workshop because they were saying ah they'll do this for a while and then get fed up with it. But it was massively successful, and then to be fair they [the NIPS] gave us a big, big, big workshop and we all learned furniture-making. It was amazing. We learned an awful lot there, it was really, really good. So the Republican women had the morning session and the ordinary women, who weren't political they had the afternoon session, and then if there was the time prisoners who were kept in confined solitary, would have had a session as well.

The subsequent chapters will examine acts of resistance and how the gendered body became used as weapon in the armoury of warfare (Carlton 2007). The women's experiences detailed in the following chapters chart how they negotiated, subverted and resisted the total institution (Goffman 1961). Chapter 7 examines how incarceration was transformed into an area for political resistance, with a particular focus on the women's escape attempt and its repercussions. Chapter 7 and subsequent chapters examine how disciplinary control encoded the female body in a gender-specific way, setting the scene for discussing the women's experiences of the no wash protest and the punitive use of strip searching by the prison authorities.

References

Adams, K. (1992). Adjusting to prison life. In M. Tonry (Ed.), *Crime and justice: A review of research* (Vol. 16). Chicago: University of Chicago Press.

Brady, E., Patterson, E., McKinney, K., Hamill, R., & Jackson, P. (2011). *The footsteps of Anne: Stories of republican women ex-prisoners*. Belfast: Shanway Press.

Carlton, B. (2007). *Imprisoning Resistance – Life and Death in an Australian Supermax*. Sydney: Institute Of Sydney Criminology Press.

Challis, J. (1999). *The Northern Ireland prison system 1920-1990: A history*. Belfast: Northern Ireland Prison Service.

Corcoran, M. (2006). *Out of order: The political imprisonment of women in Northern Ireland, 1972-1998*. Cullompton: Willan.

Darragh, S. (2012). *'John's Lennon Dead': Stories of protest, hunger strikes and resistance*. Belfast: Beyond the Pale.

Goffman, E. (1961). *Asylums: Essays on the social situation of mental patients and other inmates*. New York: Anchor Books.

House of Commons Debate. (1986, November 17). *Journals of the House of Commons from November the 12th, 1986, in the thirty-fifth year, to May the 15th, 1987, in the thirty-sixth year, of the reign of Queen Elizabeth The Second session 1986-87*. House of Commons, London.

Murray, R. (1998). *Hard Time: Armagh Gaol 1971-1986*. Cork: Mercier Press.

Northern Ireland Prison Service. (1977). *Report on the administration of the prison service for 1972–1976 (Cmnd 40)*. Belfast: HMSO.

Northern Irish Prison Service. (1988). *Annual report on the work of the prison service for 1987/88 (Cmnd 42)*. Belfast: HMSO.

Rolston, B., & Tomlinson, M. (1988). The crisis within: Prisons and propaganda in Northern Ireland. In M. Tomlinson, T. Varley, & C. McCulagh (Eds.), *Whose law and order?* (pp. 155–192). Belfast: Belfast Sociological Association of Ireland.

Taylor, P. (1980). *Beating the terrorists? Interrogation in Omagh, Gough and Castlereagh*. London: Penguin.

Wahidin, A., Moore, L., & Convery, U. (2012). Prisons and the legacy of conflict in Northern Ireland. In A. Wahidin (Ed.), *The legacy of conflict and the impact on the Northern Irish criminal justice system. Howard Journal of Criminal Justice, 51*, pp 442–457.

Women Against Imperialism (WAI). (1980a). *Women Protest for Political Status in Armagh Gaol*, Belfast: WAI. *(pamphlet)*.

7

Nor Meekly Serve My Time: 'A' Company Armagh

Republican political prisoners held in Long Kesh have a culture of resistance to British colonial rule in Ireland … they understand their imprisonment as just one more arena of struggle in which they can wage war against the British. The war doesn't end with their capture. (McKeown 1998, pp. 45–46)

This chapter provides a theoretical discussion as to how women ex-combatants resisted and created spaces in prison to continue the struggle that they were committed to beyond the walls. It sets out to examine the contours of their prison experience and to chart key moments of the continuum of resistance from individual acts to collective resistance. Political resistance is a constituent of their sense of identity as freedom fighters and is reflected in the constant dialectic of resistance and institutional response that is mapped in this and subsequent chapters. Resistance is presented and understood as the collective assertion of the political status

'Nor Meekly Serve My Time'—a song written by Francie Brolly during the Hunger Strike protest to highlight the situation of the political prisoners.

© The Editor(s) (if applicable) and The Author(s) 2016
A. Wahidin, *Ex-Combatants, Gender and Peace in Northern Ireland*,
DOI 10.1057/978-1-137-36330-5_7

of prisoners and, by extension, the political character of the Conflict: it is argued that escape, the no wash protest and the hunger strikes, violence and the use of law have been key elements of that assertion. The present chapter explores the complex interplay of power and resistance as both are shaped by and reconfigure the spacialities of the prison, focusing on the importance of politically motivated prisoners' self-organising and military discipline in controlling space and in maintaining their collective identity as combatants. It goes on to describe the women's escape attempt and the reprisals which set the stage for the heightening violence, which increasingly positioned the physical body of the female combatant as the focus of power and the site of resistance.

In the prison context, while the material conditions within the prisons cannot completely determine forms of resistance, they do influence, shape and constrain the operation of both power and resistance.

As Scott (1985, p. 299) has suggested, the parameters of resistance are also set, in part, by the institutions. It is not just that 'where there is power, there is resistance'. Rather, resistance and the exercise of power are mutually shaping, defining, and changing in an ongoing dialectic. Foucault (1990, p. 95) asserts that 'where there is power, there is resistance, and … this resistance is in a position of exteriority in relation to power'. However, the tendency to present power and resistance as binary opposites has been challenged by Buntman (2003, p. 265), who suggests that power should be seen in its 'myriad of bodies' and 'ranges of operations'. She further argues that the term 'dialectic' is not apposite but that 'the relationship between power and resistance is closer to a continuum than a relationship between opposites' (ibid., p. 267).

By the very nature of being a politically motivated prisoner, the ideology and shared cause provided the female politically motivated prisoner with a meaningful social group and identity within which she could *be* identified and *by* which she could identify; this mitigated the usual prison regime of individualising and isolating prisoners (see also Sykes 1958, p. 107). Politically motivated have historically asserted their collective status and identity, and this is no different to the paramilitary prisoners in Northern Ireland who, through their political actions, fought to be treated as collective factions rather than as individuals. In Northern

Ireland, since 1969, prisoners have organised themselves into paramilitary groupings with hierarchical command structures, functional roles and responsibilities, norms and values, support structures and policing mechanisms. In the case of the IRA Volunteers, they conceptualised the state as the colonial enemy, the struggle against which required a disciplined and organised community. Even when the actual organisation of that community is materially difficult, such as during the no-wash era (see Chap. 8) when prisoners spent large amounts of time confined to their cells, the conceptualisation of themselves as *being* and *belonging* to an organisation, a nation or a prison community was itself an act of resistance. The collective resistance process, and the sense of community formed, was, to an extent, an extension of paramilitary structures within which, as Volunteers of the IRA, they had operated while on the outside.

Central to their collective identity was that they were—and should be seen and treated as—distinct, other, and apart from those classed as 'Ordinary Decent Criminals'[1], as well as from members of opposing political factions. Sparks et al. (1996, p. 81) recognise, 'it is precisely the struggle to maintain a sense of personal agency in the face of institutional constraint which motivates and sustains some of prisoners' resistance'. This is not to argue that the actor should be understood as the centred author of social practice but, instead, it enables a consideration of the diverse forms of knowledgeability and techniques of power exercised by prisoners and staff. When history is spatialised, it is possible to realise that people occupy many spaces simultaneously, and that resistance might exist in any of them, but also *'in-between'* them (to invoke Bhabba's phrase 1990). The women come to the carceral prism with different cartographies, and it is because they have drawn places through a nexus of power relationships between nation state, soldiers, nationalism, they also exceed these confinements by creating new possibilities, unfolding new spaces, creating new geographies of resistance and, in turn, creating new futures (Yuval-Davis and Anthias 1989). The notion of 'technologies of the self' can offer a sense of the dynamic ways in which subject positions might be lived and become expressed through specific techniques and practices (Butler 1993). Yet, I would add that subjectivity will always involve a pro-

---

[1] Are prisoners convicted of non-scheduled offences.

cess of translation and is never a straightforward enaction, or imitation, of a discursive subject position. In fact, the very notion of translation can render visible the historically contingent nature of discursive formations.

In the context of prisons in Northern Ireland, such spaces and geographies within the confines of the prison walls, wings and functional areas became controlled by paramilitaries, or faced with increased surveillance (during the hunger strikes/no wash protest prisoners were largely confined to their cells). The mouths and body cavities of prisoners became receptacles in defying the prison officers gaze by carrying 'comms'[2] (see Horgan and Taylor 1997). Such places of resistance are never completely fixed or unfractured but, rather, they may be viewed as 'third spaces' (Bhabba 1994)—spaces uncolonised by intersecting with and subverting practices of domination.

'A' Company Armagh: Liberty and Strength

From the beginning of 1973, Republican women inside Armagh Prison worked to establish a military structure based on the same model as that operating outside. The Officer in Command (OC) was nominated by the women and then approved by the IRA Council and, in the majority of cases, was drawn from those who were sentenced. After selecting an OC, a full Army battalion staff was appointed, including an adjutant wing officer, welfare officer, press release officer, quartermaster, training officer, intelligence officer and education officer.

> We ran our own wings. We had our own command structure.

> AW: And what did that look like?

> Well you had the overall jail OC and the Adjutant so it was run along military lines, like the way armies would have been run. For each wing, a Wing OC and a Wing Adjutant. You would have had a Training Officer who was someone who did the drilling and the training.

---

[2] Comms/Teac: Abbreviation for 'communication'; a note written on cigarette paper or prison-issue toilet paper and wrapped in cling-film. Information was carried within body orifices from one part of the prison to another as a means to communicate with the outside world.

You would have had a Information Officer and you would have had a Press Release Officer who would do the letter writing. The screws [the prison officers] basically left us to our own devices. I mean if they'd have tried we would challenge them through our structure. I'm not saying they didn't try … well they did. Well, obviously they did the cell searches, they did that.

The women political prisoners adhered to an Army structure and formed what became 'A' Company, which had an army regime and their own flag, which read 'Unity and Strength'. As the number of women grew, the company was divided into three sections, one for each Wing, and named after female IRA Volunteers who were killed on active service: Julie Dougan from Portadown, who had died in August 1972 Vivienne Fitzsimmons from Downpatrick, who had died in August 1973; and Ethel Lynch from Derry, who had died in 1974.[3]

He [Governor Cunningham] respected our way of running things as Republican prisoners and he only dealt with the OC, Eileen Hickey, and she would say: 'this is what we're doing. We're running this as: 'A' Wing, 'A' Company, in Armagh jail'. *We* were still *soldiers* even if *we were in prison*. (Emphasis in original)

The OC Eileen Hickey was the first OC for 'A' Company. She was highly respected and there is still respect and admiration for a woman who became OC at the age of 23[4] and continued in this role until she was released in 1977 at the age of 27. She sadly passed away in 2006, but made a huge impact on the lives of the women she commanded.

Discipline and routine within 'A' Company was expected. Each woman was given the Armagh Women's Code of Practice and routine cell inspections were carried out. Meetings were held weekly, cell inspections

---

[3] Julie Dougan was the first female to die on active service and was from Portadown. She died in August 1972. Vivienne Fitzsimmons died in a premature explosion whilst preparing a device and Ethel Lynch died in an explosion in her flat in what was described as a 'bomb-making factory'((McKittrick et al.1999:330 1999, pp. 330, 505).

[4] Eileen Hickey was arrested in 1973 and sentenced to 9 years' imprisonment. She was a Volunteer in Óglaigh na hÉireann (Irish Volunteers), 2nd Battalion Belfast Brigade, and was an active member of 'D' company. She was released in 1977.

were carried out by Eileen Hickey every morning except on Sunday, and drill took place in the yard. All aspects of the daily life of the women in prison were organised and implemented by the women with the exception of holding keys. The women worked out their own routine, minimising contact with prison staff, and every morning the OC negotiated and conveyed the requests and needs of comrades with the Governor (see D'Arcy 1981, p. 59).

> The way it worked, was if a screw [prison officer] asked you to do something you tell them to go through Eileen. You just simply did not cooperate with them unless it was through your OC. So they [the prison officers] gave up. It was very easy. They gave up.
>
> Eileen was *our* OC. We didn't really do what the screws [the prison officers] told us, it was Eileen, we followed. *Her rules. Her company* and the screws [the prison officers] sort of just sat at the bottom of the wing. (Author's emphasis)

The OC was also the main link to the outside IRA leadership. This structure enforced bonds of solidarity and comradeship that went far beyond the confines of the prison walls. This structure made the women strong, defiant and undefeated in their acts of resistance.

At the height of interment, Eileen Hickey oversaw 230 women in the jail (Brady et al. 2011, p. 15), most of whom were young. The ages ranged from the mid-teens through to their late fifties. The women were drawn from both urban and rural areas, but shared the common goal of creating the conditions for the formation of a united Republic of Ireland.

> Eileen Hickey kept us so well organised and disciplined in everything we did. She emphasised the importance of the daily routine cell checks, the cleaning rota for each wing, educational classes and our contribution to the Green Cross[5]. She conducted herself at all times with great determination but also with a quiet dignity and respect for all.

Another woman attests to Eileen Hickey's leadership:

---

[5] The Green Cross was a charitable trust for families of IRA members.

She had such a great way with her. She *kept all of us in line* and in *doing* drill, cleaning the cell. She kept everybody *in* a routine. That was necessary, because if you didn't you might get depressed. There was something organised *every* single day that you had to adhere to and do. This structure lasted the whole time I was in. That routine was *kept every day*. (Emphasis in original)

Darragh, in her seminal book, recounts that:

Before 10 am, the whole Wing had to be cleaned. Bins taken down. Cells tidied up for inspection by the OC at 10.30am. Once cell inspection was over we went out to the exercise yard where they paraded in military formation for 10 to 15 minutes observed by the prison officers. Classes were organised, with quite a few prisoners taking official exams. (2012, p. 26)

Another woman recounts the level of military discipline:

A typical day—we were under the structure of the OC in Armagh jail. We didn't take our orders from the Governor. We took them from Eileen Hickey, the OC.

So you started your morning, you got up, got washed, got your cell cleaned out and then every morning at 10 o'clock the OC inspection would take place. There were different wings. The wing I was on, there were three wings, that was B wing, B1, B2, and B3. So the OC of each wing would come round and checked that your cell was clean and then you would have gone out for drill in the yard.

We were in an Army so we were out drilling in the yard. You came back in and had your breakfast. Most of the day was then up to yourself. There was a small gym and there was education. I took up education. (Emphasis in original)

Drill and military parades visibly confronted the prison structure and challenged the regime, solidifying their identity simultaneously as a politically motivated prisoner and as a soldier.

We went out to the exercise yard and did drill. I loved drill. I loved that. X was the drill sergeant and she was brilliant and she certainly took no prisoners when it came down to it. We used to do the formation drill as well, which was lovely. And then at Easter we would have put on our uniforms. We crocheted black berets and we would have had black jumpers and we would have had black jumpers, black skirts, black tights and black shoes, which you could get in. You know, we were allowed to wear our own clothes and it wouldn't look out of place. So you would have had your full uniform in there.

AW: And what would drill involve?

Well, that would have been like in any army. You would have your Training Officer and she would have called us all to fall in. We would have lined up. We would have been called to attention and then marched round the yard as an Army. And that was an important part of the day because that set the tone for the rest of the day, and you were forever reminded that you were part of an army.

The Armagh women, unlike their male comrades in prison, wore their own clothes and could improvise by creating a black Army uniform, which was worn at the special parades which were organised on Easter Sunday, St. Patrick's Day and every first Sunday of the month. The women would drill for a special commemoration parade which has been defined as a 'solemn occasion' (Brady et al. 2011, p. 67).

We also carried out parades and commemorations, particularly at Easter, and we all would have black skirts, black ties, white shirts and we all had black berets which we would use for the likes of the parades. And this at the time was a thorn in the side of the prison service that we *did* this. But we deliberately paraded. We had to *fall in* and *fall out* in the morning and in the evening. It was to differentiate ourselves from the other women. *We were not criminals. We were political prisoners and part of a major struggle.* (Emphasis in original)

This act of drilling and the wearing of the Army uniform symbolised and reasserted their political identity (Aretxaga 1997, pp. 10–12). Eileen Hickey recalls 'it was very important', in keeping the women together. It kept them aware that they were soldiers. In Armagh, you could feel so far removed from the Movement, from the struggle outside'.

Everyone has to act together in solidarity, keeping moving along as one body. Otherwise you fall off. So we learned to do many things together and as one.

Discipline, routine, order was essential in sustaining and fortifying the identity of being a soldier/freedom fighter in the Irish Republican Army. The next section charts the key moments of resistance in the history of Armagh.

'Prisoners Are Supposed to Try and Escape': Armagh—The Great Escape!

Escapes from prison were not only a feature of resistance, but also an aspiration shared by all the politically motivated prisoners I interviewed. Escapes were ostensibly a less expressive, covert form of resistance. They were, at least in the planning stages, a 'hidden transcript' (Scott 1990) of resistance. In such circumstances, the prisoners' apparent acquiescence in their domination by the prison officers is often crucial for success. Escapes from prison are both metaphorically (and, in the case of tunnels, literally) resistance practices happening beneath what De Certau called 'the apparatuses of the panopticon' (De Certeau 1984, p. 48).[6]

The reasons for a prisoner's desire to escape may be varied and complex. At a basic level, it is the natural desire of anyone incarcerated to want their freedom. As Mathiesen (1965, p. 75) suggests (and as is presumably self-evident), prisoners may seek to escape because they see themselves in the prison context as 'deplorably deprived as compared with the (often exaggerated) pleasures of the outside'. Amongst politically motivated prisoners, as Cohen and Taylor argue (1972, p. 129), a prisoner is expected to 'try to escape, join with [his/her] fellows in making life as difficult as possible for the authorities'. For paramilitary prisoners, escape offered a ready-made template for assertion of their status as prisoners of war. In

---

[6] In this context, the panopticon is used as a model to describe the disciplining and normalising discourses of the prison and, by extension, society in general. For a fuller exposition of the usefulness of the panopticon as a conceptual device, see Mathiesen (1997).

this context, of course, the objectives of the escape attempt are not limited to the goal of liberty, as even a 'failed' attempt will have achieved its goal of creating difficulties for the running of the prison, as well as establishing a definition of the prison as a site of continuing struggle.

In the context of Northern Ireland, Republican prisoners were keen to stress their identity as a political identity and, as such, their perceived duty to attempt escape. The escape signified the opening up of a 'gap' or 'space', where strategies of the powerful were rendered vulnerable, subverted by challenges and tactics of the 'non-powerful'. This recalls the statement of Buntman (2003) that power and resistance are less a relationship between binary opposites than a continuum; for the escape attempt (and, indeed, all other forms of non-cooperation with the carceral regime) represents more than a mere resistance of the disempowered and, instead, constitutes in itself an effective act of power *against* that regime (*regardless* of whether the attempt results in the actual liberty of the participants).

The Plan

AW: So what led to the escape and what actually happened?

> Well, the escape, funny enough we had been watching Colditz.
> So the three of us were sitting there and I looked up at the window and unknown to me, X was doing the exact same thing, and I was going to myself, well, if a big Brit can get through a wee air vent, we can get through that'. And I just went to say to X, and X, simultaneously said 'I think we could get out that window'. And that's how it started.

The Execution

> We had a wee system going and we had turned our radio up so nobody could hear the bars being sawed. So that's what we did. We sawed the prison bars but then you could slot them back in and then you only had to saw the bottom of the bar because when you lifted it up there was a hole at top. It slotted out. But the danger always was when they came into raid

your cell. Some screws [prison officers] were okay. Some of them just threw everything on the floor without a care. They would toss your bed up and whatever, but they came in periodically with a big stick and tapped the window. But we always kept our ham and cheese there. We called that our fridge. We tried to live off our parcels.[7] We didn't expect our people to send you up a big parcel. I wouldn't have asked. *My mother had lost three wages. Nobody thinks of the economics of war.* (Author's emphasis)

AW: So how did you get to scale the wall?

We made a big giant rope out of wool. It was over 20 ft. long.

The screws [the prison officers] got so accustomed to this wool coming in and then everybody started to knit soft toys so there were more bags of wool coming in. So that's how we used the wool.

So we plaited the wool and then we made another plait and then we made another plait and somebody would go out onto 'A' Wing and watch for the guard, because during the day all the girls were out walking about. We had to plait the wool and then run each plait through each other. Then we did the same again and again until it was about that thick. The thing was where to hide it. So we were coming back and we were looking up at the wire and sort of going, 'can this definitely really happen'. That's how they caught us, because we had no wire cutters.

So we made the small rope and we were actually all dressed in black and we put our makeup and all on, because the cars that were coming to take us. They had a change of clothes for us. We were all dressed in black. We were like panthers, because when you came out of the cell you had to go past the circle, the door where you were taken out to the yard, that was from the circle and it was always the male screws [the prison officers] that patrolled there. So we had to get past that.

We got up into the army post but it was that German wire, not that razor wire, and it literally tore into your clothes and tore into your skin. We were pretty badly cut. So we were going up through the hatch but it was covered in wire. But we got up into it anyway and X … it was only when you were up there you realised how much wire there was.

---

[7] The political prisoners were allowed to receive a parcel of food on a monthly basis.

AW: You were like the female version of James Bond!

[We all laugh]

Not able to go any further, and surrounded by the Army, they were caught. Governor Cunningham asserted that the women were under his control by stating: 'there'll be no recriminations against my girls'.

The Aftermath

We were all locked in separate cells because the jail wasn't too packed at that stage. That was March '73. So although there were more girls coming in, the jail still wasn't packed. So we were all separated and put in separate cells, and then the screws [the prison officers] opened the door and came in and wanted you to go down to what they call the medical room. It was a cell and that's where 'Dr Death' was to see if we needed medical treatment. And then the next day all hell broke loose.

Next morning we got opened up. One at a time to go to the toilet and it was only then I discovered that all the Brits ... not the screws [the prison officers] were all on the wing. It was just the male and female Brits. They were all over 'A' Wing. So when you were getting brought to the toilet a whole lot of them were lined up so you had to walk past them all to go to the toilet. And that's when they started raiding all the cells.

In response to the women's escape attempt, the state reacted the following day with a level of violence and brutality that heightened the Conflict both inside and outside the prisons.

As the following chapters reveal, the bodies of the women became an instrument of resistance in the complex securocratic dialectics of the exercise of power. Frank (1991, pp. 49–50) has suggested that the human body can be conceptualised as an equilateral triangle, at the points of which are institutions, discourses and corporeality.[8] Nietzsche argues

---

[8] The example Frank uses to illustrate his point is that of fasting amongst medieval holy women. In that example, the institution is the medieval Church; the discourses include not only those doc-

(1968, p. 492) that the body becomes a site for agency when there is a clash between two unequal opposing forces. Foucault (1979) offers an analysis of the body as an object of the exercise of power and refers specifically to any 'prison revolt' beginning with the body. As Feldman argues, for prisoners, the body is the place to which power is directed and which also defines the place for redirection and the reversal of power.[9] For Feldman, in revolt the prisoner 'objectifies the body as an instrument of violence' (Feldman 1991, p. 178). As the women experienced new levels of harassment and violence, the female body had to be reinvented as actively defiling, resisting, thus restoring the political potency of the prisoners in resisting the power of the prisons. In the context of a prison where other forms of resistance are narrowed and may become obfuscated by the isolation of the setting (Scott 1990), the body may move to 'the centre of a political struggle' (Turner 1984, p. 39).

The creation of new spaces illustrates how spatialities are constitutive not only of domination, but also of resistance; that struggles for power are spatialised and constituted in space and time in specific ways—from opposition to repositioning; that power relations intersect in specific ways, and resistance occurs in spaces beyond those defined by power relations (Benjamin 1988). Thus, acts of resistance have to be understood not only in terms of their location in power relations, but also through their intended and received meanings. It has been shown that political subjectivities are constituted through political struggles, but also that there are many spaces of struggle through which people become political.

Resistance re-territorialises prison space in various ways, transforming its meanings, to undermine territory as a natural source of power, and reconfigure it as a space for citizenship, democracy and freedom—within limits. Territories involve location, boundary and movement—and they will therefore overlap, be discontinuous and shift, as people seek alterna-

---

trines of the Church which eulogise the virtues of fasting, but also discourses on medieval marriage and the role of women. The corporeality of the body poses the practical questions of how much self-starvation and so forth the body can endure (Frank 1991, 1990).

[9] Bettelheim also offers an instructive example of how the limits of endurance of the human body may become an instrument for the reversal of power, particularly when that power is applied disproportionately (see Bettelheim 1986).

tive ways of living and communication by moving—in this case—beyond the confines of the cell.

The spatiality of struggle allows what Mohanty calls a 'paradoxical continuity of self, mapping and transforming since the subject of resistance is neither fixed nor fluid, but both and more' (1996, p. 26). And this 'more' involves a sense of resistance to both fixity and to fluidity, as an intensely knowingly ambivalent location.

The voices of the women reveal that various manifestations of discipline and power do not in any way comprise an unchallengeable or unchanging system of control and domination (Scott 1985). As Willian Bogard (cited in Rhodes 1998, p. 286) contends, 'discipline always creates gaps, spaces of free play which embody new possibilities for struggle'. Moreover, 'an escalation or intensification of discipline and control' often results in the emergence of correspondingly extreme forms of resistance (Rhodes 1998, p. 288).

For some prisoners, resistance served as a bargaining tool and a means of resolving what Carter (2000, p. 365 cited in Carlton 2007) refers to as the 'crisis of visibility'. For others it served as a vehicle for self-expression, or a way of venting feelings of frustration and desperation. For most, the act of resistance was a key component of short-term survival.

It is within such a context that the prisoner's mind and body come to form sites of struggle on which the institutional dynamics of power and resistance are played out. Rather than preventing or limiting resistance, each strategy of discipline and control opened up new spaces, tactics of subversion and possibilities for prisoner expressions of resistance. These tactics served numerous and diverse personal objectives for the politically motivated prisoners but, above all, they constituted necessary responses for resistance and survival within the confines of a securocratic prison regime.

Violent Repercussions: The Day After the Escape

> When they brought us into the yard, me and X had been doubled up, so they locked us all in separate cells and then the next morning all hell broke loose. Our cell was wrecked.

We woke up and they were letting you out one at a time to go to the toilet, and when we came out they had moved the Army in. So it was out of Cunningham's hands. They took him and all the female screws [prison officers] off the wing and moved the British Army in.

There were a couple of women in the Army as well. So they led you down to the toilet one at a time. But a couple of girls, whatever way they got out of their cell, they were beaten up and their story is in the book [*In The Footsteps of Anne*, see Brady et al. 2011]. So we were sitting in our cell and then they took us out of a separate cell and they put us into one cell. The only thing in it was a locker and we sort of went: what the hell are they doing this for?

This section has examined how the prison become a place of opposition to British rule (McConville 2003) and detailed the prison's response to the 'The Great Escape'. What the voices of the women reveal is the unremitting control at the hands of the state, yet their collective resistance and commitment to organising against the authority or legitimacy of the state provided mutual support and mobilisation against a common enemy (see Campbell et al. 1994; McKeown 2001). Although the next chapters will focus on experiences of incarceration as such, the meaning of the act of imprisonment derives from the context whereby an authoritarian state employs its discretionary power to use prisons as a coercive weapon in a political struggle. As Tomlinson eloquently argues:

Since the emergence of modern prison systems in the nineteenth century, penal policies and prison regimes in Ireland have been strongly influenced by the containment of political disorder, specifically militant Irish Nationalism and Republicanism. While it is quite possible to describe the prison systems in Northern Ireland and the Republic of Ireland in administrative and managerialist terms … this would miss the extent to which contemporary prison systems have been shaped by the political struggles of a range of movements concerned with ending British sovereignty in Ireland. (Tomlinson 1985, pp. 1–2)

The following chapters show how the Conflict on the streets continued behind the prison walls, examining the increased use of violence by the prison and discusses how the female body was targeted in gender-specific ways. Chapter 8 focuses on how and why women were compelled to go on the no wash protest and the responses to this form of political protest.

References

Aretxaga, B. (1997). *Shattering the silence: Women, nationalism and political subjectivity in Northern Ireland*. Princeton, NJ: Princeton University Press.

Benjamin, J. (1998). *The bonds of love: Psychoanalysis, feminism and the problem of domination*. New York: Pantheon Books.

Bettelheim, B. (1986). *The informed heart: A study of the psychological consequences of living under extreme fear and terror*. London: Peregrine Books.

Bhabba, H. (1990). *Nation and narration*. London: Taylor & Francis.

Bhabba, H. (1994). *The location of culture*. London: Routledge.

Brady, E., Patterson, E., McKinney, K., Hamill, R., & Jackson, P. (2011). *The footsteps of Anne: Stories of republican women ex-prisoners*. Belfast: Shanway Press.

Buntman, F. (2003). *Robben Island and prisoner resistance to apartheid*. Cambridge: Cambridge University Press.

Butler, J. (1993). *Bodies that matters: On the discursive limits of sex*. New York: Routledge.

Campbell, B., McKeown, L., & O'Hagan, F. (1994). *Nor meekly serve my time: The H-Block struggle, 1976-1981*. Belfast: Beyond the Pale.

Carlton, B. (2007). *Imprisoning resistance – life and death in an Australian Supermax*. Sydney: Institute of Sydney Criminology Press.

Cohen, S., & Taylor, L. (1972). *Psychological survival: The experiences of long-term imprisonment* (1st ed. 1972). Harmondsworth: Penguin Books.

D'Arcy, M. (1981). *Tell them everything: A sojourn in the prison of her majesty Queen Elizabeth II at Ard Macha (Armagh)*. London: Pluto.

Darragh, S. (2012). *'John's Lennon Dead': Stories of protest, hunger strikes and resistance*. Belfast: Beyond the Pale.

De Certeau, M. (1984). *The practices of everyday life*. Berkeley: University of California Press.

Feldman, A. (1991). *Formations of violence: The narrative of the body and political terror in Northern Ireland*. Chicago: University of Chicago Press.

Foucault, M. (1979). *Discipline and Punish – The Birth of The Prison: Translated by A. Sheridan*. New York: Vintage, Random House.

Frank, A. (1990). Review Article-Bringing Bodies Back in A Decade Review in Theory, *Culture and Society 7*, 131–162.

Frank, A. (1991). *The body: Social processes and cultural theory*. London: Sage.

Horgan, J., & Taylor, M. (1997). The provisional Irish Republican Army: Command and functional structure. *Terrorism and Political Violence, 9*(3), 1–32.

Mathiesen, T. (1965). *The defences of the weak: A sociological study of a Norwegian correctional institution*. London: Tavistock.

Mathiesen, T. (1997). The viewer society: Michel Foucault's "Panopticon" revisited. *Theoretical Criminology, 1*(2), 215–234.

McConville, S. (2003). *Irish political prisoners 1848-1922: Theatres of war*. London: Routledge.

McKeown, L. (1998). *Unrepentant Fenian bastards: The social construction of an Irish Republican Prisoner Community*. PhD thesis, Faculty of Arts, Queen's University Belfast.

McKeown, L. (2001). *Out of time: Irish republican prisoners Long Kesh 1972-2000*. Belfast: Beyond the Pale.

McKittrick, D., Kelters, S., Feeney, B., & Thornton, C. (1999). *Lost lives: The stories of the men and women that died as a result of the troubles*. Edinburgh: Mainstream Publishing.

Mohanty, T. C. (1996). Feminist encounters: Locating the politics of experience. In L. Nicholson & S. Seidman (Eds.), *Social postmodernism: Beyond identity politics*. Cambridge: Cambridge University Press.

Nietzsche, F. (1968). *The will to power*. New York: Vintage Press.

Rhodes, L. (1998). Panoptical intimacies. *Public Culture, 10*(2), 285–311.

Scott, C. J. (1985). *Weapons of the weak: Everyday forms of peasant resistance*. Newhaven: Yale University Press.

Scott, C. J. (1990). *Domination and the arts of resistance: Hidden transcripts*. Newhaven: Yale University Press.

Sparks, R., Bottoms, A. E., & Hay, W. (1996). *Prisons and the problem of order*. Oxford: Clarendon.

Sykes, G. M. (1958). *The society of captives: A study of a maximum security prison*. Princeton, NJ: Princeton University Press.

Tomlinson, M. (1985). Imprisoned Ireland. In V. Ruggiero, M. Ryan, & J. Sim (Eds.), *Western European prisons systems: A critical anatonomy*. London: Sage.

Turner, B. (1984). *The body and society: Explorations in social theory*. London: Sage.

Yuval-Davis, N., & Anthias, F. (Eds.). (1989). *Women nation state*. London: Macmillan.

8

Parthas Caillte: The Politics of Resistance and the Role of the Gendered Incarcerated Body

This chapter and Chap. 9 draw on events that became a focus of political protest both within and beyond the walls of Armagh Prison: the no wash protest the hunger strike and the use of strip searching. These two chapters examine the pivotal position of resistance and the significance of gendered identity as the violence of incarceration intensified (Coady 1986), foregrounding the testimonies of the women which, to date, have been conspicuously absent in many of the accounts and popular iconography of prison resistance.

Background to the Events of 7 February 1980

The events that triggered the woman's involvement in the dirty protest, otherwise known as the no wash protest began with what was a normal day at Armagh Prison. At this stage, the 32 women were on the no-work protest, as an act of resistance to the removal of special category status in 1976

Parthas Caillte is Irish for Paradise Lost.

© The Editor(s) (if applicable) and The Author(s) 2016
A. Wahidin, *Ex-Combatants, Gender and Peace in Northern Ireland*,
DOI 10.1057/978-1-137-36330-5_8

and in solidarity with their comrades in Long Kesh/the Maze. Relations between prisoners and prison officers had worsened as a result of the criminalisation policy, with assassinations of prison officers by the IRA, and an increased incidence of violence by prison officers against male prisoners at Long Kesh/the Maze, resulting in the men commencing the 'dirty protest' there. In Armagh, tensions and the general harassment of the women by the prison officers were also intensifying, culminating in the violent events of 7 February 1980.

> The atmosphere had already been developing to a kind of different level. The whole level of atmosphere of the prison was changing because of the loss of political status, and you've had hostility rising among the prison officers. You had vigorous searching you know, not only as you *came in* but when you were *going out*, and *going from* one wing to another and *all* that. So that was beginning to affect the atmosphere.
>
> We refused to do prison work with the result that you were locked in your cell during the working hours. (Emphasis in original)

The events of 7 February revolved around the ongoing struggle for political status symbolised by the wearing of paramilitary uniform. All women prisoners at this time were allowed to wear their own clothes, and women Republican prisoners would use these to fashion a black paramilitary-style uniform to symbolise their membership of the IRA. The uniform was worn, for example, to commemorate the loss of a comrade and on parades held outside in the yard, in support of their male comrades' struggles for political status (at that time, the 'blanket' and 'no-wash' protests) within Long Kesh/the Maze.

A week before 7 February, the Catholic Church had refused to allow the body of a dead IRA Volunteer, Hugh Delaney, to rest overnight in the chapel. As his three sisters had been interned in Armagh, the Republican prisoners decided to hold a commemorative parade for him wearing clothes, approved by the prison authorities, from which they improvised an IRA uniform. This activity in the encoded world of the prison not only signified to the prison authorities the women's defiance towards the prison regime, it also asserted their political status, their collective identity as Volunteers/soldiers in an Army.

As one woman states:

> So it was *all about us being soldiers*. It was about us being an army faction. We would always remind them [the prison officers] that *we were an army within the prison*, and that they had to negotiate and respect that structure as political prisoners. They [the prison officers] always thought they knew better and then they would *go up against us* and then you had a *game* of survival. You know, Azrini, it was just *a constant battle*. (Emphasis in original)

The wearing of the uniform was crucial in reinforcing their collective identity, an identity that the British government sought to strip from them with the removal of special category status. As Eileen Hickey comments: 'it kept [the POWs] aware that they were soldiers. In Armagh you could feel so removed from the movement, from the struggle outside' (Women in Struggle/Mná I Streachailt, 1994; 12).

'Screws on the Landing': Events of 7 February 1980

Drawing on interviews from the women involved in the events that took place on 7 February, feminist journalist Nell McCafferty writes, 'before noon, all social workers, education officers and religious ministers were cleared off the premises of Armagh jail ... A high ranking officer of Armagh prison came onto the wing, and some 25–30 male officers were with him and formed a semi-circle round us' (1981, pp. 8–11). The prison officers had surrounded the prisoners during lunch. The women recount how an unusually appetising meal of chicken, chips and apple pie was used by the prison personnel to lure them from their cells to an open visible space on the ground floor.

> The funny thing is that in Armagh prison food was so horrendous. It was atrocious. But they knew when to get us. There was apple crumble and chips.

On the 7th of February, the lunch was brought up onto the wing, onto 'B' Wing and we discovered it was chicken and chips, which was very rare because we'd never got good food to be honest with you. I don't know, obviously it was probably deliberate but the cook in Armagh, *cooked good food and ruined it*, and that's basically what he did, *he ruined it*.

The door that connected 'A' and 'B' Wings opened and 30 to 40 of male screws [prison officers] came out and formed a semi-circle in front of the stairs. They blocked off access to the stairs. Blocked off access to the ground floor cells, so we were surrounded. (Emphasis in original)

The women were beaten by the prison officers until they were separated into two association rooms, where they were held until the searches of their cells were completed. After their cells were wrecked, the women were allowed to return to their cells one at a time, but only after each prisoner was searched individually.

Another woman recalls:

It turned out that the search was for all the uniform gear. They herded us all into what was called The Association Room. We were held there for hours until we were allowed back into our cells. After they had searched us, I mean, stripped us. Took everything that they felt was contraband. But as we [the women] started to ask to use the bathroom we were refused and the word quickly spread.

They could have taken the black clothes out at any cell search at any time, because they did that regularly. But no, they came in, and it was all men and it was a very unnerving time. Just for those gates to open and come in with full length riot shields and the hard helmets. They begin beating the women up and throwing them about the place. I remember getting thrown over this big male screw's [prison officers] head on to the landing and when I looked up, X was standing over me and she had been shaking me and I was going 'what's wrong?' and she went 'you were knocked out. Are you okay?' And I went 'yep' and I got up.

Another woman states:

They could have taken [the black clothing] at any time, that's true ... I believe that he [the Governor] wanted to assert his authority and for us to toe the line and for us to do what we were told. He wanted to *break* our comradeship. To *break* 'A' Company and to stop us having our own leadership.

It worked the opposite way because then nobody would have anything at all to do with them [the prison officers] except through Mairéad [the OC], which is what we always did do but even more forcefully. It wasn't easy for the women at the time. We were moved over onto A1 and for the following year we were on the no wash protest. (Emphasis in original)

In addition to reinforcing the political status of the Republican women, the paramilitary uniform contests the legitimacy conferred by the state on the prison officers through the official signifier of their own military-style uniform. For the prison officers to derive any power from the uniform, they must be part of a monolithic disciplinary field. Alternative legitimacies, such as that established by the paramilitary uniform, questioned the prison's power to punish and therefore were not tolerated. It could be argued that the politicised identity of the women seemed doubly threatening to prison officials because of the political prisoners' gender: the paramilitary uniform foregrounded the subject position of 'soldier', thereby disrupting traditional gender roles.

Another ex-combatant reiterates the view that the sole purpose informing the intensity of the violence used against the women was to 'break the strength of the comradeship [of the women]':

The Governor, wanted to show his power and to try and *break* the strength of the comradeship that we had and the strength of the Company. We were 'A' Company and we *stuck together*. (Emphasis in original)

Another woman remembers the intensity of the violence and the bewilderment caused by the unprovoked attack.

I mean I don't know what they'd been led to believe whether they'd hyped themselves up, or whether they've been told to expect trouble or what, I don't know. But they obviously were geared for it because they moved as one.

It wasn't that one male screw [prison officer] was grabbing a woman and then the others followed. It was just like; it's merely on cue that they [prison officers] moved together. *It was bedlam. It was madness.* I mean there were women being thrown. I can remember vividly Q, going up the stairs, if you've been there you'll know there are big metal handrails and there's a middle handrail, and I can remember Q's throat being against the middle handrail and the screw had a hand on her head, pushing her against it.

You know, no-one was in any great physical shape, and they [the women] certainly weren't in any physical shape to take on big six foot men who were well fed and well exercised.

One woman recounts the events:

This screw [prison officer] had his two knees on my chest, and another screw holding my arm and another at the bottom. It was like being raped.

You could feel the tension in the air, and we then explained to the women, you know, you've no chance. I mean we had nothing to hit them with, you know, we didn't want anybody injured for the sake of a cell search. That's what precipitated the no wash protest then in Armagh Jail. From that day forward until the end of the no wash protest there were always male screws in Armagh Jail.

The prison officers eventually locked the women in their cells and refused to allow them access to any prison facilities.

Father Faul Faul describes the situation in detail:

Men in riot gear were sent into the cells armed with batons and shields. They beat and dragged the girls to the guardroom, twisting their arms and pulling their hair. They showed no regard for the fact that their jumpers and skirts were pulled up around them and they were nearly naked. The girls were then starved of food and drink and the toilets were locked. The girls were not allowed to go to the toilets. (Faul 1980, p. 15)

They, like the men, incurred disciplinary punishments (Brún 1988). Several of the women were assaulted by male prison officers who forcibly dragged them in varying degrees of nudity down to the prison Governor for adjudication (Coogan 1980). The following quote from a report smuggled out of jail by one of the prisoners illustrates the sexual overtones of the assault:

At around 3.45pm on Thursday February 7th, numerous male and female screws [prison officers] invaded my cell in order to get me down to the

Governor. They charged in full riot gear equipped with shields. I sat unprotected but aware of what was going to happen as I had heard my comrades
screaming in pain. I was suddenly pinned to the bed by a shield and the
weight of a male screw on top of me. Then my shoes were dragged off my
feet. I was bodily assaulted, thumped, trailed, and kicked. I was then trailed
out of my cell, and during the course of being dragged and hauled from the
wing both my breasts were exposed to the jeering and mocking eyes of all
the [prison officers]. There must have been about twenty of them. While
being carried, I received punches to the back of my head and my stomach.
I was eventually carried into the Governor, my breasts were still exposed.
While I was held by the screws the Governor carried out the adjudication,
and I was trailed back and thrown into a cell. (Republican News 1980)

The Aftermath of 7 February: The No Wash Protest

The events of 7 February became the catalyst for the protest in Armagh.
The extraordinary form of this political action—coupled, on the one
hand, with the strong emotional reactions that it provoked and, on the
other, with its gendered character— makes the no wash protest a particularly suitable case for the exploration of how subjectivity, gender,
the corporeal body, resistance and power are articulated in situations of
heightened political violence (Bosworth and Carrabine 2001).

I mean, you see a few months previous the first time they'd allowed TV
cameras on the Blocks[1] and we'd seen the men on the no wash protest on
the news. God. And I was personally, Sweet Jesus, Mary and Joseph, how
are they [the Blanket men] living like that? God love them, how can they
do that?

Who would have thought, that a couple of months later I'd be doing the
same thing.

The women of Armagh Prison were subjected to beatings and placed
in solitary confinement for 23 hours each day for several weeks (NCCL
1986; United Campaign Against Strip Searching 1987).

---

[1] The term 'Blocks' was the colloquial term referring to the H Blocks. See Chp 3, f.n 30 and 31.

The testimonies of the women reveal how the Republican women in Armagh Prison felt forced into the position of joining their male comrades in the no wash protest. Up to this point, the women had also been resisting the change of status from political prisoners to criminals since 1976 by refusing to do mandatory prison work, and were also enduring similar disciplinary measures to those their male comrades were facing. The accounts show that there was a growing tension between the prison officers and the politically motivated prisoners. Different levels of punishment were employed against the women and the withdrawal of privileges depended on whether you were on remand, sentenced, on the no work and then on the no wash protest.

> On remand you were allowed cigarettes and you were allowed foodstuffs and toiletries. On the no work protest you were still allowed a parcel a month, but it was fruit and toiletries, tissues and that was it. Once the no wash protest began, there was no parcels.

AW: Nothing?

No, just one visit a month.

The aftermath of 7 February as depicted in the women's testimonies illustrates the level of state violence:

> The prison authorities refused to let us use toilet facilities. They beat us up. We had been lying in the cells during that time with cuts and bruises, battered basically, and … you know … And then they moved us from 'B' Wing at that time back to A1.
> I mean we didn't go on it. *We were forced on it because the bathrooms were locked.* (Emphasis in original)

AW: For those who are not aware of what the no wash protest is, could you just explain how and why you went on it and what it involved?

It wasn't a decision that we made to go on it. It was *forced* upon us. From the 7th of February, we were locked into our cells. We didn't get any exercise from the 7th of February and by the 8th of February they [the prison officers] were coming around and handing food into the cells to us.

We *weren't* unlocked to wash. We *weren't* unlocked to go to the bathrooms. We *weren't* unlocked to go for exercise, and it wasn't until late in the afternoon of the 8th that they decided to let us out for exercise. (Emphasis in original)

The Beginning of the No Wash

The crisis started when the prison officers insisted on finding and destroying all the pieces of black clothing in the women's cells. It was reported in the Irish Press on 9 February 1980, that 'paramilitary clothing and flags' were discovered during a search. The prisoners were moved to a different wing of the prison on February 13 with very few personal belongings. According to Mairéad Farrell (cited in McCafferty 1981, p. 28), 'within a week we were given back a few items of personal property—comb, toothbrush and a few photos of relatives'.

> They were housed in 'A' wing, two to an eight-by-twelve-foot cell with two beds, two pillows, two chamber pots, two plastic mugs and plastic knives and forks. In response to the rising public awareness and concern for the women prisoners, the NIO[2] responded by publically stating that a number of women had been confined to their cells and deprived of toilet facilities, except for their 'slop-pots' [sic]. With the lack of toilet facilities, the cells' chamber pots overflowed (*Irish News* 1980).

Initially, the women threw the contents of their slop buckets out of the window, but the prison officers boarded up the windows. This led to the women throwing the contents of their slop-buckets out onto the landings and at the prison officers when they opened their cells doors. This was done to prevent the prison officers from throwing contents of the 'po' all over the cell when the women went for exercise (see Brady et al. 2012, p. 215). Once the women had no way of emptying their chamber pots,

---

[2] Northern Ireland Office.

they resorted to smearing excrement all over the walls of their cells in protest. As a result, Mairéad Farrell, the IRA commanding officer at Armagh Prison, described the circumstances of the no-wash as the women being 'forced into a position of a "dirt strike" as our pots are overflowing with urine and excrement. We emptied them out of the spy-holes into the wing. The male officers nailed them [the spy-holes] closed, but we broke them off using our chairs' (cited in McCafferty 1981, p. 18).

A woman recounts that:

> There were no toilets in the cells in them days. It was a chamber pot and it only held so much, you know, and so we started pouring it out through the door but the screws [prison officers] came along and brushed it back into the cell.

Later, the NIO issued a statement denying the claims that women were forced onto the no wash protest and saying that, by the following Monday, 'most of the women were washing themselves and that the claims that they were forced onto the no wash protest were a fabrication … They were being allowed to leave their cells and eat meals, take daily exercise and visit the washrooms each morning. But they were refusing to work, hand over their sheets for cleaning or read books from the library although facilities were still open to them' (*Belfast Telegraph*, 14 February 1980).

Father Faul described the no wash protest as follows:

> Once you walked into the wing and you were just met with the smell of urine and excrement and all that sort of thing and in the early stages there were pools of urine where the girls had thrown it out the cell door when they were let out for one hour. You were hop stepping in the corridor over this urine etc., and when I visited the cells there was all the hardened excrement on the walls. They [the prison officers] had blocked the windows to a great extent because they thought the girls would throw it out of the window, so the girls were in semi-darkness. They were locked in for 23 hours a day. They had no showers. No washing. (Faul 1980)

Mairéad Farrell [the OC] led the women on the 13-month campaign of the no-wash resistance, which the press termed the 'Dirty Protest' (Sinn Féin Women's Department 1985). The following testimonials demonstrate that the Armagh women had no option but to go on the no wash protest, which they used to highlight prison conditions and the current situation in Northern Ireland.

A woman who was on the no wash protest, details her account:

> There was *nowhere* to empty your chamber pots. There was *nowhere* to get washed. There was *nowhere* to go to the toilet.
>
> I was given the directive to get rid of the chamber pots in any way that the women could and some women rolled up religious magazines. There was a spy-hole in the door. It's a round circle and someone had made them into funnels and poured it through the hole. You used to pour it down the window and it went out into the yard, but the effective thing to do was to advise people to throw it down and on to the suicide wire or when the screws [prison officers] arrived to hand out food or anything like that the women would stand with their chamber pot and she would step forward and throw it. If you'd been in Armagh the suicide net caught everything.
>
> You've been on 'B' Wing somewhere on 'B3' which is the top wing and you know there's a walkway that comes round and there's the suicide wire between the walkways. It wasn't just urine. It was faeces. It was tampons. It was tissues. It was left over food. Oh yes, and this was just falling onto the suicide wire. It was horrible and the screws [the prison officers] were livid about it. What were we supposed to do? There *wasn't* a choice. We didn't decide to go and start a no wash protest.
>
> It was a situation that *we were just forced* onto it. (Emphasis in original)

In a letter smuggled out, Mairéad Farrell writes:

> We were then locked up 23 hours a day and we were denied access to books in the library and denied access to the toilets.
>
> So for 23 hours a day, from February 1980 until March 1, 1981 when Bobby [Sands] went on hunger strike, 'we were on a no slop-out protest with our cells covered in excreta, denied washing facilities and denied dignity'. (Whalen 2007, p. 75)

Living Conditions

The no wash protest meant that the women did not wash their bodies, brush their teeth or wash their hair.

> It was February, when we started the no wash. We sent all our stuff out. We had only one set of clothes—the clothes we were standing in.
>
> It was stupid putting all clean clothes on to your dirty body. So we decided to turn out what little stuff we had anyway, and we got a set of clean clothes then every three months. We divided this among ourselves.

Another women states:

> We thought fuck em. We will put it on the walls and not wash ourselves and that's when it escalated. That's was when the no wash came in, and it was fierce.
>
> They [the prison officers] blocked the bottom of the door so we couldn't pour the urine out, and then we poured the urine out the window and they boarded up the windows. So you were living in semi-darkness. In this fetid, stinking, shit … and it went on for months and months and months you know.

The only natural light the women had escaped from the cracks between the glass and the boards that were placed in front of the windows to stop the women from throwing the contents of their chamber pots onto the yard. Living in semi-darkness, with only one hour for exercise, the women would reach up to the windows to breathe what little air was coming through the space between the glass and the boarded windows.

> We stood up on top of the bed and you climbed up to where the wee bit of the window was, and although they had it boarded up, there was still enough space that you could have shouted out the window.

AW: So you were in complete darkness then?

> There was a light, but yes, the light was very, very dull. The cells were always dull and then if you can imagine the excrement all over the walls and ceiling. So yeah, it was pretty gloomy.

Mairéad Farrell's mother wrote in 1980 about the terrible conditions: 'I think it's inhuman that the girls are being forced to live in these conditions. I think it's absolutely desperate that such conditions are allowed to continue. Mairéad says, the flies are terrible and there are some kind of fleas and other insects hopping about the cell' (*An Phoblacht/Republican News* 1980).

Another woman describes the process of being moved so that their cell could be cleaned.

> We got moved after three months to a clean cell and that's when the flies came in. I think it was because the cells were all bleached down and they used ammonia to clean the cells out. You were moved in. Everything was wet. It was damp. It was the clean cells actually that had the flies and the flies used to actually be swirling in the middle of the cell. So you'd spend your first day getting rid of them. The strange thing was when all the cells were covered in shit, the cells very rarely had flies.

The smell of the faeces was replaced by the potent smell of chemical detergents which encouraged flies to settle, and caused respiratory problems amongst the women from which some still suffer. In this enforced move from one cell to another, the women were forced into the gaze of the prison officers, exposing them to verbal and physical abuse. The cell movement represented a space in which the women not only became visible but were vulnerable to violence and prison disciplinary control and power:

> They [the prison officers] boarded up the windows and then they moved us across the ground floor in 'A' Wing and put us in the cells and boarded up the windows. It was easier to *control us*. (Author's emphasis)

In trying to devise ways of surviving these new living conditions, the women initially sought ways to deal with the revulsion of applying faeces to the walls of their cells.

> We were so naïve and so stupid that we actually pulled the wardrobe out and stuck the poo on the wall behind the wardrobe and pushed the wardrobe back, thinking that if we can't see it, it didn't happen.

Like the Republican male prisoners at Long Kesh/the Maze who embarked on the no wash protest in 1978, maintaining a level of cleanliness was important to the women and this method of application not only reduced the chances of bacteria and maggots, but also the smell.

We put our excrement on the walls because that way it smelt less. It dried up quicker and there was less chance of it turning into maggots.

AW: So it is true, that the smell disappears once it's on the wall?

Absolutely, yeah. The urine smell actually was worse. It sort of never disappeared. Another thing that disappeared would have been body smells, for some strange reason. We thought they disappeared. I think we basically became immune to them. You never became immune to the conditions because it was *disgusting*. It wasn't where we wanted to be but we felt closer to our comrades in the H Blocks. (Emphasis in original)

Although, the women described the cells as '*fetid*', and they were not allowed to have a television, radio or reading material to break the monotony, they found ways to subvert and reclaim the regime of isolation by writing and singing in Gaelic and writing political slogans. The act of speaking and writing in Gaelic was a 'symbolic weapon of resistance in the wider struggle for national self-determination' (Mac Ionnrachtaigh 2013, p. 42). By reclaiming the faecal cell and reclaiming the body through dirt, the women created a context of cultural separatism (Turner 1984). This act divorced the prisoners from the sign systems of captivity.

The prison cell, already imprinted with a scatological writing of the political prisoners, relinquished part of its wall space to the graphics of Gaelic language acquisition. The prisoners scratched their accumulated learning alongside the faecal matter on the walls. Alongside the scatological history of domination, the prison cell now bore the secret history of language acquisition and of other women before them. The prisoners who were physically absent from each other, who may have never seen each other, were present with each other through the cell wall. Thus, the 'use of the Irish language as a means of resistance had a "transcendental power" that was first and foremost directed at the prison itself', transforming 'the cell into a pedagogical space' in an 'act of personalised political appropriation' as strong as that of the defilement of the cell with excreta (Mac Ionnrachtaigh 2013, p. 195). The reading of old Gaelic graffiti on the cell wall by each new inhabitant and the addition of new inscriptions became an act of sociation and a means for reproducing knowledge that defied and circumvented the disciplinary gaze, transforming the prison space into a spectacle of alternative representation, meaning and political power.

> Yeah, we all made designs. We drew wee flowers. We did flowers or we wrote 'up the IRA' and we had our names on the back of the door and stuff. During the no wash protest they wouldn't let us associate and at one point the only way to do it was to take the iron bed off the bottom part of the bed and dig it into the wall during the night until we all had holes from one cell to the next one.

In order to make the cell conditions more bearable and make a tangible link with the outside world, the women also drew scenes of places outside the prison that had a significant meaning to them. The meanings and experiences of life beyond the walls connected the women to the outside world, enabling them to manage the meanings and nuances of the time discipline of the prison world. Identity management is vital in order to survive the reduction of identity to that of 'inmate', by providing a means to recede from the prison gaze. This tacit knowledge recreates the prisoner as a knowing agent within a system which attempts to suppress the sense of self by recreating meaning with the aim of 'producing and shaping an obedient subject' (Foucault 1977, p. 152).

As one commentator has suggested:

> Although their world was reduced to four cramped walls, within that tiny space self was everywhere (Ellman 1993, p. 99).

The smearing of cells also represented an attempt to take greater control over space and territory, albeit within the limited confines of the cell, by prisoners experiencing extreme vulnerability to staff assaults. Resistance was enacted by re-territorialising space in order to transform its meanings, undermining the totalising control of territory by means of which the prison both enacts and symbolises its power, and turning the prison into a space of messages, covert communication and sharing lives with others, albeit within the limits of the disciplinary gaze.

> What would have happened was that … you see when a cell was covered in shit, and even part of that, I mean after a while myself and X thought we can't live like this. So we would decorate the cells and we used to decorate it with lovely scenes of Donegal and we used to use the poo … because our diet was so bad the poo was like hard crayons, you know what I mean? What a conversation to have, but it was, and we used to decorate everything from X—to Wonder Woman on the walls. So we used to have the cell decorated, and the smell was bad, you got used to the smell, you did.

Through the Gaelic and the scatological writing, the cell became a historical membrane that secreted a record of prison experience and knowledge. The cell ceased to separate, isolate and de-socialise the political prisoners. The Gaelic writings had become an archaeological artefact, a liberation of memory, comradeship and solidarity. An entire genealogy of resistance was etched with pain and endurance into the material of imprisonment (Arendt 1970), as both the minds and the bodies of the prisoners passed into this cell membrane through the medium of their writing and faecal transcription of their political condition.

The composition of networks inside and outside the prison enabled calculated action on conduct through discursive formations and, in time, the cell became the extended body of the prisoners and their bodies become their temporary prisons.

Cell Movement

Just as none of us is outside or beyond geography, none of us is completely free from the struggle over geography. That struggle is complex and interesting because it is not only about soldiers and cannons but also about ideas, about forms, about images and imaginings. (Said 1993, p. 7).

The women on the no wash protest were moved every three months and the process of moving brought with it further beatings. The knowledge that they would be beaten increased their anxiety about being forced out of the shadows of the semi-darkness that they were used to, reflecting the heightened vulnerability of the women and the intensified disciplinary measures of the regime seeking, in some way, to force the women to conform.

Any excuse to put their hands on you. So I remember this morning there was a cell search. They were going to move us from my cell to another, and my cell was dirty. Every six weeks they'd clean your cell and it was cleaned with Jeyes Fluid and they'd come with a big steamer and clean your cell.

We had *nothing*. Just what we were wearing. The same clothes for months, so we had nothing. I had one photograph. I had a daughter, a baby in Armagh jail. My child was born in Armagh jail. I had a photograph of her and I would take it with me when I moved cell, and I would try to keep it clean, and they [the prison officers] were pulling and hauling at me and they were searching me and she took the photograph of my daughter and dropped it on the cell floor and put her foot on it. She destroyed the photograph of my child, and I grabbed her by the throat. The screw [the prison officer] blew the whistle and hit the alarm. They all piled in and I was trailed out into the centre of wing you know.

I was spread-eagled, in the crucifix position, lying on my stomach in the urine and the shit that was floating down that wing. They had my arms and legs and they got a male officer in and you know the stairs particularly from B1 to B2—the second level carrying like me in a crucifixion pose and the male officer just grabbed me here and with my bra and pulled my shirt up and my breasts were dangling down. It was really humiliating you know and they were kicking and beating me.

We knew there were consequences to every action you took. You lost a day's remission for every day that you refused to work, and then they double charged you. How could I lose another day's remission when I've already lost it? But they go through this fucking stupid process. We used to go and stand in front of the Governor, the screw told him the story. You were found guilty. You know, no one's ever found not guilty.

Moreover, the cells were cleaned by Loyalist men from Long Kesh/ the Maze, although 'the NIO denied that male 'Loyalist orderlies' had been given extra remission as an incentive, if they cleaned the Republican

wings in Armagh, stating that they were selected because they 'were willing to do the work, are considered suitable for it, and for no other reason'
(*Irish News*, 9 September 1980). As the women looked increasingly dirty,
the prison officers tried to counteract defilement by increasing their care
in making themselves up and having their hair done. The British government reinforced the idea that the women on the no wash protest required
special measures, such as the constant change of cells and separation
from the other prisoners, because they potentially posed an 'unacceptable
health hazard to other prisoners and staff'.

> The women came off because the no wash protest ended in both the H
> Blocks and in Armagh on 1st March 1981, when the second hunger strike
> commenced with Bobby Sands.

The no wash protest lasted 13 months, during which more attention
was focused on Armagh Prison than at any other time during the decade
(Armagh Co-ordinating Group 1981). The no wash protest embraced
the struggle for better prison conditions and shared with the protest of
the men in Long Kesh/the Maze the united objective of winning the five
central demands:

- The right not to wear a prison uniform (applied to the male prisoners
  only);
- The right not to do prison work;
- The right of free association with other prisoners, and to organise edu-
  cational and recreational pursuits;
- The right to one visit, one letter and one parcel per week;
- Full restoration of remission lost through the protest.

While in many ways the women's protest mirrored that of the men,
representing the shared objective of asserting their political status and
identity, the voices of the women clearly illustrate that the responses they
received by going on the no wash protest was specifically gendered in
the experience itself, the disciplinary consequences for the women on
the protest and the changes in their subjectivity as women through this

experience. The weaponising of menstrual blood was seen as 'shocking' in a manner which depended on received notions that women's bodily functions should be hidden.

As one ex-combatant states:

> I think it's the same thing as the periods. No-one spoke about women having periods; no one spoke about that kind of experience. In Catholic Ireland there were a lot of things that had happened that really didn't make for a comfortable sitting in meetings. Unfortunately, because of the norms in society, they weren't ... I'm not justifying it; I'm trying to analyse and reflect upon as to why this was the case. One could say the same about many of the experiences that some people have come through with the Catholic Church—they weren't spoken about.

It therefore had the secondary effect of challenging aspects of the Republican cultural identity itself, which found much of its expression through idealised notions of womanhood (largely as promoted by the Catholic Church). While all the (male and female) prisoners re-appropriated, through their weaponising of the 'dirty' body, the racist notion of the Irish as 'primitive' and animalistic (see Neti 2003), the fact that the women also used their menstrual blood in this way also served to subvert the ideals of feminine modesty and, indeed, to reinsert the sexed body into the military struggle from which it had largely been erased.

The women could be seen both as doubly 'victimised' not only by the forced dismantling of their 'feminine' identity, but also as being necessarily and unintentionally drawn into a confrontation with the cultural misogyny of both their own communities and the dominant culture of the imperial power.

The previous section examined the conditions which precipitated the no wash protest and how the women found ways of subverting the prison regime. The no wash protest continued until the second hunger strike commenced at Long Kesh/the Maze on 1 March 1981, when the no-wash protest ended at both prisons in order to focus attention on the men on hunger strike. The following section focuses on the women's involvement in the first hunger strike of late 1980, during which the no wash protest continued.

The Hunger Strike

On 27 October 1980, seven men, led by the late Brendan Hughes, OC of the H-Blocks at the time, began their hunger strike. On 1 December, three women went on hunger strike for 19 days: Mary Doyle, aged 24, from Greencastle, Co. Down; and Mairéad Nugent, aged 21 and Mairéad Farrell,[3] aged 23, both from Andersonstown, Belfast. Mary Doyle had been charged with possessing incendiary devices and sentenced to eight years' imprisonment. Mairéad Nugent was convicted of attempting to bomb the house of the then Governor of Armagh Prison, Governor Whittington, and Mairéad Farrell was sentenced to imprisonment for possession of explosives and membership of the IRA. This was the second and the last of the hunger strikes the women were to undertake. Farrell believed that the involvement of women in the hunger strike would 'create an additional source of pressure on the prison authorities', and would place 'a moral pressure' on the British government to concede to the demands of the Republican prisoners.

> What happened was the men had decided to go on hunger strike with Brendan Hughes and Sean McKenna and the others. Meanwhile the women had suffered on the no wash protest and we were saying 'this is going nowhere'. The screws [the prison officers] were stepping things up, the Governor was getting worse, and they [the prison officers] didn't care. And we thought we have to step this up. But when the men went on the hunger strike, the women then began discussing with the men and also with the leadership whether they should follow. We decided that the women should join as well.
>
> We were there for the *same* reason as the men. We'd went through the *same* conditions at that time as the men and we felt that we needed to be taking the *same* road. So people put their name forward at that time. (Emphasis in original)

On 1 December, Mairéad Farrell, Mary Doyle and Mairéad Nugent joined the fast. They remained on the Wing, confined in an excreta-

---

[3] Mairéad Farrell was the IRA OC in Armagh Prison from December 1979–1986.

covered cell for almost two weeks, before they were transferred to the Hospital Wing of the jail. The women ended their protest on 19 December 1980.

> So the first morning we informed the screws [the prison officers] that we were on hunger strike. They put the three of us together in a double cell which was brilliant you know to be together and to keep one another going.

In an attempt to break the women's resolve, the prison officers loaded their plates with appetising food:

> The plates were overflowing with food. Steaming hot—when we always got cold food. And it was always wee small portions, but our cell was never left without food you know. It's was like they thought that the smell of the food in the cell would break us.

She goes on to say:

> God help their [the prison officers] wit. I mean when the supper was left in all night and then they brought in breakfast. They took that out, brought in lunch, took that out. That's the way they went. You know, and it was just so petty of them.
> The other thing I mean we got our hate mail okay, from England. Post marked England, where we got called Provie[4] murdering bastards and that they hoped we would stay on hunger strike for a long time and that we would die in great pain etc. Now the screws [the prison officers] were able to get those letters to us but not the ones from our family.

For the remaining women, the impact of seeing their friends deteriorate added to the sense of helplessness and foreboding of what was yet to come.

> Three women on hunger strike. It was absolutely *terrible*. Absolutely terrible. Each day you were watching them and you wanted to be on it yourself.

---

[4] Colloquial term for members of the Provisional IRA.

It was like we're *all* in this together. We're *all* comrades. We're *all* working towards the same goal. There was a lot of feeling for them but a lot of guilt and also each day watching them getting weaker and becoming more emaciated. You see, 19 days. After a week … and if you remember, after a year being on the no wash protest everybody had already lost so much weight. So it was bad. It was really bad. (Emphasis in original)

In December 1980, the prisoners were presented with a document which seemed to be conceding to the demands of the hunger strike. On 18 December, the hunger strike was called off by Brendan Hughes, motivated by the belief that a settlement would be delivered and his concern for his comrade Sean who was near to death.

On the eighteenth night we heard on the news … The hunger strike was over in the Block, and we looked at one another. Did I hear that right? So we waited for the following news and it confirmed it again. So it wasn't until the following day then until a visit was granted that we were told, you know, that it was called off. Obviously, we thought we had achieved the 5 demands, you know?

I mean, and the first thought for me was you know, nobody was dead, you know, and that we had won, basically. But I mean it was days and weeks to come, that you know, that we realised that the Brits reneged on the 5 demands.

The women came off the hunger strike on the 19th night when they heard that the men's hunger strike was over. The women heard on the radio that the men had called off their hunger strike; unbeknown to them, Danny Morrison had been refused access to the women by the NIO to inform them of the recent developments. The British reneged on the settlement and, on 1 March 1981, Bobby Sands, then OC of the H-Blocks, began the hunger strike which ultimately resulted in the death of 10 men. By September 1981, with 23 men still on hunger strike, some of the families had begun to authorise medical intervention. On 3 October 1981, the end of the hunger strike was announced. The outcome of the second hunger strike was that one of the five demands—the right not to wear the prison uniform—was met.

The protesting prisoners applied a new strategy and declared they were available for work. The work provided by the prison authorities was sabotaged by the prisoners and, eventually, the prison authorities broadened the definition of prison work to include education and the right of the prisoners to be responsible for keeping their own areas/units clean.

However, the special category status for politically motivated prisoners was never reinstated. Nevertheless, as a result of these events, 'criminalisation was proven to be a failed policy' (Brady et al. 2011, p. 185) and, in fact, the response to criminalisation not only raised awareness of the plight of the political prisoners to a global level, but also resulted in a more politicised and mobilised Republican community. Although 'the conditions at the H-Blocks improved, the conditions in Armagh deteriorated, with the use of strip searching introduced in an attempt to make the women conform to the prison regime' (ibid.).

I went on to what was called the no wash protest and I was on that for several years, and you had obviously the hunger strike period and you had all what happened during the strike period in the jails. When the hunger strike ended in the Kesh the conditions actually got better.

Whereas in Armagh the conditions actually got worse, and Governor Thomas Murtagh introduced strip searching. In terms of the strip search, and I'll just go into it in detail, it hadn't been in Armagh before then. Through all the years of all the protests, all the years of all that, it was never introduced.

It wasn't introduced until 1982, late '82. It was different for women than it was for men because we were never used to getting strip searched and then all of a sudden this policy came in, a blanket policy. Every time you were going out of the reception of the jail or coming back you had to be strip searched and we were a very, very, small number and we always wore our own clothes, so there was never any blanket protest. The Republican women were mostly affected by this policy because we had to go in and out to court every week.

So what happened was the women refused to be searched and then they were forcibly stripped, and what that actually meant was the screws [prison officers] got you down to reception and whilst it was female screws that were in the room to do this, the male screws were on the outside and the RUC men who took you to court were there as well. So it was all within hearing of this happening. And they would have put a towel round the woman's head so she couldn't identify who was doing it and force her down, and Catherine Moore, I don't know if you have read Catherine Moore's description, this girl from Derry who was on remand at the time. And they would have held them down spread-eagled and literally tore their clothes off, sanitary towels and everything. So that was the type of strip search that was introduced.

In some instances the women were blindfolded, and unable to see their assailants. This process is indicative of the state's power to punish, in which 'being surveyed required the removal of their vision and the monopolisation of that sense by the state, (Feldman 2006, p. 432).

After that ordeal:

> When she returned to the prison wing she was given six weeks' confinement for assaulting the 20 prison officers.

It is clear from the women's testimonials that they had not only been assaulted by prison officers, but were also suffering in conditions that Cardinal Tomás Ó Fiaich characterised as being worse than the slums of Calcutta (Faul and Murray 1979). The women survived through a complex system of managing the lived body, which was achieved through a variety of practices entailing the use of props; that is, symbols, constraint, containment, concealment, bodily function governance and the experience of embodiment as fleshy, sensate bodies (Edwards and McKie 1996). As described above, the women living in these abnormal extreme conditions of permanent semi-darkness and limited communication with the other women carved out spaces and meaning. The women rewrote the individualisation of prison punishment by creating methods that reconnected them with others and with the outside world. Pile and Keith (1997, p. xi) argue, 'these resistances are embedded in the "politics" of everyday spaces through which identities are constantly in a state of flux'. It is through the creation of new identities that new spaces are formed in response to these shifts in meaning. The resistant identities open up further possibilities; new landscapes and new meanings (Glenholmes 2014). Thus, the carceral gaze seeped into 'somatic surveillance', which is integral to self-surveillance, to physical survival; and, subsequently, the body becomes inscribed into the organisational body to which the women were resistant.

This chapter clearly highlights the inscription of femininity and time onto the rhythms of the body. It illustrates how the body operates within fields of power and within a realm of signs (cf. Baudrillard 1982, p. 180). It has been argued that time and identity in prison consist of a multiplicity of discursive elements that come into play at various times, thereby existing in 'different and even contradictory discourses' (Foucault 1967, pp. 100–102). The Foucauldian lens allows an analysis that goes beyond domination and subordination and truth or deception. The prison inscribes an invisible code similar to the body idiom described by Goffman (1961); the body resists, negotiates and is a receptor, generator and interpreter of the social meanings produced externally and also internally by the women in the study.

As sensate, fleshy bodies, some women suffered from infections while on the no wash protest and, as result of their experience of incarceration, have had ongoing gynaecological, respiratory and mental health problems.

The following chapters will address how the gendered body through the politics of menstruation (O'Keefe 2006) and difference came to the fore in a way that was not applicable to the men in the H-block struggle. Chapter 9 will examine how women found ways to undermine the violence they experienced as women and as politically motivated prisoners. The quote below demonstrates the liquid landscape of the prison in relation to how punishment and control was used in an attempt to undermine the solidarity between the women, their commitment to Republican ideals/beliefs and self. As Mandela argues:

The challenge for every prisoner, particularly every political prisoner, is how to survive prison intact, how to emerge from a prison undiminished, how to conserve and even replenish one's beliefs. The first task in accomplishing that is learning exactly what one must do to survive. To that end, one must know the enemy's purpose before adopting a strategy to undermine it. Prison is designed to break one's spirit and destroy one's resolve. To do this the authorities attempt to exploit every weakness. Demolish every initiative, negate all signs of individuality—all with the idea of stamping out that spark that makes each of us human and each of us who we are Mandela (1994, pp. 340–341).

References

An Phoblacht/Republican News. (1980, November 22). *Armagh prisoners, decision final. Women join the hunger strike.* www.Anphoblacht.Com/Contents/13890.

Arendt, H. (1970). *On violence.* London: Allen Lane and Penguin.

Armagh Co-ordinating Group. (1981, May). Women behind the wire.

Baudrillard, J. (1982). *In the shadow of the silent majorities (Foreign Agents) (Semiotext (E)/Foreign Agents)*, MIT Press, Cambridge, Mass.

Bosworth, M., & Carrabine, E. (2001). Reassessing resistance, race, gender and sexuality. *Prison in Punishment and Society, 3*, 501–515.

Brady, E., Patterson. E., McKinney, K., Hamill. R. & Jackson. P. (2011). In The Footsteps of Anne: Stories of Republican Women Ex-Prisoners. Belfast: Shanway Press.

Brún, B. (1988). Women and imperialism in Ireland. *Women Studies International Forum, 11*(4), 323–328.

Campaign Against Strip Searching. (1987). *Stop strip searching.* Dublin: Parnell Square.

Coady, C. A. J. (1986). The idea of violence. *Journal of Applied Philosophy, 3*, 3–19.

Coogan, T. P. (1980). *On the blanket: The H-Block story.* Dublin: Ward River Press.

Edwards, J., & McKie, L. (1996). Women's public toilets: A serious issue for the body politic. *European Journal of Women's Studies, 3*, 215–232.

Ellman, M. (1993). *The hunger artists: Starving, writing and imprisonment.* London: Virago.

Faul, D. (1980). *Black February Armagh prison: Beating women in prison.* Pamphlet, Armagh D. Faul.

Faul, D., & Murray, R. (1979). *H Blocks: British Jail for Irish political prisoners.* Dungannon: D. Faul.

Feldman, A. (1991). *Formations of violence: The narrative of the body and political terror in Northern Ireland.* Chicago: University of Chicago Press.

Feldman, A. (2006). Violence and vision: The prosthetics and aesthetics of terror in states of violence. In F. Coronil & J. Skurski (Eds.), *States of violence* (pp. 425–469). The University of Michigan: Michigan Press.

Foucault, M. (1967). *Madness and civilization: A history of insanity in the age of reason* (R. Howard, Trans.). London: Tavistock.

Foucault, M. (1977). *Discipline and punish: The birth of the prisons* (Translated from the French: A. Sheridan, Trans.). London: Allen Lane.

Glenholmes, E. (2014). *We broke Armagh: It never broke us.* Belfast: Tar A nall (Unpublished, Personal Letter).

Goffman, E. (1961). *Asylums: Essays on the social situation of mental patients and other inmates.* New York: Anchor Books.

Irish News. (1980, February 8). Former IRA freed.

Mandela, N. (1994). *Long walk to freedom: The anthropology of Nelson Mandela.* New York: Little Brown.

Mac Ionnrachtaigh, F. (2013). *Language, resistance and revival: Republican prisoners and the Irish language in the North of Ireland.* London: Pluto.

McCafferty, N. (1981). *The Armagh women.* Dublin: Co-op Books.

National Council for Civil Liberties (NCCL). (1986). *Strip searching: An inquiry into the strip searching of women remand prisoners at Armagh prison between 1982 and 1985.* London: NCCL.

Neti, L. (2003). Blood and dirt: Politics of women's protest in Armagh prison, Northern Ireland. In A. Aldama (Ed.), *Violence and the body.* Bloomington: Indiana University Press.

O'Keefe, T. (2006). Menstrual blood as a weapon of resistance. *International Feminist Journal of Politics, 8*(4), 535–556.

Pile, S., & Keith, M. (Eds.). (1997). *Geographies of resistance.* London: Routledge.

Republican News. (1980, February 23). Republican Press Centre. http://newspaperarchive.com/cgi/Republican-In-1980/

Said, W. E. (1993). *Culture and imperialism.* London: Vintage.

Sinn Féin Women's Department. (1985). *Women in struggle: Revolutionary struggle women's bulletin. Series 2: A women's place is in the struggle* (p. 3). Interview with Mairéad Farrell.

Turner, B. (1984). *The body and society: Explorations in social theory.* London: Sage.

Whalen, L. (2007/2008). *Contemporary Irish republican prison writing: Writing and resistance.* London: Palgrave Macmillan.

9

The 'Norms of Our Conflict': The Use of Strip Searching as Gendered Punishment

The aim of this chapter is to examine how strip searching was used against women in a gender-specific way. In so doing, it will draw attention to the disjunction between official policy relating to strip searching and the way it was used and conducted in practice, and to the way the issue of security was used by the prison authorities to legitimise the practice of strip searching. The chapter will challenge the official discourse around the use of strip searching by examining how the women experienced and responded to this particular type of gendered punishment, and how it was used to control and discipline the bodies of politically motivated prisoners.

> Two wardresses walk in. They ordered you to stand up. They took off your clothes. They started by inspecting your shoes as you stood naked. They went through your panties, your bra, and every seam of every garment. Then they would go through your hair and inspect your vagina.
> Nothing is more humiliating. And you are all alone in the cell.

© The Editor(s) (if applicable) and The Author(s) 2016
A. Wahidin, *Ex-Combatants, Gender and Peace in Northern Ireland*,
DOI 10.1057/978-1-137-36330-5_9

Another woman recalls:

> You had to take your pants off and you had one of these big long sanitary towels, it wasn't like the stuff we have now. You would have been standing there with the pad out. I felt like lifting it and sticking it in her face! '*This is your shame, it's not mine*'. 'I'm sorry X, I have to do this. You know it's my job'. You know, Azrini, I'm proud of everything I have done, and I would do it again. (Emphasis in original)

She later goes on to say in relation to growing up in the North of Ireland and the constant searching, that:

> After a while an *abnormal* situation becomes the *norm* of everyday life: so being stopped and searched was like the norm. There's *nothing* normal about it. But Azrini, *it was the norms of our Conflict*. (Emphasis in original)

The women's stories, and this chapter in particular, reveal that 'the instruments with which the body is abused in order to break the spirit tend to be gender differentiated and, in the case of women, to be sexualised' (Cockburn 2001, p. 22). For example, Martina Anderson and Ella O'Dwyer endured over 400 strip searches while on remand in HMP Brixton between 1984 and 1985 (a top security, all-male prison in the UK), where they were held in solitary confinement. This obliges us to question the purpose of strip searches, in a situation where the women had never left the presence of a prison officer and were held in isolation. These two particular women endured, on average, 25 strip searches each month (Scraton et al. 1991, p. 150). Martina Anderson had one search after gynaecological examination (London Armagh Group 1984).

Ella O'Dwyer poignantly describes the high levels of fear and anxiety induced by the process of moving from isolation into the gaze of the prison officer, and thus becoming visible through the strip search. It will be argued throughout this chapter that, by placing the body in a position of compulsory visibility, the process of the strip search becomes pregnant with the potential for gendered violence. This act of violence becomes a metonym for dominance over others: power 'lies in the totalising engorged gaze over the politically prone body and subjugation is encoded as exposure to this penetration' (Feldman 2006, p. 427). In Northern Ireland, visibility can be aggressive and the weapons of aggression, in turn, become instruments of political image-making: 'weaponry makes ideological objects and scenography appear' (Feldman 2006, p. 428).

The following statement by an ex-combatant, Ella O'Dwyer, forcibly conveys the punitive intention and psychological impact of this enforced objectification of the prisoner's body:

> I stand like an embarrassed child watching her [the prison officer] dangle my bra and panties about. For increased effect, I am ordered to turn around slowly to give them a peep at everything. They [the prison officers] order me to lift the gown that I have been given to wear. I have only been allowed to wear the gown since September. Before that I had to stand naked while they checked my clothes. Prison officers rub my hair and ears like an animal and I have to lift my feet.
>
> The awful dread is that I will be touched so I am stiffened to resist. They have told me that they can lift my breasts forcibly, if they decide to, and even probe my body folds. They can touch any part of me at all. It is horrible to have four eyes staring at me over the top of a blanket. While two other officers stand behind this blanket another may stand in front. I know that every part of me is being touched accidentally or deliberately since I arrived here. The gown I was wearing slips off when I fumble, to rush into my clothes. (Women's Equality Group/London Strategic Policy Unit 1986, p. 164)

The practice of strip searching and the high levels of psychological brutality involved continued when the ex-combatants were transferred to Durham prison, a 'Category A' women's prison in the North of England. The process of the strip search—that is, the level, detail and method by which it is conducted—is discretionary; it can range from 'frisking' to 'skin searches to an intimate body search'—that is, a 'search of the body's orifices, including the anus and vagina regardless of menstruation' (ibid., p. 38).

While the degrading and humiliating process of strip searching is not itself a provision under emergency law, it was used during the detention of women under emergency legislation (CAJ 1987; The Community for

Justice 1987, 1985). Strip searching has most notably taken place within Armagh and Maghaberry women's prisons, but also when women have been detained in police custody (Loughran 1985). However, it was used primarily against remand prisoners (Loughran 1983, 1986).

> They [the women] were cuffed.[1] Straight out of Armagh prison, straight into a van, and this was completely secured and locked. Straight out of the van into another cell in the court. No contact with anyone, other than those prison screws [prison officers]. Straight from that cell, up into the court, surrounded all the time by police officers, screws and the judge. No contact with anyone. Then straight into the cell. Back into the van. Back into the prison. *Strip Searching was a weapon in the arsenal of the prison service.* (Emphasis in original)

This meant that female remand prisoners endured systematic strip searching twice a day, before and after each court appearance or visit. Sentenced prisoners were strip searched on any occasion they had to leave the prison (for example, for hospital visits), as well as for 'security reasons'. The use of strip searching escalated and was used more widely after the end of the no wash protest and the hunger strikes of 1981, a time of increased political confrontation between Republicans and the state (*Irish Times* 1980; Scraton 2007; Tomlinson 1980). Its introduction into the women's prisons in June 1982 has been attributed to the general strategy of attempting to break female Republican prisoners and the Republican movement in general:

> The British Government is using *women's nakedness to tyrannise us*. We feel that our bodies are used like a *weapon to penalise us*, with the intention of making *us* collapse under the pressure. If we haven't collapsed by now, I don't think that we will. (Martina Anderson, 22 April 1987, IRIS) (Emphasis in original)

Hatred and bigotry in the North of Ireland towards Republicans, and towards Catholics more generally, also fuelled a specific type of engendering of punishment (see Scraton and Moore 2005, 2007). Those con-

---

[1] Cuffed is a colloquial term for being hand-cuffed.

ducting the strip searches did not discriminate on the basis of age or circumstances, as both young and old were forced through the process, as were women who were menstruating, pregnant, had just given birth or were recovering from a hysterectomy (Irish Prisoners Appeal 1986; hristian Study: A Community Problem 1997).

Evidence points to strip searching being less a genuine 'security measure' than a instrument of war that terrorised, punished and degraded Republican women (McCulloch and George 2009), rendered more brutal by exploiting the fact of menstruation to intensify the enforced sense of degradation and vulnerability (Aretxaga 2001; Scrambler and Scrambler 1993; Smith 2009). A menstruating woman was 'forced to remove her sanitary protection and hand it over for inspection. During this process she remained totally naked, exposed and 'unprotected' until the visual body inspection and search of her clothing was completed; only then is her sanitary protection returned' (Maghaberry Republican Prisoner's Statement 1987, p. 17; Roche 1985). Speaking of their experiences of menstruating while being strip searched, female prisoners proclaimed:

> There is no degree of decency preserved throughout the strip search. It is simply a debasing and revolting practice. (Prisoner's Statement 1986, p. 6)

It is well-documented that the British state forces repeatedly singled out Republican women (Harris and Healy 2001; Pickering 2001), to intimidate, humiliate and reinforce women's sense of powerlessness in the hope of breaking the Republican movement. The discretionary nature of penal policing was brought into play to support mechanisms of regulation, disciplinary power and the power to punish.

A shared theme from the ex-combatants was that the strip searches were about:

> Humiliation. I mean it's about control.

Another woman says:

> I believe it was just part of trying to *break the struggle from within*. There's no other reason.

All the women in the study experienced strip searching as a brutal, intimidatory, sexualised and degrading practice which was viewed as being targeted specifically at Republican prisoners to force them not only to conform to the prison regime in a way that wasn't applied to the Loyalist women.

As the following testimonies reveal:

> Their [the prison officers'] sole aim at times was to, what they believe, *is to break you psychologically* and they think that they can do this through strip searching and *firing* at you all the kind of draconian measures that they can to try to prevent one from surviving.

She goes on to say:

> Anytime you *moved* anywhere or anytime you went up to the bathroom they [prison officers] just *stopped you*. This is how they operated. In Brixton, they seconded officers. HMP Durham is a male prison but up to 2005 held women. They came in from Durham or came in from HMP Holloway is a closed category prison for adult women and young offenders. It is the largest women's jail in Western Europe. In 2015, it was announced that the prison will close. Holloway all tanked up because they had heard of us. They wanted to be the group that *was going to break you and that was what their sole purpose was that month, to apply as much pressure on you as they could.* (Emphasis in original)

The role of strip searching was to '*other*' them by rewriting the coloniser's gaze on the body of the occupied through the enactment of pain and suffering. The women's accounts demonstrate that, while the regime within the prison was not gender-specific, the type of punishments were (Scraton 2007; Scraton and Moore 2005; Moore and Scraton 2014). This type of punishment was gender differentiated, in that it was sexualised:

> There was something more of a sexual connotation attached to the searches, particularly where women were held down by men to be stripped. There was something more psychologically severe in that, than it was for men.

The process of entering the closed world of the prison immediately serves to reinforce an awareness of powerlessness through the loss of privacy and bodily integrity (Elias 1994; Kowalski and Chapple 2000; Laws 1985). The testimonies shared demonstrate the deliberate 'ramping up' of this aspect of prison violence and control, in an ongoing power struggle centred on the control of women's bodies.

The next section will landscape the policy and practice surrounding strip searching and how the issue of security was used to justify the practice.

Kafka-esque Landscape of the Strip Search-The Disjuncture between Policy and Practice

The Northern Ireland Office describes the strip search procedure as follows:

> The prisoner is shown into an enclosed cubicle where, in complete privacy, she removes her clothing and passes them out to a woman prison officer for searching. While she is in the cubicle she may put on a prison-made top and skirt or if she prefers, a sheet which she wears while her clothes are being searched. She is then briefly visually examined, while still in the cubicle by one female prison officer to ensure that she has not hidden any item on her person. She does not have to stand about naked, as has been suggested, nor is she seen by other prisoners or groups of staff.
>
> In March 1983, in response to women's accounts, the then Minister of State for Northern Ireland, Lord Gowrie, rejected the allegations of brutality and stated: 'there is no question of internal searches being carried out, nor is there any prodding and poking—the officer conducting the search does not touch the prisoner at all'.

Such denial of moral culpability indicates the disjunction between policy and practice, as discussed below.

Strip searches were first introduced in 1982 and were carried out as a matter of 'routine', which meant that every prisoner leaving the prison for whatever reason would be strip searched. In 1983, in response to considerable public condemnation of the practice, it was announced that 'routine' strip searching would be abandoned but 'random' strip searching would continue for 'obvious' security reasons (Sinn Féin Women's Department 1993; Liberty 1992). From 2 March 1983, following a review, the searches became random and this practice continued when the women were transferred to a new maximum security prison, HMP

Maghaberry, on 18 March 1986. Since 1983, 'random' strip searching has continued, determined only by the agenda of the prison authorities and the government's appraisal of the political climate. This strategy was in evidence in March 1992, when a mass forcible strip search was carried out by officers in riot gear against 21 women prisoners in Maghaberry Prison.

Strip searching in the North of Ireland is defined in the Prison Rules (Northern Ireland) 1982, made under the Prison Act (Northern Ireland) 1953 (cited in Matthews 1988). The Prison Rules state that strip searching is to be authorised by the Governor: 'subject to any direction by the Secretary of State'. It stipulates that:

1. Every prisoner shall be searched when taken into custody by an officer, on his/[her] reception into a prison and subsequently as the Governor thinks necessary or as the Secretary of State may direct.
2. A prisoner shall be searched in as seemly a manner as is consistent with discovering anything concealed.
3. No prisoner shall be stripped and searched in the sight of another prisoner, or in the sight of a person of the opposite sex.
4. Any unauthorised article found during the search shall be taken from the prisoner.

The government has stated that they have no policy on strip searching and the frequency of strip searching is a matter for the discretion of the governor. Thus, the onus of authorising strip searching falls entirely on the governor of the prison. This means that, in practice, the Chief Officer has sole responsibility. The NCCL comments that 'we saw no reason to disbelieve the Governor's statement about current practice. We do, however, find it difficult to accept that all strip searches carried out after the decision to randomise in March 1983 were being done solely at the instigation of the Chief Officer or any of her staff' (NCCL 1986). Even if this were the case, it raises questions as to whether current practice is in accordance with the Prison Rules, and as to where responsibility and accountability lies.

NIACRO Policy Papers Strip Searching (n.d.) provides the following definitions as to what the differences are between the searches and how the actual process should be conducted.

> **Strip Search**: The subject removes clothing from the top half of the body. That clothing is searched by hand, and the naked part of the body is examined visually. The subject replaces clothing and the process is repeated for the lower half of the body.
>
> **Rub Down Search**: A search, by hand, of the clothed body. The searcher runs his or her hands over the clothing of the subject using a continuous motion. Hair and footwear are usually given a visual examination.
>
> **Pat Down Search**: Prior to 1998, this denoted a search of pockets to check they were empty. It now refers to a less detailed form of rub down search.
>
> **Intimate Search**: A physical search of a bodily orifice. This practice is called a full search.
>
> **Reception Searches**: A visual check of the body is made on all prisoners entering Northern Irish prisons for the first time and must be distinguished from the practice of strip searching female remand prisoners leaving and re-entering the prison before and after court appearances. The practice of strip searching was introduced in November 1982, after a cell search during which a set of keys which had been smuggled in by two remand prisoners were discovered. (Cited in NIACRO Policy Papers Strip Searching)

There has been considerable debate regarding the definition of 'strip search'. The above distinctions and practices are not reflected in the women prisoner's accounts (see also Scraton and Moore 2005, 2007). They consider the removal of clothes and the visual inspection of the body (prisoners instructed to open mouths, lift breasts and open legs) as a strip search.

> Being a sentenced prisoner meant we weren't getting out of the prison, we weren't being strip searched. The remand prisoners resisted. They must have went on resisting for about a year and they were being badly beaten and humiliated, and talking to some of them at Mass: they actually used to say they felt as if they were *raped*, such as X. It was a disgusting practice. There was *no need for it*. If you think that people can have detectors of one sort of another, there is just no need for stripping people. (Emphasis in original)

Gendered Suffering: The Denial of Harm and State Sexualised Violence

Women have systematically reported the fear and reality of sexual violence and sexual harassment by British soldiers and the Royal Ulster Constabulary during the Conflict. Research has shown that sexual harassment of women by security forces was, indeed, widespread and systematic outside as well as inside the prisons (Pickering 2001). However, this section focuses specifically on the experiences of systematic intimate violence against imprisoned women combatants at the hands of the state.

AW: And how many prison officers would be in the room with you?

> There would have been probably about I'd say between a half a dozen—ten, because you had to be literally held down, forcibly held down and forcibly stripped.
>
> You can imagine what that was like.

More violent, frightening accounts are provided that contradict the government's statement in which there is a shameful denial and silence as to how the women's bodies/nakedness were surveyed, prodded and intimate surfaces inspected. The process whereby the women were strip searched was particularly humiliating and invasive (see Moore and Scraton 2014; Scraton and McCulloch 2009).

The next testimony highlights the sexualised and ritualised nature of the searches.

> Well *it's sexual assault*. You know when they strip searched you they are looking in your body cavities. And if you look at the record of the number of strip searches. Strip searches were horrendous things, but very few of us ever liked to talk about it you know.
>
> It got horrendous, I mean the strip search. If you had not taken a visit in six months, and some girls wouldn't because you'd have a strip search going on your visit, and strip searched coming back, right, but if you hadn't been out of your cell for three months and your locked up 24 hours a day, *what contraband could you have on you*? They [the prison officers] have been look-

ing at you for 24/7 for three months, and yet they come and strip search your cell. You've absolutely nothing in your cell.

I think you know that the women would say they were unfairly strip searched. They will say that. I presume you know—I mean if you know what happens when a man is strip searched, why it would be any different for a woman?

I mean they're not going to strip search you just to … they're going to have to search your body. I think there's *a good deal of shame attached to it, and that you don't want to make it public that someone had been putting their fingers inside your body. This was very deeply felt among the women*. It's just— it's just like the girl who was sexually molested by the British Army and the RUC when she was being interrogated but she didn't want to speak about it because it's *very shameful*. They find it *very shameful*, and I don't think our society, when you say strip search and I'd say our parents and *our* people know exactly what that means. *We know exactly what that means for a girl.*

My brother was in prison the same time as I was, and he went mad when he heard I'd been strip searched. '*Them bastards put their hands on you*' and I know why he was upset. I know he was thinking right searching his anus, right, and he knew that a woman had a vagina as well and, but he would *never* say those words 'vagina', being stripped, but our people know. It's just to go into those details of your body orifices women just don't do it. I think it's a *shame* thing. I mean I used to say I was strip searched, end of. But the physical side is that you're anally and vaginally searched so, people just don't want to talk about it, and it is a very hard and difficult thing actually.

I think this is the first time when I've been interviewed, and I've said, yeah someone put their fingers inside my body. (Emphasis in original)

In looking in particular at the word, 'shame' in this context, it 'involves the intensification not only of the bodily surface, but also of the subject's relation to itself, or its sense of itself as self' and arises in the moment of our 'wounding exposure to others' (Ahmed 2004, pp. 104–105). As such, shame is intra-psychic and attaches to what one is (Sedgwick 2003). Yet, it is also in the act of 'speaking out' which challenges the shame by refusing the definitions imposed by the (sexist) public gaze (Sedgwick 2003). Shame's power resides in its ability to transform or intensify the meanings of parts of the body, a prohibited identity or other people's behaviour towards the self (Sedgwick 2003). For the woman quoted above, and those she calls: '*our society, our people*', the violation of private intimate zones of women's bodies speaks to the undermining of the power of the political struggle as women's bodies are relentlessly searched inside and out without any possibility of rescue. Such continuous wounding exposure meant that the physical, psychic and relational aspects of shame were 'very deeply felt among the women'. They feel shame because of what they had to endure: a procedure that was, indeed, meant to induce *shame, pain* and *terror*, to keep the women in their place, to produce compliance with prison regimes, to break resistance, estrange the women from themselves and from who they once were, and induce a future estrangement from communal ties because of the silence produced by shaming experiences (Bettelheim 1986).

In the Northern Irish case, it is well documented that the British, the RUC and the Prison Service repeatedly singled out Republican women (Pickering 2001; Harris and Healy 2001). In particular, the state forces targeted female bodies in a sexual manner. The women in the study repeatedly compared strip searching to being raped (McCulloch and George 2009; Walsh 1988), unlike the descriptions provided by the men in the study. Viewing strip searching as part of ritualised state violence against women (United Campaign Against Strip Searching 1989) reveals the process of strip searching is a form 'of sexual coercion' (McCulloch and George 2009, pp. 121–122). The process of entering the closed world of the prison immediately serves to reinforce an awareness of the loss of privacy, bodily integrity and one's inability to protect oneself by preventing pain itself (Sinn Féin n.d.). As the woman cited above explains, strip searching is a form of sexual assault that very few of 'us ever liked to talk about'.

She later goes on to say that to minimise the possible harm to the body, the women 'deployed passive resistance'.

> Well, if you were really stroppy sometimes, they [the prison officers] would get the riot squad up. They [the prison officers] would come up with the riot gear with their shields. The glass shields and you know push you in the corner and hold you down with their shields while the women screws [prison officers] would search you. Quite rapidly, we decided it was worse with having a man there present so you would just not struggle so much.

Plus you were frightened. You were frightened of getting *torn down there or getting hurt down there*. It was sort of *passive resistance* when it came to the searching because you were *terrified of them really hurting you down there, you know hurting your internal organs*. You know that's the first time I've spoken about that. (Emphasis in original)

These experiences show just how easily the regulations forbidding strip searching in the presence of 'a person of the opposite sex', and setting out the acceptable limits of bodily invasion could be circumvented and over-ridden, simply by redefining the situation—at the female prison officers' 'discretion'—as one which required enforcement by male officers equipped for violence. They further demonstrate how the *threat* of this violence makes presence the permanent material element in the strip search regardless of whether the male officers were actually present or not.

Fear transformed into terror of being hurt, of feeling pain from injury to the genitals or anus, in turn leading to passive resistance. How can one be passive and resistant at the same time when the body is being violated? Fear led to a closing off of the part of the body being violated from the self, so that it could be sensed only as a part of oneself which did not determine the contours of the self. In this involuntary act of psychosomatic resistance, the anus and genitals were converted into weapons against state terror and brutality through estrangement from the self throughout the continuing regime of the strip search, as well as in the very moment of its occurrence. This passive resistance, the absorption of pain by the body, also led to silence, of only speaking about this for the first time in an interview and of not being fine at all emotionally. These acts of resistance by the women demonstrate a crisis which disrupts the normal repertoire of behaviour. Such repression of pain—through not rehearsing its passage through the body by not speaking about it to others—is a self-induced silencing which produces its own estrangement. That is, the woman's refusal of pain's production of who she is coexists with the knowledge that pain's production of her will always be a part of the body that she inhabits, an integral part of what she sees and feels as her 'self'. Estrangement is entangled within her as doubly effective through a denial and acceptance of pain as part of who she would—or, indeed, could—claim to be. The women then live within a melancholia

(Cheng 2001; Khanna 2003) based on pain's repression but unexpected and unwanted emergence. The unwanted misery and subjection of pain and denial of recognition of one's right to dignity because of the designation 'political prisoner' has been swallowed whole only to return sporadically in memories of one's brutalisation in which the terror is relived. Pain bubbling to the surface of the abject leads to what Fanon (1967) describes as an aberration of affect. In this instance, it is such aberration that produces estrangement from the self. The prison environment inculcates a level of vulnerability, a visceral uncertainty where bodies become subject to the violence of incarceration through estrangement.

This brings to mind Scarry's (1985) account of the pain of torture and Fournier's (2002) work on pain, evisceration and the fleshing out of gender. Scarry (1985, p. 52) speaks to the *extraneare* of pain; that is, the most essential aspect of pain is its sheer averseness. Pain is a pure physical experience of negation, an immediate sensory rendering of 'against', of something being against one and of something one must be against. Even though it occurs within oneself, it is at once identified as 'not oneself', 'not me', as something so alien that it must right now be got rid of. The psychic pain of incarceration produces daily negation which women struggle against in their attempt to recapture 'the me' from the 'not me', through medication to numb the pain or other coping strategies in order to counter the feeling of being about to explode. The psychic pain of incarceration produces an almost obscene conflation of private and public. It brings with it all the solitude of absolute privacy with none of its safety, all the self-exposure of the utterly public with none of its possibilities for camaraderie or shared experience (Scarry 1985, p. 53). As the testimonies of the women indicate, these psychological effects persist far beyond the cessation of incarceration and the here-and-now experience of violence.

There has been widespread international condemnation of strip searching as inhumane and degrading treatment, which violates the right of people held in detention to be treated with respect for the dignity of the person (Liberty 1995, 1992).

The conducting of strip searches is obviously intimidatory, humiliating and invasive, and a form of physical and sexual terrorism; it lacks a utility (other than as an act of aggression designed to break resistance) and affects women both physically and mentally. Invariably, women reported the profoundly traumatic impact of strip searching:

That meant they [the prison officers] opened your cell in the morning before it was time for unlock and they would have come in and searched your cell and stripped you, and at that stage you were stripped completely naked with your hands above your head. There would be eight screws [prison officers] around you passing comments about your body. They would have lifted your boobs and look inside your mouth and examine the inside of your ears.

The following section will develop the question as to whether the purpose of strip searching was used purely to address possible breaches in prison security or whether this technique of punishment was, rather, used merely to exacerbate 'the pains of imprisonment' (Sykes 1958).

The Issue of Security: An Oxymoron

In the policy documents issued by the prison service, security was given by the Northern Ireland Office and prison authorities as the main reason for the use of strip searching. In a letter to the NCCL in April 1984, Nicholas Scott's[2] office stated that women prisoners were strip searched:

in the interests of maintaining security at the prison.

The same letter makes the point that:

Both the Governor and the prison authorities have a statutory duty to maintain the security of the prison and the safe custody of all prisoners; they must take appropriate steps to achieve this objective. Both the Secretary of State and Mr Scott are satisfied that it was necessary to have recourse to this form of searching on occasions in the interests of security.

A second important reason provided by the government in support of the use of strip searching was self-defence, with regard to both the safe custody of the other prisoners and the protection of the prison officers, either from attack or allegations of brutality. The increased use of strip searches at Armagh Prison (other than the strip search and bath on

---

[2] Sir Nicholas Paul Scott PC JP was a British Conservative Party politician. He served as a Minister for Social Security, Disabled People, northern Ireland and Employment.

initial reception/committal to the prison) began in November 1982. In October 1982, two remand prisoners, both young offenders (not political prisoners), had been found in possession of two keys which they had picked up in Armagh court house and taken back to the prison with them.

According to Mr James Prior,[3] 'the implications of this breach of security were carefully considered and it was decided to replace the routine rub-down searches with strip searching which is in regular use in prisons in Great Britain' (*Hansard*, 15 March 1983, Column 120).

The Minister's point is reiterated in the Northern Ireland Office's published pamphlet entitled: *Strip Searching: The Facts*, where it is stated that: 'The keys incident had demonstrated in a serious way that a rub-down search accompanied by the use of metal detection equipment was not necessarily an effective safeguard' (Northern Ireland Office 1985).

Representatives of the Northern Ireland Office pointed out several times the particular high-security nature of the prison due to the very serious offences for which some prisoners have been convicted (Prison Officers' Association 1987).

That experience indicates that many prisoners are of the nature to use extreme methods. Against this background, it would be curious if it were decided that they [strip searches] are not necessary.

From November 1982–1983, the following items have been found during strip searches:

April 1983—15 valium and sleeping tablets
September 1983—£5.00 and a bottle of perfume.
October 1983—Uncensored letter.
June 1985—Tranquillizers.
(*Hansard*, 29 July 1983, col. 631 and 5 December 1983, col. 84)

---

[3] Mr James Prior was Her Majesty's Principal Secretary of State for Northern Ireland from 1981–1984.

In the Northern Ireland context it cannot be argued that these items present a risk to security or in any way threaten prison officers or the safe custody of others. In light of this the stated aim of strip searching fails to be supported.

Rolston and Tomlinson point out:

The thousands of searches which have been conducted since 1982 have not been entirely successful as a deterrent against smuggling but they have netted a few items. In April 1983, 15 Vallium and 2 sleeping pills were found under a prisoner's foot in the search cubicle. In September, a £5 note and a small phial of perfume were discovered, and in October the searches found an uncensored letter. Two years later in June 1985, 47 assorted Librium, Libraxam, and Ativan were found among prisoner's clothing and in the reception area. (1988, p. 175)

In Armagh, between November 1982 and November 1985, 'the average number of strip searches per prisoner per month was approximately 25' (Rolston and Tomlinson 1988, p. 189). This figure indicates that these searches were used disproportionately against imprisoned Republican women in Northern Ireland. A report produced by the Stop Strip Searching Campaign in Northern Ireland in 1987 maintained that over 4,000 searches had been carried out in the five years since their introduction in 1982 (Stop the Strip Searches Campaign 1987; see also Faul 1980, 1983).

The report states:

Since 1982 and almost four thousand strip searches later, nothing which would constitute a security risk has been found on the prisoners. The only items the authorities can claim to have found are: £5 note, a bottle of perfume and two letters, all of which were found during ordinary rub-down body searches. How then can strip searching be justified when these statistics unquestionably [sic] confirm that strip searching is of no security value to the authorities whatsoever? (Stop the Strip Searches Campaign 1987, p. 8)

The force of public pressure led the authorities to relax the practice to its current level of random searches only. But why did it ever exist? Armagh closed in 1986 and the women were transferred to Mourne House, the women's prison in the newly built high-security Maghaberry Prison complex. 'The prison was constructed on new generation principles, with intensive security and technological surveillance integral to its operation' (Scraton et al. 1991, p. 152). This included, for example, electronic doors, television monitors, observation cameras; control rooms with 'banks of switches and lights'. These are contained in a 'soulless, low complex of buildings wired in and fenced in on an eerie, featureless stretching plateau'.

The relevance of gender was again highlighted in March 1992, when prison officers in riot gear violently conducted a mass forcible strip search on all of the 21 political women and 13 of the 14 ordinary prisoners. The women experienced a brutal raid by prison officers which involved the women having their clothes torn and forcibly removed by prison officers while in their cells. While neither reduced to total passivity, nor completely incapacitated, the women's voices were effectively silenced; their self-esteem, physical and mental health, femininity and sexuality was permanently undermined by the possibility of recrimination, violence and abuse.

It was reported that up to six prison officers held down each individual woman to initiate a search—again, not discovering anything of political value (Liberty 1995, 1992; *Women's News* 1993).

The women resisted the attack by prison officers:

> I was there and it was the most frightening experience of my life. We had made the decision to resist because it hadn't happened before, coming into your cells, and stripping you in your own cells. This is your own living space. It *was like being raped.* It was an invasion of your privacy. Your cell was your home and I mean we said we're not subjecting ourselves to that. (Emphasis in original)

These testimonies are bleak reminders of the destructive force of imprisonment and the authoritarianism of the state. The cells in Maghaberry had become a place which the women personalised with photos, paintings and so on. In a similar way to a bedroom in wider society, the cell provided shelter, escape from the intrusion of the prison gaze. Scarry argues that 'in normal contexts, the room, [provides] the simplest form of shelter, expresses the most benign of human life' (Scarry 1985, pp. 38–39). In total institutions where surveillance is all encompassing and penetrates flesh as well as psyche, one has to be 'seasoned' into the category 'prisoner'. The voices of women demonstrate how strip searching and physical brutality mean that there was nowhere to hide, as even your cell, which you see as your home, can be invaded, and you can experience rape, terror and the trauma of listening to other women's suffering.

Another woman recounts the incident:

> They [the prison officers] came onto the wing, and door by door they started to open the doors. Ten or twelve screws [prison officers], held down the women, Sat on them. Stripped them. At this stage there was a lot of physical stuff going on and heads being banged off the walls, the floor, being trailed down the wings, you know, being hurt, arms being twisted because you are fighting them.
>
> So at this stage then we all started to barricade our doors because we knew what was going to happen and it went on for 10 or 12 hours. I never experienced anything like it in my life and I think what was more *traumatic was the screaming* of the women, being trailed up the wing, half clothed and being put into the recreational space. (Emphasis in original)

After the event:

> I sat on the bed and they [the prison officers] told me to get dressed and I wouldn't get dressed. I told two of the screws [the prison officers], I said, 'Yous', but I was screaming, I said, 'Yous took my clothes off, you put them on', and then do you know what they done? I tell you what—she was probably, she must have been near to the age of my mammy, and she was sat on the bed and my clothes were all round the place and she was scrambling onto the bed buttoning my bra and I was just sitting like that and her hands were shaking. She was trying to do the clasp and I didn't give a fuck. The other women were saying, 'Oh I couldn't have done that because I just wanted to get them out', and I just said, 'No, you're seeing to me'. She was humiliated having to dress me, somebody must have said to her, 'Are you serious? Leave her in there, come on'. So then they left me, but I was screaming like mad, oh God, and it went on right through the night. It went on for 10 or 12 hours to get round all the cells.

AW: Do you think that sort of experience has affected the women mentally and physically…?

Yes, I mean … do you know what—that's probably the first time I've ever talked about it without crying.

In a situation where their power was already greatly diminished by the fact of being in detention, the women readily saw the need to control at least some of the most basic aspect of their person. Primarily, this was achieved by controlling access to their physical body. Barricading themselves into a confined space was often futile, but was seen as the only way to hold off the inevitable and not submit one's body, self and identity readily to degradation. As their testimonies reveal, women in prison vehemently resisted efforts to strip search them, which usually resulted in them being forcibly held, beaten up and having their clothes torn from their bodies. Such confrontations often resulted in serious assaults on women who refused to submit. The prison authorities would respond to the women resisting the process of the strip search with coercive disciplinary measures, and issue subsequent punishments such as loss of remission, solitary confinement and withdrawal of visiting orders.

In Pickering's seminal study (2002, p. 179) detailing accounts of women political prisoners, she records women's resistance, 'which usually resulted in them being forcibly held and clothes torn from their bodies'. The physical assault and emotional trauma of the forcible strip search was exacerbated by women being charged with breaches of prison rules and/or assaulting staff. The use of force individually was matched by the use of punishment institutionally. Women prisoners, political or 'ordinary', were constantly reminded that they were powerless to resist the authority of the prison. Pickering concludes:

> Strip searching came to epitomise, for many, the resolve of the security services to have women submit to the process of criminalisation and surveillance by taking control of women's nakedness. This form of visual surveillance authorises other forms of bodily invasion. The objective of 'breaking women' was understood by women in this study who had experienced strip searching as being particularly vicious with the sole purpose of breaking their collective resistance against the regime (ibid., p. 181).

The voices of the women heard in this chapter bestow a level of visibility on the violation of private bodily space. By entering the private realm of the prison, their bodies at once become the public property of Her Majesty's Prison Service. The bodies of politically motivated prisoners are interpolated as agentic weapons against the state yet, conterminously, their bodies become bearers of pain and suffering. Furthermore, this type of lived experience of pain is amplified in the sense that it is objectified, made visible to those outside the person's body. Finally, the objectified pain is denied as pain and read as power (Scarry 1988, pp. 12–15), completing a sequence which places the body in a continuum of systematic violence (Aijner and Abbink 2000; Fawcett et al. 1996; Kelly 1987) directed and operationalised by agents of the state.

In a letter dated 17 March 1992, one woman recounts the nightmares and the suffering which still continue 22 years later after the strip search at Maghaberry Prison.

Nightmares

My waking nightmare begins as I recall what happened the night here in this cell on Monday 2/3/1992.

I was informed at 9.30 am that I, and every other female prisoner was to be formally strip searched, if I did not comply with the order to remove my own clothes. Almost 2 hours later, after having listened to the screams of X as she was being brutally attacked and stripped, my cell-door was flung open and the riot squad surged forward. Three or four of them wore visors and wielded shields and batons, the other two, clad in overalls. A shield was rammed straight into my face, forcing me back against the bars on my window, while another two attacked me from either side. I was seized, flung face down on the floor and sat upon, while my arms were twisted and locked up my back.

Having satisfied themselves that I'd been immobilised, my assailants proceeded to pull my clothes off from the waist down. They then proceeded to pull all the clothes from my upper body before getting up and leaving me. As I raised myself onto my elbows, feeling shocked and disorientated, I looked at my clothes strewn all around my cell and saw the backs of my attackers passing out through the door.

> From my window, I watched helplessly as Y was seized and tortured by those violent screws [prison officers], her cries for help bringing tears to my own eyes. I listened to the two women in the cell next to mine being attacked and beaten. Being a witness to the horrifying treatment of another person was actually worse than my own experience, probably because the scene could be envisaged too vividly.
>
> The events of that awful day are still haunting me. I can no longer fully relax as the threat of another attack has become my waking dread. Sleep offers me no comfort either, because that's when the nightmares start. Life, for me can *never, ever,* be *the same again.*

Although this account was written 14 days after the attack, the women are still haunted today by waking nightmares of past events. In this woman's account, she clearly demonstrates the enduring legacy of pain. The very threat of pain was immobilising and, in itself, a form of punishment—having to listen to the suffering of another when what was happening could be visualised and felt viscerally. Pain does not have to be administered to one's own body to be deeply felt and to continue to haunt one's life into the future. Painful memories construct a link to the body of the other through the empathetic connections forged through common experience, even though it is not exactly the same experience because it is sensed by another body. Pain's estranging individualisation can thus be undone in this moment where pain is felt as removed from one's body but, nonetheless, creates a vicarious connection to others. Thus, the creation of new identities and new spaces are formed in response to these shifts in sensing pain as the pain of the other, which forms the connective tissue of resistance. As resistant identities open up further possibilities of connection through shared pain which resists estrangement, new landscapes within the carceral walls are produced.

To conclude, what this section demonstrates is the continuing domination of punishment and retribution which lies at the core of penal policy. This chapter clearly demonstrates how violence was institutionalised in the prisons in the study and, as Poulantzas argues, operates through strategies 'about which people seldom talk: *namely the mechanisms of fear*' (Poulantzas 1978, p. 83). At the same time, the violence and torture the women endured demonstrates that the self extends beyond the boundaries of the body (Calamati 2002, p. 87). Moreover, the experiences the women endured during the different phases of reactive confinement (1969–1975); criminalisation (1976–1981) and managerialism (1981–2000) show how bodies become potent weapons of war, demonstrating women's resistance, the centrality of their role in the Republican movement and the processes whereby collective consciousness and communal suffering transgress the carceral walls of the prisons.

The routine use of strip searches against prisoners, particularly female prisoners, means that '[s]exual abuse is surreptitiously incorporated into the most habitual aspects of women's imprisonment' (Davis 2003, p. 81; 2005). The state is 'directly implicated in this routinisation of sexual abuse, both in permitting such conditions that render women vulnerable to explicit sexual coercion carried out by guards and other prison staff and by incorporating into routine policy such practices as the strip search and the body cavity search' (ibid.). While strip searches are normalised within prison, prisoners, especially female prisoners, experience them as a form of sexual violence of coercion (Radford et al. 2000; Riches 1986; Stewart 1997). Outside of the prisoner–prison officer relationship, the coercive removal of clothes would constitute sexual assault (George 1992, 1993). A significant issue is the relationship between what comes to be normalised in the context of prisons and what is represented as aberrant (Carlton 2007). Redefined as sexual assault, the strip and/or cavity search constitutes one of several interlinked 'circuits of violence' connecting the 'ordinary' to the 'extraordinary' (ibid., p. 62). The 'ordinary' is characterised by the routine violence permeating all prisons: the 'extraordinary' extends the continuum of state violence to sexual violence to state torture. What this chapter clearly demonstrates is that, as Goffman has argued: 'total institutions disrupt or defile precisely those actions that in civil society have the role of attesting to the actor and those in his [her] presence that he [she] has some command over his [her] world—that he [she] is a person with 'adult' self-determination, autonomy and freedom of action' (1968, p. 47).

Chapter 10 discusses some of the wider processes which have influenced the nature and scale of the transition from conflict to compromise (Bew 2007). Yet, it must be said that this transitional journey that promises opportunities is, at times, thwarted by processes that reveal deep institutional and political rigidities. Chapter 10 will show that the road to peace has been driven by a 'combination of the politics of devolution, the needs of victims and survivors, struggles for truth and justice, and state-managed reforms' (Tomlinson 2012, p. 44).

References

Ahmed, S. (2004). *The cultural politics of emotion*. Edinburgh: Edinburgh University Press.

Aijner, G., & Abbink, J. (Eds.). (2000). *The meanings of violence: A cross cultural perspective*. Oxford: Berg.

Aretxaga, B. (2001). The sexual games of the body politic: Fantasy and state violence in Northern Ireland. *Culture, Medicine and Psychiatry*, 1–27.

Bettelheim, B. (1986). *The informed heart: A study of the psychological consequences of living under extreme fear and terror*. London: Peregrine Books.

Bew, P. (2007). *Ireland: The politics of enmity 1789-2006*. Oxford: Oxford University Press.

Calamati, S. (2002). *Women's stories from the North of Ireland*. Belfast: Beyond the Pale.

Cheng, A. A. (2001). *The melancholy of race: Psychoanalysis, assimilation and hidden grief*. Oxford: Oxford University Press.

Christian Study: A Community Problem. (1997). *A Christian response to strip searching*. Belfast: Christian Response to Strip Searching Group.

Cockburn, C. (2001). The gendered dynamic of armed conflict and political violence. In C. Moser & F. Clark (Eds.), *Victims, perpetrators or actors? Gender, armed conflict and political violence*. London: Zed Books.

Committee on the Administration of Justice (CAJ). (1987). *Strip searching and the Irish community* (Briefing Paper). Belfast: CAJ.

Committee on the Administration of Justice (CAJ). (1987). Strip Searching and the Irish Community: Briefing Paper. Belfast: CAJ.

The Community for Justice. (1987). *Strip searching: A moral issue*. Belfast.

Davis, A. (2003). *Are prisons obsolete?* New York: Seven Stories Press.

Davis, A. (2005). *Abolition democracy: Beyond empire, prisons and torture*. New York: Seven Stories Press.

Elias, N. (1994) [1978, 1982]. *The civilizing process* (Vols. 1 and 2, E. Jephcott, Trans.). Oxford: Blackwell.

Fanon, F. (1967/1970). *Black skin, white masks*. London: Pluto.

Faul, D. (1980). *The stripping naked of the women prisoners in Armagh prison 1982-83*. Armagh: D. Faul.

Faul, D. (1983). *The stripping naked of the prisoner in Armagh prison 1982-83*. Armagh: Prison Officers' Association.

Fawcett, B., Featherstone, B., Hearn, J., & Toft, C. (1996). *Violence and gender relations*. London: Sage.

Feldman, A. (2006). Violence and vision: The prosthetics and aesthetics of terror in states of violence. In F. Coronil & J. Skurski (Eds.), *States of violence* (pp. 425–469), The University of Michigan: Michigan Press.

Fournier, V. (2002). Fleshing out gender: Crafting gender identities on women's bodies. *Body and Society, 8*(2), 55–77.

George, A. (1992). Strip searches: Sexual assault by the state. In P. Weiser Easteal (Ed.), *Without consent: Confronting adult sexual violence*. Proceedings of a Conference held 27–29 Oct 1992, Jan 1993, Australian Institute of Criminology, Canberra. http://www.aic.gov.au/publications/revious%20 series/proceedings/1-27/20.html. Accessed 18 Feb 2014.

George, A. (1993). Strip searches: Sexual assault by the state? *Alternative Law Journal, 18*(1), 31–33.

Goffman, E. (1968). *Asylums: Essays on the social situation of mental patients and other inmates*. New York: Anchor Books.

Harris, H., & Healy, E. (Eds.). (2001). *Strong about it all: Rural and urban women's experiences of the security forces*. Derry: Northern Ireland North West Women's/Human Rights Project.

House of Commons Debate. (1986, November 17). *Journals of the House of Commons from November the 12th, 1986, in the thirty-fifth year, to May the 15th, 1987, in the thirty-sixth year, of the reign of QUEEN ELIZABETH THE SECOND session 1986-87*. London: House of Commons.

Irish Prisoners Appeal. (1986). Stop strip searches of Irish women prisoners in Armagh and Brixton. *Irish Republican Information Service (IRIS)* No. 17.

The Irish Times. (1980, August). No wash protestors: August.

Kelly, L. (1987). The continuum of male violence. In J. Hanmer & M. Maynard (Eds.), *Women, violence and social control*. London: MacMillan.

Khanna, R. (2003). *Dark continents-psychoanalysis and colonialism*. London: Duke University Press.

Kowalski, R., & Chapple, T. (2000). The social stigma of menstruation. *Psychology of Women Quarterly, 24*, 74–80.

Laws, S. (1985). Male power and menstrual etiquette. In H. Homans (Ed.), *The sexual politics of reproduction*. Aldershot: Gower.

Liberty (National Council for Civil Liberties). (1992). *Broken covenants: The violations of international law in Northern Ireland.* London: Liberty.

Liberty (National Council for Civil Liberties). (1995). *Northern Ireland: Human rights and peace dividend.* London: Liberty.

London Armagh Group. (1984, February). Strip searches in Armagh jail. *Women Behind the Wire*, No. 2.

Loughran, C. (1983). Armagh and feminist strategy. In T. Lovell (Ed.), *British feminist thought.* London: Blackwell.

Loughran, C. (1985, Summer). Strip searchers continue. *Women's News*, No. 11 (Summer).

Loughran, C. (1986). Armagh and feminist strategy: Campaign around republican women prisoners in Armagh jail. *Feminist Review, 23*, 59–79.

Maghaberry Republican Prisoner's Statement. (1987, April). *Women's news*, No. 25, p. 17.

Matthews, R. (1988). Alternatives to and in Prison: A Realist approach. In P. Carlen & D. Cook (Eds.), *Paying For crime.* Milton Keynes: Open University Press.

McCulloch, J., & George, A. (2009). Naked power: Strip searching women in prison. In P. Scraton & J. McCulloch (Eds.), *The voice of incarceration.* Oxford: Routledge.

Moore, L., & Scraton, P. (2014). *The incarceration of women: Punishing bodies, breaking spirits.* Basingstoke: Palgrave Macmillan.

National Council for Civil Liberties (NCCL). (1986). *Strip searching: An inquiry into the strip searching of women remand prisoners at Armagh prison between 1982 and 1985.* London: NCCL.

Northern Ireland Office. (1985). *Armagh prison: Strip searching.* Belfast: The Facts, Northern Ireland Office.

Northern Irish Prison Service. (1988). *Annual report on the work of the prison service for 1987/88 (Cmnd 42).* Belfast: HMSO.

Pickering, S. J. (2001). Engendering resistance: Women and policing in Northern Ireland. *Policing and Society, 11*(3–4), 337–358.

Pickering, S. (2002). *Women, policing and resistance in Northern Ireland.* Belfast: Beyond the Pale.

Poulantzas, A. N. (1978). *State, power, socialism.* London: Verso.

Prison Officers' Association. (1987, January). *Strip searching: The fact and the fiction.* London: A Report by the Prison Officers' Association (January).

Prisoner's Statement. (1986, November). Strip searching: Violence against women. *Women's News*, No. 2, p. 6.

Radford, J., Harne, L., & Friedberg, M. (2000). Introduction. In J. Radford, M. Friedberg, & L. Harne (Eds.), *Women, violence and strategies for action: Feminist research, policy and practice*. Buckingham: Open University Press.

Riches, D. (Ed.). (1986). *The anthropology of violence*. Oxford: Blackwell.

Roche, D. (1985). *Strip searches at her majesty's prison for women, Armagh, Northern Ireland*. Belgium: Irish Information Partnership.

Rolston, B., & Tomlinson, M. (1986). Long term imprisonment in Northern Ireland: Psychological or political survival? In B. Rolston & M. Tomlinson (Eds.), *The expansion of European prison systems: Working papers in European Criminology*. European Group for the Study of Deviance and Social Control: Belfast.

Rolston, B., & Tomlinson, M. (1988). The crisis within: Prisons and propaganda in Northern Ireland. In M. Tomlinson, T. Varley, & C. McCulagh (Eds.), *Whose law and order?* (pp. 155–192). Belfast: Sociological Association of Ireland.

Scarry, E. (1985). *The body in pain: The making and unmaking of the world*. New York: Oxford University Press.

Scarry, E. (Ed.). (1988). *Literature and the body: Essays on populations and persons*. Baltimore, MD: Johns Hopkins University Press.

Scrambler, A., & Scrambler, G. (1993). *Menstrual disorders*. London: Routledge.

Scraton, P. (2007). *Power, conflict and criminalisation*. London: Routledge.

Scraton, P., & McCulloch, J. (Eds.). (2009). *The violence of incarceration*. London: Routledge.

Scraton, P., & Moore, L. (2005). Degradation, harm and survival in a women's prison. *Social Policy and Society, 5*(1), 67–68.

Scraton, P., & Moore, L. (2007). *The prison within: The imprisonment of women at Hydebank Wood 2004-06* (1st ed.). Belfast: Northern Ireland Human Rights Commission.

Scraton, P., Sim, J., & Skidmore, P. (1991). *Prisons under protest*. Milton Keynes: Open University Press.

Sedgwick, E. (2003). *Touching, feeling: Affect, pedagogy, performativity*. London: Duke University Press.

Sinn Féin Prisoner of War Department (SFPOW). (1993). *Memorandum on discrimination against women prisoners in Mourne House, HMP Maghaberry*. Belfast: Sinn Féin.

Sinn Féin Women's Department. (n.d.). *Strip searching: Violation of women's rights goes on*. Dublin: Sinn Féin.

Sinn Féin Women's Department. (n.d.). *Women in struggle/ Mna I Streachailt.* Dublin: Sinn Féin.

Sinn Féin Women's Department. (1993). *Maghaberry fact file* (2nd ed.). Dublin: Sinn Féin.

Smith, C. (2009). A period in custody: Menstruation and the imprisoned body. *Internet Journal of Criminology.* www.internetjournalofcriminology.com.

Stewart, M. (1997, Summer). Institutionalised sexual violence: Condoned by the state. *Scottish Labour Briefing*, No. 46:11.

Stop the Strip Searches Campaign. (1987). *Stop strip searching.* Dublin: Pamphlet.

Sykes, G. M. (1958). *The society of captives: A study of a maximum security prison.* Princeton, NJ: Princeton University Press.

Tomlinson, M. (1980). Reforming repression. In L. O'Dowd, B. Rolston, & M. Tomlison (Eds.), *Northern Ireland: Between civil rights and civil war,* Belfast: CSE books.

Tomlinson, M. (2012). From Counter-Terrorism to Criminal Justice: Transformation or Business as Usual. In A. Wahidin (Ed.). The Legacies of Conflict on the Criminal Justice System in Northern Ireland in the Howard. *Journal of Criminal Justice, 51*(5), 442–457.

United Campaign Against Strip Searching. (1989). *An Enquiry into the Psychological Effects of Strip Searching.* London.

Walsh, D. (1988). The Royal Ulster Constabulary: A law unto themselves? In M. Tomlinson, T. Varley, & C. McCullagh (Eds.), *Whose law and order?* Dublin: Sociological Association of Ireland.

Women's Equality Group/London Strategic Policy Unit. (1986). *Working together to end strip searching conference.* London Strategic Policy Unit, Conference Papers, 5 Dec, Unpublished Papers.

10

There Is No Glory in Any War

This was very much a *people's war* and [...] *the whole community would have been involved.*

There is no such thing as a nice war or a clean war, that's balls! War is horrendous. It's terrible. It's vicious. It's all of those. It's disastrous for the generations who experience it.

I think in all war, there are periods of reflection and I *think there's no glory in any war.* I think for all of those that have been involved in war—we reflect on the barbarity of it. *There's no war that's nice.* So I think, you know, as we reflect on that—we reflect on the human cost to all sides that were party to Conflict.

I think war made politics possible and I think that's where I come from.
(Reflections of ex-combatants)

The Rocky Road to Peace: The Good Friday Agreement

In this chapter, the focus shifts to the peace process in Northern Ireland and, in particular, the Good Friday Agreement of April 1998 (otherwise

© The Editor(s) (if applicable) and The Author(s) 2016
A. Wahidin, *Ex-Combatants, Gender and Peace in Northern Ireland,*
DOI 10.1057/978-1-137-36330-5_10

known as the Belfast Agreement). The intention is not to describe in detail the provisions of the Agreement, or the twists and turns of the peace process, as these have been well-documented elsewhere (McEvoy 2007; Shirlow et al. 2005; Vaughan and Kilcommins 2008). Rather, the chapter explores the attitudes towards the peace process of the women ex-combatants in the study, providing insights into the subjective legacy of the Conflict and sets the scene for exploring the women's subsequent experiences. The women's reflections are set alongside a discussion of some of the principles underpinning the Good Friday agreement, in the context of a broader debate about the nature of transitional justice, the role of penal reform and social justice in the transition from Conflict to peace.

The general view of all the participants in the study was that the Good Friday Agreement was: '*Inevitable*', '*Necessary*', '*Good*' and '*Progressive*'. As this chapter makes clear, the transition from conflict to a post-conflict society is developmental: a 'negotiated compromise'. It is only by acknowledging the fragile process to peace that the spectre of the past can be exorcised (Wahidin 2012, p. xi).

This was a long war.
I think that the British knew that they couldn't defeat us and they didn't. We brought the British to the negotiating table. So I think, you know, when you have that, I think there was a realisation that we [the IRA and the Republican Movement] were in a stalemate situation.

When we came to the Good Friday Agreement, the Good Friday Agreement was ultimately an agreement between the British Government and the IRA and the Republican movement. I think there was a stalemate situation there, if I could describe it like that.

We were looking for different ways of moving this forward and I think, as I reflect on it, I think the British couldn't defeat the Movement, with all their resources.

AW: So why do you think, it was the Volunteers, the combatants, who were open to exploring ways out of the war in the 1980s?

I think acceptance came about in '74, '75. There was an acceptance that the Brits couldn't defeat the IRA, but likewise the IRA couldn't defeat the British Army.

AW: So what happened was there needed to be a *negotiated settlement.*

I mean, morally you have to sit back and say to yourself, do we continue a war just for the sake of continuing a war, knowing that it is not going to bring us to a particular juncture? Or do we develop a strategy, a campaign, where we can actually bring a Government that doesn't want to negotiate to the table. Do we force negotiations?

    We'd force negotiations, but there would be disengagement of the British state from this part of Ireland, because there wasn't a military solution to this. The Brits knew that. The IRA knew that, but the Brits *were not ready* for negotiations and hence the reason for the continuation of the war. (Emphasis in original)

The 1998 Good Friday Agreement promised an end to the protracted Conflict. By incorporating the principle of the right to self-determination, the 1998 Agreement set in train a whole series of transformative possibilities for *how* justice is done and *seen* to be done in Northern Ireland and, to a lesser extent, in the Republic of Ireland (Vaughan and Kilcommins 2008). Only 1 % of the Northern Irish Catholic electorate voted against the Good Friday Agreement in the 1998 referendum (Hayes and McAllister 2001, p. 81), reflecting an acknowledgement not only of the legacy of the past, but also of the social and political trajectory of a society in transition. This is echoed in the following statement:

The tragedies of the past have left a deep and profound regrettable legacy of suffering. We must never forget those who have died or been injured, and the impact on their families. But we can best honour them through a fresh start, in which we firmly dedicate ourselves to the achievement of reconciliation, tolerance, and mutual trust, and to the protection and vindication of human rights for all. (Belfast/Good Friday Agreement 1998)

The Good Friday Agreement[1] (GFA), otherwise known as the Belfast Agreement, followed the 1994 and 1997 paramilitary ceasefires which formed the basis of a negotiated settlement for the future of Northern

---

[1] *Agreement Reached in Multi-Party Negotiations* (Cm 3993, 1998). For further details of the parliamentary stages of the legislation and all the legal preparations for devolution, see http://www.nio.gov.uk/implemact.htm. The Agreement was translated into legislation in the form of the Northern Ireland Act 1998.

Ireland. The signatories to the Agreement committed the participants to resolving the protracted Conflict through democratic and non-violent means, as well as to the promotion of social inclusion, equality and 'community development and the advancement of women in public life' (Section 6, paragraph 1). The Agreement was concluded on 19 April 1998 and became law with the passing of the Northern Ireland Act 1998. The 1998 Agreement provided the broad template for the reconstruction of criminal justice in the context of new constitutional relationships between Northern Ireland, Great Britain and the Republic of Ireland. 'One of the most controversial aspects of the peace process' included the provision for the early release of those paramilitary prisoners ('politically motivated prisoners') whose organisations were on ceasefire for politically motivated ('scheduled') offences (McEvoy 1998, p. 55; 2001).

The GFA created a *framework* for change and for continuing progress towards peace, as recognised in the following comments:

> So our job is to ensure that *change* takes place.
> The Good Friday Agreement isn't a settlement. It's a work in progress—and that's what people shouldn't forget.

The piecemeal nature of the transitional process owes much to the lack of political agreement over the causes of the violent Conflict and the reasons why it endured for so long.

> So in terms of going far enough, I don't know what that means. The point about it is *you have to create the circumstances for a process* which can lead to the achievement of your objectives, and I believe that has been done. I believe that there are some very serious outstanding problems to be resolved but I *believe that they can be resolved*. (Author's emphasis)

And why do you think Republicans were so open to exploring different ways out of the war?

> Because we didn't want it! *It's our country*. It's our people. Who wants to fight a frigging guerrilla war and risk death and killing people and imprisonment forever? We only went to war to get a solution. The solution mightn't be perfect but if it's going in the right direction—*take it*. Get on the train and try and get it going in the direction you want. (Emphasis in original)

In societies transitioning from conflict, a core defining feature is an absence of confidence in criminal justice organisations and the lack of legitimacy of the criminal justice process to deliver justice *for* all (Davis 2005). This is often characterised within transitional justice discourse as an absence of the 'rule of law'. It is argued within the transitional justice framework that the reconfiguring of state institutions such as the police and the courts through legal redress is a central element in the facilitation of social healing (Huntingdon 2000). A lack of confidence in the criminal justice process was evident in the case of Northern Ireland throughout the Conflict. Thus, the Good Friday Agreement called for a review of the criminal justice system focusing on institutions such as the police, the courts and the prosecution service, and created provision for the early release of politically motivated prisoners (see Annex B of the GFA) convicted in the special jury-less Diplock Courts (Wahidin et al. 2012). The above are all evidence of an apparent belief in the capacity of state institutions to meet the aims associated with transitional justice, and to place human rights at the heart of policy and practice.

The next section will provide an overview of the key debates within the transitional justice literature, exploring efforts to restore the legitimacy of criminal justice in societies emerging from conflict (Eriksson 2009; McEvoy 2001).

Defining Transitional Justice

The concept of transitional justice acknowledges dealing with past human rights abuses as a step towards building a more positive future. As stated by Kofi Annan, then Secretary General of the United Nations, it is through addressing the: 'spectrum of violations in an integrated and interdependent manner' that transitional justice has the potential to 'contribute to achieving the broader objective of prevention of further conflict, peace building and reconciliation'[2] (UN 2007). While acknowledging significant differences in approach underpinning the ever-expanding field of transi-

---

[2] United Nations rule of law and transitional justice activities include developing standards and best practices, assisting in the design and implementation of transitional justice mechanisms, providing technical, material and financial support, and promoting the inclusion of human rights and transitional justice considerations in peace agreements.

tional justice, a common assumption is that it characterises a *transitional moment* between two regimes: from one which was oppressive, dictatorial or illegitimate towards a democratic one (Huntingdon 2000; Teitel 2000). However, this idea of a 'moment' during the transition from an authoritarian regime to a democratic one should be questioned. As Lundy and McGovern (2008: 273) argue, Northern Ireland was a democracy *within* which conflict existed. Thus, the orthodox transitional justice framework:

> Ignores the problem that human right abuses may continue to take place in circumstances where in theory at least, the norms of liberal democracy accountability prevail. It also therefore permits a radical critique of implicit liberal versions of transition that may otherwise struggle to deal with the subversion of the rule of law, under the guise of law itself, in ostensibly liberal democratic states.

In the light of the above criticism, I will adopt the UN's somewhat broader definition of transitional justice as follows:

> The full range of processes and mechanisms associated with a society's attempt to come to terms with a legacy of large-scale past abuses, in order to ensure accountability, serve justice and achieve reconciliation [...] striving to address the spectrum of violations in an integrated and interdependent manner [...]. (UN 2010)

Transitional justice is, nevertheless, a contested term and varies in shape and nature depending on the society transitioning from conflict to peace (Ditch and Morrissey 1981). However, there are shared principles and discourses that have influenced the development of a transitional justice template in the delivery of prosecutorial styles of justice, truth recovery and a programme of criminal justice reform (Shirlow et al. 2005). Within transitional justice discourse and practice, there is also an increasing acknowledgement that the transitional process must centrally place social justice and human rights protections as a foundation for sustainable peace (see Lundy 2011; Moore and Wahidin 2015; Wahidin et al. 2012).

The next section examines the meaning of 'peace' and the reasons why, in Northern Irish society, the process has been approached with caution.

The Fragile Nature of the Peace Process: The Challenge to Change

A ex-combatant explains:

> I don't think anybody of our generation accepted or believed that we would entirely defeat the British Army but I think there was an acceptance that through our actions it would bring the Brits to a viewpoint that they had to negotiate. But they had to negotiate about dis-engagement. Is this a continuous process? Of course it's a continuous process. It is about us developing our strategy and continuing to drive it forward.

All too often, 'peace' can be understood narrowly to mean the ending of violence and, hence, fail to address wider issues of justice. Lasting peace cannot be imposed by physical force or the physical relocation of the population; this can only be achieved by a series of negotiated settlements that form a compromise deal. It thus involves both negative peace (the cessation of violence) and positive peace (social redistribution, the pursuit of equality, fairness, and a sense of flourishing and well-being. War and peace are relational, for the possibility of a resolution is always implicit in conflict, and it is only through conflict that the conditions for peace may become attainable (see Brewer et al. 2013).

The movement from war to peace has to take account of and address the management of emotional dynamics. It must be accountable to past pains arising from historic social injustice and, so, must address issues such as social redistribution, the introduction or restoration of equality and fairness in the allocation of scarce resources, and the opening up of life opportunities that were once closed to some groups (Brewer 1991). The inevitability of a piecemeal approach to creating a sustainable environment for peace to emerge emanates from a resistance by those parties who wish to maintain the status quo.

The peace strategy would fall tomorrow only for the involvement of Sinn Féin, because Unionism doesn't want it. Unionism is about stopping change. It is about slowing change down. They know it has to change but *all they're doing is resisting change and to* try and slow process down. (Emphasis in original)

AW: Why?

Because Republicans would benefit most from change. Anti-progressive people benefit most from stalemate and stasis and *just no change*. So progressive people are always looking for change and this was just another mechanism for change. To bring about change or to create the conditions for the potential for change. So because Republicans have always had that *outward international progressive looking approach to things*, whereas many of our *opponents have had an inward approach of least change possible*.

AW: What in your view is stopping the peace process from progressing quicker than it is?

Insecurity. (Emphasis in original)

The above testimonial points to the reality that peace, as much as violence, provokes emotions that need to be managed. For example, peace comes with an ontological cost: the conditions required for peace threaten feelings of security because they require the overthrow of familiar ideas and ways of understanding the world (Brewer 2003, pp. 86–89). Peace poses what Lederach (cited in Knox and Quirk 2000, p. 26) calls the 'identity dilemma': people who have defined their group identity, tradition and loyalties for so long in terms of 'the enemy' suddenly find they have to reshape their sense of who they are and what groups they feel loyalty towards.

The peace process can be called into question and derailed by renewed violence, identified by Darby (2006) as 'spoiler violence': the deliberate intent to undermine the peace agreement in Northern Ireland. The peace process has an uncertain future which from the outset is based on negotiated compromises, rather than a shared vision (Moore and Wahidin 2015).

Positive peace is not met simply by parties agreeing to the accord itself; signing the Belfast Agreement is the beginning, not the end, of a peace process (Bew and Gillespie 1996). As Rex (1981, p. 18) discusses with respect to the sociology of conflict generally, a settlement can only be achieved when protagonists are persuaded that the costs of continuing the struggle are greater than any gain that might be realised from continuing it.

Despite the possibilities it opens up, there is a general awareness amongst ex-combatants of the limitations of the Good Friday Agreement. Those ex-combatants released from prison faced huge discrimination, in terms of adoption rights, travel and insurance, to name a few. A salient criticism of the prisoner release mechanism based on early release, rather than on amnesty, is that it preserves the principle of accountability and criminalisation for all those involved in politically motivated activity (McEvoy 1999; McEvoy et al. 2010). The continued detention of some Republican and Loyalist prisoners, and their continued resistance within the prisons, demonstrates that, in the transition to peace, the overspill of the legacy of Conflict is far from over.

> We're still considered criminals. We still can be refused access to all goods and services in society. We're the only section of society that can be legally discriminated against, and it's not right. *I'm not a criminal.*

The Republican combatants whose voices are heard in this book do not believe they have any reason to feel either shame or guilt for their actions in creating the conditions for a negotiated peace settlement. Shame-guilt is not an emotion that helps to realise peace; it is permissible after it. However, many in the study talked about personal *regrets* that have impacted on the next generation.

> Yeah, everyone's got regrets. People killed people, you know. People were killed. There are loads of regrets. People abandoned their children, left them literally. You were too fucking busy being on the run and running around.

AW: Looking back, do you have any regrets?

Of course you've regrets in the sense that you regret that people you know are now dead and that sort of loss. Of course there's regrets around that. But again, it's a *struggle* and we *came through it* and when you're involved in *armed struggle—you're going to lose lives. People are going to end up in jail.* A few nights ago, I was at a 1981 play about the hunger strikers and we were just talking and we were saying it's hard to believe that's what we lived through. We actually *lived through that and now it's unbelievable that period actually existed.* But it did.

So when you look back and you think about regrets, personally I've no regrets in the sense that I'm here today, and there are *many, many people who aren't.* So I don't think I've any sort of right to regret anything. For me, I'd been imprisoned. *It was still a struggle. You were there. You were still part of the struggle and you used it as best you could to further the struggle.* So personal regrets, none.

But regrets for those who aren't with us now and those whose families that have been broken. People who can't deal with it anymore or people who are sore because of what they came through, certainly there are those regrets for that.

But in terms of the armed struggle itself, what we came through personally: I think that's *struggle.* You come through it and you're lucky to be here. (Emphasis in original)

The management of emotions must address two problems: finding the balance between the need to acknowledge what happened in the past and moving forward, and encouraging people to see the truth from someone else's standpoint. Positive emotions such as hope that envision the future are as important here as negative ones that allow the packaging and re-packaging of the past.[3]

Addressing post-violence adjustments, an ex-combatant had this to say:

AW: What help should there be for ex-combatants?

---

[3] There are lessons here from many societies around the world which can be categorised as 'post-violent societies', (for example, Rwanda, Sierra Leone, Southern Sudan, South Africa, Sri Lanka, the Philippines and much of Latin America).

In terms of a care package where people are helped through that sort of transition, I'm not talking about just people coming out to you and trying to fit you into society again and whatever else, that is not an issue for us in that sense, for our communities, but dealing with the transition in life and some of this is about, you know, people with Post Traumatic Stress Disorder and stuff like that.

We have to move away from the debate about who's the perpetrator and who's the victim, because every time ex-combatants or ex-prisoners look for some sort of services—the issue comes down to who deserves all this.

Well, if you're involved in struggle *we all deserve* it. It's not about saying you were right and you were wrong. *It's about saying we've come through struggle.* (Emphasis in original)

Once again, the issue comes down to the classification of combatants as 'criminals' as opposed to (ex) politically motivated prisoners: the approach of '[fitting] you into society again' is essentially informed by the philosophy of conventional rehabilitation services which view the ex-prisoner as having become an outsider to a law-abiding society by virtue of their offending behaviour and imprisonment and, hence, needing to be 'reintegrated' in order to prevent re-offending. The ex-combatants view this approach as inappropriate because the actions for which they have been imprisoned have not so much estranged them from their communities as formed a continuity with the wider struggle with which their communities identified. Such an approach attempts to reaffirm their definition as 'criminal' and, hence, deny the state of war which formed the context for their actions, which in other contexts might simply entitle them to services aimed at helping them with the trauma resulting from their involvement in combat. Thus, in the post-conflict experiences of combatants we see a continuation of the struggle for political status which has formed the central theme in the preceding chapters devoted to the experience of imprisonment.

The peace process has been protracted and fragile (Brewer 2003). The piecemeal nature of the transitional process in Northern Ireland reflects the lack of accountability by the British government and political consensus as to the causes of the Conflict (Moore and Wahidin 2015). Through the voices of both female and male Republican combatants, this book acknowledges the legacy of the Conflict and how the spectre of the past influences the direction and speed of the peace process. Although the trajectory to conflict resolution has been slow, a space has emerged in which to engage in a dialogue, and policy and practice that provide an alternative to the inefficient and violent system that has historically failed a section of society (Brewer et al. 2013; Wahidin 2012). In the propitious move towards conflict resolution, the changing contours of Northern Irish society provide the opportunity to re-imagine and work towards a peaceful society, 'one which is set free from the legacy of the past' (Ashe 2007/2009; Wahidin 2012, p. xi).

Chapter 11 will examine the role of Disarmament, Demobilisation and Reintegration (DDR), and will examine how ex-combatants come to understand the past through making 'private troubles public issues' (Mills 2000:2).

References

Ashe, F. (2007/2009). From paramilitaries to peacemakers: The gender dynamics of community-based restorative justice in Northern Ireland. *British Journal of Politics and International Relations, 11*(2), 298–314.

Belfast/Good Friday Agreement. (1998). *Agreement reached in the multi-party negotiations*. Belfast and Dublin: British and Irish Governments.

Bew, P., & Gillespie, G. (1996). *The Northern Ireland peace process 1993-1996: A chronology*. London: Serif.

Brewer, D. J. (1991). Policing in divided societies: Theorising a type of policing. *Policing and Society, 1*, 179–191.

Brewer, D. J. (2003). Northern Ireland. In M. Ceijka & T. Bamat (Eds.), *Artisans for peace*. Maryknoll, NY: Orbis Books.

Brewer, D. J. Mitchell, D., & Leavey, G. (2013). *Ex-combatants, religion and peace in Northern Ireland*. Basingstoke: Palgrave Macmillan.

Carlton, B. (2007). Imprisoning resistance – life and death in an Australian Supermax. Sydney: Institute of Sydney Criminology Press.

Darby, J. (2006). A truce rather than treaty? The effect of violence in the Irish peace process. In M. Cox, A. Guelke, & F. Stephens (Eds.), *A farewell to arms: Beyond the Good Friday agreement*. Manchester: Manchester University Press.

Davis, A. (2005). *Abolition democracy: Beyond empire, prisons and torture.* New York: Seven Stories Press.

Eriksson, A. M. (2009). *Justice in transition: Community restorative justice in Northern Ireland.* Cullompton: Willan Publishing.

Hayes, B., & McAllister, I. (2001). Sowing dragon's teeth: Public support for political violence and Para-militarism in Northern Ireland. *Political Studies, 49*(9), 901–922.

Huntingdon, S. P. (2000). *Transitional justice.* Oxford: Oxford University Press.

Knox, C., & Quirk, P. (2000). *Peace building in Northern Ireland, Israel and South Africa: Transition, transformation and reconciliation.* London: Macmillan.

Lundy, P. (2011). Paradoxes and challenges of transitional justice at the local level: Historical enquiries in Northern Ireland. *Contemporary Social Science, 6*(1), 89–106.

Lundy, P., & McGovern, M. (2008). Whose justice? Rethinking transitional justice from the bottom up. *Journal of Law and Society,* 265–292.

McEvoy, K. (1998). Prisoner release and conflict resolution: International lessons for Northern Ireland. *International Criminal Justice Review, 8*(1), 33–61.

McEvoy, K. (1999). Prisoners, the agreement and the political character of the Northern Ireland conflict. *Fordham International Law Journal, 22,* 1–27.

McEvoy, K. (2001). *Paramilitary imprisonment in Northern Ireland: Resistance, management, and release.* Oxford: Oxford University Press.

McEvoy, K. (2007). Beyond legalism: Towards a thicker understanding of transitional justice. *Journal of Law and Society, 34*(4), 411–440.

McEvoy, K., Shirlow, P., & McElrath, K. (2010). Resistance, transition and exclusion: Politically motivated ex-prisoners and conflict transformation in Northern Ireland. *Journal of Terrorism and Political Violence, 16*(3), 647–670.

Mills, C. W. (2000). *The Sociological Imagination.* Oxford: Oxford University Press.

Moore, L., & Wahidin, A. (2015b). Transition, women and the criminal justice system in Northern Ireland. In C. O'Dwyer & A. McAlinden (Eds.), *Criminal justice in transition: The Northern Ireland context* (pp. 227–301). London:Hart Publishing.

Morrissey, M., & Ditch, J. (1981). Social policy implications of emergency legislation in Northern Ireland. *Critical Social Policy, 1*(3), 19–39.

Rex, J. (1981). *Social conflict: A conceptual and theoretical analysis.* London: Palgrave Macmillan.

Shirlow, P., Graham, B., McEvoy, K., Purvis, D., & O'hAdhmaill, F. (2005). *Politically motivated former prisoner groups: Community activism and conflict transformation*. Belfast: Northern Ireland Community Relations Council and Northern Ireland Human Rights Commission.

Teitel, R. (2000). *Transitional justice*. Oxford: Oxford University Press.

United Nations (2007) Human security in theory and practice. An overview of the human security concept and the United Nations Trust Fund for Human Security. Human Security Unit United Nations.

United Nations. (2010). Guidance Note of the Secretary-General: United Nations Approach to Transitional Justice. https://www.un.org/ruleoflaw/files/TJ_Guidance_Note_March_2010FINAL.pdf.

Vaughan, B., & Kilcommins, S. (2008). *Terrorism, rights and the rule of law: Negotiating justice in Ireland*. Cullompton: Willan.

Wahidin, A. (2012). The legacy of conflict in Northern Ireland. In A. Wahidin (Ed.), *The legacy of conflict and the impact on the Northern Irish criminal justice system. Howard Journal of Criminal Justice, 51*, 437–441.

Wahidin, A., Moore, L., & Convery, U. (2012). Prisons and the legacy of conflict in Northern Ireland. In A. Wahidin (Ed.), *The legacy of conflict and the impact on the Northern Irish criminal justice system. Howard Journal of Criminal Justice, 51*, 458–473.

11

Conclusion: Compromise After Conflict—Making Peace with the Past

The armed struggle had its way and it brought us to a certain stage.
(Ex-combatant)

Introduction

The focus of this final chapter is to capture some of the complexities of the disarmament, demobilisation and reintegration (DDR) process, foregrounding the centrality to the peace process of the treatment and status of ex-combatants, and the roles which their experiences equip them to play in the building of a post-conflict society.

In the transition from armed conflict to peaceful political struggle, ex-combatants faced a number of obstacles, all of which can be broadly related to the continuing struggle over the definition of their activities as part of a *war*, as opposed to actions which mark them as criminal and as deviant. This struggle was, in part, played out through the determined retention by the various paramilitary organisations of control, throughout the process, of decisions regarding the nature

© The Editor(s) (if applicable) and The Author(s) 2016
A. Wahidin, *Ex-Combatants, Gender and Peace in Northern Ireland*,
DOI 10.1057/978-1-137-36330-5_11

and timing of the decommissioning of arms (see Bairner 1999, p. 13). A further obstacle was the resistance of the British state to providing for the accountability of security agencies colluding in political killings and regarding the state's involvement in the Conflict.[1] The degree of collusion and of political cover-ups, and the precise agencies involved, therefore remained unclear. In addition, the lack of political status means that, despite the provision in the Good Friday Agreement for early release from prison, the ex-combatants 'are still considered criminals'. This chapter will examine how residual criminal status is expressed in the continuing exclusion of ex-combatants from full citizenship rights, which in turn presents them with barriers to social and economic integration.

The testimonies of the women and men ex-combatants in this study demonstrate a commitment to constructive reconciliation driven by their deep embeddedness in the Conflict and their intimate understanding of the individual and communal sufferings involved. Their insistence on the importance of a non-blame approach to support the *'casualties of war'* contrasts with the 'hierarchy of deservingness' permeating the allocation of resources for community-based support and reconciliation projects. Yet, it is only by gaining an understanding of the motivations and contexts for the struggle, and through the sharing of communal suffering, that this knowledge may become one of the many mechanisms which contribute to preventing the return of a violent past (Hackett and Rolston 2009) and, in turn, help drive the recovery process forward.

---

[1] In 2011, it was announced that Prime Minister David Cameron accepted that there had been state collusion in the killing of a leading human rights lawyer Pat Finucane—while simultaneously announcing that there would be no public inquiry into his death. For the full account, see 'Afternoon [Prime Minister's] Press Briefing for 11th October 2011. Go to http://www.number10. gov.uk/news/afternoon-press-briefing-for-11-october-2011/ (accessed 26 November 2014). Another example of state collusion was evidenced in 2007. Statement by the Police Ombudsman for Northern Ireland on Her Investigation into the Circumstances Surrounding the Death of Raymond McCord Junior and Related Matters. Statement under Section 62 of the Police (Northern Ireland) Act of 1998 (22 January 2007), www.policeombudsman.org/PONI/files/9a/9a366c60-1d8d-41b9-8684-12d33560e8f9.pdf (accessed 26 November 2014).

The Political Process of Disarmament, Demobilisation and Reintegration

The role played by ex-combatants in the process of DDR is widely acknowledged as a prerequisite for post-conflict stability and for preventing the recurrence of armed conflict (McEvoy and Shirlow 2009). The DDR programme as part of the peace-building enterprise is structured as a process of transition from war to peace. The UN Integrated Disarmament, Demobilisation, and Reintegration Standards (IDDRS 2006) state simply:

> The sustainable social and economic reintegration of former combatants should be the ultimate objective of [DDR]. If reintegration fails, the achievements of the disarmament and demobilisation phase are undermined, instability increases, and sustainable reconstruction and development are put at risk (United Nations 2011).

This model of DDR generally regards former combatants as a threat whereby ex-combatant dissatisfaction can return a country to war (McMullin 2004, 2014) and treats them as if they were 'individualised cases of violence in a normal peaceful society', to be seen as a 'painful symptom of the violence that needs to be disinfected and normalised' (van der Merwe and Smith 2006, p. 42). For example, the UN integrated DDR standards refer to DDR as a process that contributes to security and stability in post-conflict recovery contexts by 'removing weapons from the hands of combatants, taking the combatants out of military structures and helping them integrate socially and economically into society by finding civilian livelihoods' (UN 2006, p. xi). However, with a significant increase in DDR programmes in recent years, it has become evident that more flexible approaches are necessary when designing and implementing the various components of the programmes, particularly in terms of taking into account the type of conflict that has occurred and the socio-economic and political conditions prevailing in the post-conflict environment.

Reflecting on some of these initiatives suggests that the way in which DDR is approached is at least as important as the details of designing and implementing DDR activities. There is now increasing consensus that DDR processes are 'deeply embedded in the social, political, economic and historical context of post conflict situations, [and must] be understood in relation to the specific environment in which they are implemented' (Porto and Parsons 2003, p. 6). This environment will determine, to a large extent, 'what is possible and what is not, why developments follow a certain path rather than a different one, and how effective certain activities are opposed to others' (Porto and Parsons 2003, p. 6). This has certainly been the case in relation to the approach taken throughout the development of the peace process in Northern Ireland.

Although a range of peace-building measures was considered in the period leading up to the Good Friday Agreement, it was not until 1994 that the main armed Republican organisation, the IRA, called its first ceasefire. Six weeks later, in October 1994, and in response to the IRA announcement, the Combined Loyalist Military Command—representing the Ulster Volunteer Force (UVF) and the Ulster Defence Association (UDA) —called for a cessation to all paramilitary activity. Following a period of protracted talks, a breakdown and reinstatement of the ceasefire by IRA and intense negotiations, the Northern Ireland Peace Agreement was formally signed in April 1998.

As previously noted, the IRA ordered an end of their armed campaign in July 2005. All of the IRA's 'Volunteers' were instructed 'to assist the development of purely political and democratic programmes through exclusively peaceful means' (BBC News 2005). The statement implied that the IRA might continue to exist but more as an association of old comrades than as a fighting force (*The Economist* 2005). In September of that year, the Independent International Commission on Decommissioning (IICD) reported that it was satisfied the decommissioning process had taken place, using estimates of IRA weaponry submitted by the British and Irish governments (see the Independent International Commission on Decommissioning 2005). The only other Republican paramilitary group formally to declare a 'stand down' was the Irish National Liberation Army (INLA), which, on 11 October 2009, issued a statement announcing that its 'armed struggle is over' (BBC News 2009).

The statement by the IRA declaring the end of the 'armed struggle' was read out by former Republican prisoner Seana Walsh, in a symbolic vindication of the political achievements of the armed struggle and the central role of its politically motivated prisoners. Moreover, during the negotiation phase of the Good Friday Belfast Agreement, while still serving prison sentences, combatants played a pivotal role in securing paramilitary support in favour of this agreement. Under the terms of the Agreement, it was confirmed that the release of 'politically motivated' prisoners or 'former combatants/former prisoners' should be addressed (Powell 2008). By the summer of 2000, all remaining political prisoners from organisations which were on ceasefire and serving sentences of more than two years were released. Central to the Good Friday Agreement was a commitment to the reintegration of political motivated prisoners; however, numerous barriers to full reintegration still remain.

In 2007, the UVF re-appointed former Loyalist prisoner Billy Hutchinson to liaise with the IICD which, in turn, led to a statement by the UVF and the closely associated smaller grouping the Red Hand Commandos (RHC) that they would 'put their weapons 'beyond reach'.[2] The Ulster Defence Association (UDA) soon followed and, after a number of meetings with the IICD, issued a statement indicating that while arms would be put 'beyond use', the organisation would retain all arms (*Belfast Telegraph* 2007). By the end of 2008, the Combined Loyalist Military Command (which represented both the UVF and the UDA and Red Hand Commandos) was reconvened and, by June 2009, announced that the decommissioning of Loyalist weapons had been completed for the UVF and 'had begun [sic] for the UDA'. Finally, in February 2010, a breakaway faction, the UDA's South East Antrim Brigade, decommissioned the 'remainder' of its weaponry.

Since the 1994 ceasefires, the disarmament component of the Northern Ireland peace process has been one of the most difficult aspects of the peace process (McEvoy 1998). Attempts to coerce paramilitary organisations to disarm *before*, *during* and *after* the peace negotiations were resisted by armed groups and contributed to the Irish Republican Army ending its ceasefire in 1996 for over a year. It would be wrong to suggest that the process of DDR in Northern Ireland has been entirely smooth. Not all former combatants have engaged in either peace-building activi-

---

[2] 'UVF Calls an End to Terror Campaign', *BBC News*, 3 May 2007.

ties or community based self-help organisations. The Agreement resulted in a splintering in the Republican movement and the formation of new groups, which opposed the peace agreement (Cochrane 2011).

The process of DDR is premised on the need to create a firm economic and social foundation while, at the same time, to provide opportunities for former combatants to contribute to and participate in post-conflict peace-building and reconstruction. As we will see, from the perspective of the ex-combatants in the study these conditions have not wholly been realised.

No Return to War

It is clear from the interviews that there is no appetite for war among the participants in this study. Moreover, there was a realisation and echoing of the sentiments of Mandela, when he and other South Africans met Northern Irish politicians in May 1997, that the consequences of war next time around would be far greater.

> Whenever things threatened to fall apart during our negotiations we would stand back and remind ourselves that if negotiations broke down the outcome would be a bloodbath of unimaginable proportions, and after that bloodbath we would have to sit down again and negotiate with each other. The thought always sobered us up, and we persisted, despite many setbacks. (Quoted in O'Malley 2001, p. 276)

The testimonials reveal the historical factors that have impacted on the ex-combatants' personal biographical experiences. The legacies of colonialism, systematic discrimination and violence are, indeed, public issues—issues which the state must address to support the mechanisms of the peace process.

> I'm just telling you the reality of how things were—there was a lack of politics then, you [Catholics] weren't given any rights. There was systematic discrimination. My parents couldn't vote. I mean, you had an apartheid system where people were denied the vote. The reality is that I was a product of that society.

The losses were great:

> You would like to go back and say, well, maybe I should have gone into politics, maybe I would have made more of an impact as a young politician. But I can't turn the clock back. I do meet a lot of victims, people who have lost family members. But there were losses on both sides.
>
> I'm very much for trying to make politics work. I have been through war at a very early age and would not want to see anybody having to go through similar things or see things that I saw in my lifetime.

The outcome of war has led to a society in transformation where future generations have opportunities and life chances that were previously denied to the Catholic population.

> *I think that there is another way now.* I think that there are opportunities now for us [Catholics] that we didn't have before. We were totally discriminated against. We were imprisoned. We were murdered.
>
> We are living in a different society now and I just wish everybody could see that and for everybody to put their support and their efforts into pushing the peace process forward, because I don't believe that the *political struggle is over yet.* (Emphasis in original)

Many of the experts-by-experience in this book wanted to live in a different society than the one they were born into, and they wanted their children and grandchildren to be untainted by the effects of war.

> I wouldn't want that for my grandson, who is nine this year. I wouldn't want him being part of an army that had to do the things that I did as a kid. I was young and still doing very dangerous things daily, for years and years. So I wouldn't want that for them.

There was also consensus that the days of armed struggle are over.

> I wouldn't be going down the route of armed struggle now because *those days are over. There is the political will to work towards peace.* (Emphasis in original)

Apology

In the process of recovery and healing, many of the ex-combatants wished for the state to be accountable for their role in the Conflict. State forces were responsible for just over 10 % of all deaths in the Conflict between 1969 and the ceasefires of 1994. The British Army was responsible for 82 % of those deaths and the RUC (Royal Ulster Constabulary) for a further 15 % (Fegan and Murray 1995; Rolston 2000). The year of Bloody Sunday, 1972, was the worst for state killings, when 83 people were killed by state forces.

> One of the big things, the British Government needs to do is apologise to us. It will give an opportunity for everybody to sit down and try and move forward.

Another states:

> What we need to deal with is the legacy of the Conflict, and the British need to address that but they won't address it, because they say they were only here to protect life but yet four or five hundred people were killed by the British Army and state forces. The truth and reconciliation process is all about truth not blame. It is about compromise and reconciliation.

The above voices echo the prevailing sense of injustice and, in this context, 'the failure to focus on the State's record on human rights abuses' (Rolston 2002, p. 92).

Compromise After Conflict: Making Peace with the Past

Ex-combatants and their involvement in the peace process have been shown to be a rich resource for the effective building of bridges through their cross-community involvement. All the participants in this study were involved in some form of community work, or work that was underpinned by social justice and the politics of effecting change. Their effectiveness emanates from not only their prison experience, which provides legitimacy for their involvement in such community-led strategies of conflict transformation (McEvoy and Shirlow 2009), but also from the fact that they are indigenous to and rooted in their respective local communities (Rolston 2011). The ex-combatants have a central role to play in conflict transformation because 'their qualification, their status, and their future relate to the political and ideological struggles over the more general meaning and purpose of the Northern Ireland Conflict' (Féron 2006, p. 489). Moreover, as McEvoy and colleagues note, 'having fought on behalf of those communities … they have the credibility to engage in … real reconciliation work … [and] have arguably taken the greatest risks in the peacemaking … many of them explicitly on the basis that they do not want the next generation to go through what they've experienced' (McEvoy et al., p. 98). McEvoy and Shirlow have suggested that 'it is precisely because of their violent pasts that former prisoners and ex-combatants are ideally placed to provide such agency in moving out of conflict' (McEvoy and Shirlow 2009, p. 35).

One ex-combatant explains:

> I mean we are involved with different community relations with Unionist groups and the walls are coming down. It's very small steps but those steps are being taken. It's very slow and it is going to be slow and people just get impatient and you know they want it to happen tomorrow, but it's not going to happen tomorrow, it's going to be a long process.

Another ex-combatant reiterates the next phase of the struggle:

> By us [Sinn Féin] being in Stormont we're working from within just the way the prisoners did when we were in prison and we're taking control. It's all a means to an end … the war was easy in a lot of ways because you had it on your doorstep. You were witnessing people being shot, being beaten and people being arrested. So it's harder to sell the peace process to people but it's something that *we have to do*, and it's getting that sort of balance as well. There's a whole new understanding, I think, developing within the community as well. (Emphasis in original)

Communal violence and communal suffering provokes a broader range of emotions and is complicated by the emotions aroused by the transitional journey to peace. However, in addressing post-violence adjustments, the emphasis on the 'shame-blame-guilt' nexus has led to a narrow focus on restorative conferences and other shame-guilt management structures adopted from criminal justice settings. Thus neglecting the broader public policy framework that facilitates successful peace-making.

> Because the Republican forces are progressive forces. What we [Republicans] wanted was an equal society and it was up to us to constantly provide the energy to move the political process on towards that objective of peace. Unfortunately, when you have people who are also sitting at the table who have no vision and who only want to go back to the past, to the status quo when it was institutionalised discrimination. That's the barrier. The struggles are still here but in a different form. But to see now the equality agenda being pushed forward on all fronts—change for the better is happening but the Unionists are resistant to that.

In the push to move forward, resistance to change still exists and there are complex reasons for this. Lundy and McGovern (2008) and Lawther (2014) link Loyalist and Unionist resistance to a number of underlying factors which have affected the perception of truth-sharing, forgiveness and compromise in these communities.

Dealing with the Impact of War: The Silence and Denial of Guilt and Shame

The ex-combatants from this study understand the key role they have played and continue to play in the transition from war to peace. They themselves are well aware of the invisible scars that many former combatants carry with them (Green et al. 2007). They stress, therefore, that assistance with economic and employment issues and help with psychological trauma must be placed at the centre of the reintegration process to ensure recovery.

As one female ex-combatant states:

Very many of us have issues, both psychological and physical. We've a lot of wounded, a lot of unknown wounded who have never been reported and never been overly well dealt with. We've many, many psychologically injured personnel and we're working on that. We've our own counsellors and stuff. We've done a lot of research and we're very proactive in assisting our people. But the vast majority of our people have just gone their own way.

So there needs to be acceptance of the *casualties of war* and you deal with it effectively and correctly. There needs to be acceptance that everybody who was involved deserves the *same* response: the *same* support. And then you have, for example, our own people who come from an organisation which is a secret organisation which is very much an honourable organisation and a lot of them hold it in high regard.

She describes the feelings of shame *about asking for help* which is part of the psychological legacy of a struggle in which 'unnatural' levels of strength and endurance were called for:

The last thing that they want to do is come and speak to somebody about something's that affecting them, because they feel that they're letting down their comrades not only themselves but they're letting down the IRA, and to go and seek help is in some way seen as weak, or not coping or shameful. It is seen in some way as denigrating what you're involved in, and it's trying to get that out to people, 'Listen, Jesus Christ, remember, see what you were involved in and what hundreds of others were involved in—*It wasn't natural*'. It's an event and a period that it's truly going to have some sort of effect on you. So you need *to be honest with yourself and say: 'I need to deal with this'*, because if you *don't* deal with it you ruin everybody around you, not only yourself. In my opinion, people need to feel it's okay to seek help. To tell their stories about pain and fear. (Emphasis in original)

Other ex-combatants concur in emphasising that there is a need for greater understanding and awareness of the support needs of former combatants. Attention needs to be paid both to the specific needs of ex-combatants and to their involvement in the overall process of reintegration and peace-building.

Support for the Disarmament, Demobilisation and Reintegration Programme

Rather than devising a blueprint for DDR, the Good Friday Agreement set out certain provisions, which allowed for a more piecemeal approach to be taken. This included demilitarisation of both state and non-state parties in the form of the removal of the British Army's presence and the reduction of state military installations, the cessation of paramilitary activity and disarmament of paramilitary organisations, as well as the release and reintegration of ex-combatants.

A significant feature of the mechanisms to support ex-combatants and drive the peace process forward is the decentralised nature of the DDR programme, which has been facilitated by a fusion of both top-down and bottom-up approaches to peace-building (see Mendeloff 2004). The centralised, state-centred top-down approaches adopted through the Agreement were aimed at tackling the structural causes of the Conflict through significant political and institutional reform. In contrast, the 'bottom-up' approaches involved grassroots community-based initiatives across Northern Ireland, developed throughout the voluntary and community sectors in order to facilitate conflict transformation across all communities at the grassroots level (see McEvoy and McGregor 2008).

Although significant progress has been made in peacemaking and conflict transformation (MacGinity et al. 2007), there is much further to go. The limitations of the Good Friday Agreement have had negative implications for the ex-combatants.

> That was a major problem in the setting up of the political-cum-peace process, there wasn't an appropriate DDR situation, and it's obvious that the DDR could have been more supported.
>
> It's obvious the DDR wasn't implemented by the British Government because they would have had to acknowledge that it wasn't gang warfare going on here, and to me, that's why DDR wasn't implemented, because a prerequisite to moving into the 'political process' would be the sorting out of the then ex-military situation where all combatant groups would be dealt with and given re-assistance back into the communities. It wasn't done. It just wasn't done.

It was done arse about face. One major combatant side was bought off and the others were … well, I mean, there was £1¼ million paid out for people to leave the RUC, people who had been in the RUC for 30 years and getting a massive wage every week, who were on pensions and then retired. Whereas when I got out of prison in the 1990s I had £26 and not a penny to my name after 22 years in prison.

Still Discriminated Against

It is evident that, when considering the re-integrative needs of ex-combatants, it is important to deal with the wider issues, such as the residual criminalisation that ex-combatants face (Jamieson et al. 2010; Rolston 2011, p. 37; Shirlow and McEvoy 2008), and the additional obstacles to reintegration which result from holding a criminal record. The Good Friday Agreement set out the conditions for release of prisoners on licence and the mechanisms of prisoner recall. The early release scheme was established by the 1988 Northern Ireland (Sentences) Act, which set up the Sentence Review Commission to oversee and implement the release process. All those belonging to organisations on ceasefire were eligible for release; however, it was distinct from a blanket amnesty in that those released continued to hold a 'criminal' record and could have their licences revoked if they re-engaged in criminal or terrorist activities (Dwyer 2007; Moore and Wahidin 2015). The early release scheme as stipulated by the Good Friday Agreement was, *de facto*, a recognition of prisoners' political status; yet, the failure to quash the 'criminal' record under the Agreement has led to their exclusion from normal rights of citizenship.

Although reintegration and civic inclusion was a provision under the Good Friday Agreement, politically motivated prisoners continue to face barriers around employment, educational, psychological and emotional needs (see Jamieson et al. 2010; Shirlow and McEvoy 2008). In May 2012, a review panel reported on the various structural barriers preventing full reintegration and noted that the existence of legal barriers has continued to place ex-politically motivated prisoners in a disadvantaged position since their release (OFMDFM 2012). I would contend that, in order to achieve full reintegration as part of the wider political process and to embrace peace and reconciliation fully, numerous structural barriers need to be lifted to reflect the wider transitional process. The failure of the Good Friday Agreement to uphold to the principles of reintegration and inclusion of former political prisoners means that ex-combatants continue 'to experience labour market exclusion and legislative barriers regarding their inclusion into economic life, resulting in low income which may also predict psychological morbidity, the extension of social exclusion, poor life chances and negative impacts upon their families' (OFMDFM 2012, p. 15).

One ex-combatant shares a common sentiment running throughout the interviews:

> We've been very, very badly treated. We are *still* considered criminals. We *still* can be refused access to all goods and services in society. We can be recalled. We are the only section of society that can be legally discriminated against, and *it's not right*.
>
> I've had meetings with the American Government representatives in their embassy, both their consulate here and their embassy in Dublin, and I've asked them what's their relationships now like with Japan and Vietnam and Korea and stuff, and they go, 'What do you mean?' I said, 'they fought wars against you and you let them into your country. We fought against the British Government and you won't let us into your country. What's the big deal?' I can go to London tomorrow, nobody queries it, but I can't go to Washington, and the reason I can't go to Washington is that I fought against the British Government and I take offence at it.
>
> The British Government are vindictive by holding criminal records against us. *I'm not a criminal.* (Emphasis in original)

Ex-combatants are barred from adopting and fostering, from obtaining insurance, and from applying for taxi or bus operator licences; travel restrictions to the USA, Canada, and Australia are in place, and they have difficulty in accessing mortgage facilities.

As one ex-combatant states:

The other thing is too that we are the only segment of society who can legally be discriminated against, and that was supported by the House of Lords. I can't adopt a child. I can't foster a child. Car insurance. We can't get car insurance. We can't get home insurance. They are bringing in a law now that we can't drive a taxi which is ridiculous.

Various studies have highlighted the difficulties that many of the ex-combatants, both women and men, face in terms of accessing employment (Gormally et al. 2007; Grounds and Jamieson 2003; Shirlow 2001; Shirlow and McEvoy 2008). Research carried out in 2010 by an ex-combatant organisation found that ex-combatants are at least four times as likely to be unemployed as others in Northern Ireland (Tar Isteach 2010). Their exclusion from certain types of jobs due to their criminal record was difficult to explain, given that at least 17 members of the Legislative Assembly, local councillors and Special Advisors to Members of the Executive hold 'conflict related convictions' (Tar Isteach 2010).

It was clear that the participants in the study especially resented their social and economic exclusion in the light of what they saw as their central role as peacebuilders:

So we're the only people in this segment of society who can legally be discriminated against, and as you seen up in Stormont, we have ex-prisoners in Government- the Minister of Health, the Minister of Education, but me as an ex-prisoner, I can't get a job. So what we were saying, is that there should be a new dispensation and there's over 30,000, 40,000 people that went through the prison gates—we're part and parcel of society and the peace builders, so why is it that we are still prevented from full citizenship rights?

A male participant disillusioned with his employability prospects states:

I came out with a university degree, did youth work and community work and all the work I'm doing now and you're telling me I can't be trusted to get a job in Stormont or a job in Tesco's or Woolworth's or things like that. We are denied visas to Canada, America, Australia and New Zealand and other countries because we're ex-prisoners. *We're part and parcel of resolving issues here and we are still treated like criminals.* (Emphasis in original)

To re-dress the stigmatisation of ex-combatants, the state has to acknowledge its role in the Conflict and remove the obstacles that currently prevent reintegration and entitlement to full citizenship rights. The publication in May 2007 of guidance for employers as to best practice in recruiting people with conflict-related convictions—*Recruiting People with Conflict Related Convictions: Employers Guidance* (OFMDFM 2007)—was an acknowledgement of the barriers facing ex-combatants with regard to employment. However, the guidelines are voluntary, and a tripartite review panel set up in 2010 concluded that there was a general lack of awareness regarding the barriers facing ex-combatants and their exclusion from certain professions even though qualified.

Managing the Past

To manage the past you need to be honest. People need to be honest and upfront and say very clearly, listen, *this was a unique situation.* This was a *unique situation* in the North and in the context that young men and women who were ordinary people, who weren't brought up to get involved in armed action were propelled into it because of conditions that existed in the state.

The reality is there was a war going on in this part of Ireland and people fought that war and people died. That's fact! You can't hide away from the realities of life.

The IRA were involved in actions which resulted in civilians dying. *Wrong.* It wasn't the intention. The state was involved in some of the executions of the civilians, they [the state] see it as fighting against terrorists, if you want. The reality of it was that we were in a war situation.

I'm often asked that question, 'You spent 23 years in prison and do you think it was all worth it?' The reality was I was a product of that society and in turn the politics. When I meet victims, I always try to say to them I'm not trying to justify why I joined. I'm not trying to justify the armed struggle, because our armed struggle took a lot of lives, a lot of innocent lives, so *we can't glorify it.* (Emphasis in original)

Another states:

> I lost three family members, one of them was an IRA Volunteer, and when you look around you actually have to say to yourself ... This is a *continuation of the struggle* and the reason that you're here is because of the sacrifices that others have made, not only within the jails but obviously people who are dead. People who were on active service were killed as a result of the Conflict. If you accept that point, then the struggle continues. I think you deal with it a lot more progressively, if you want, and probably ... maybe the right word's not progressive but you deal with it a lot easier. Any loss is hard. Loss is always hard to deal with. But if you accept the role of the individuals and the movement and, if you want, the jail element to it—it was to advance our struggle, and you say listen: people lost loved ones. People had to die at a young age. But it *wasn't for nothing*. It was a continuous thing. *I think war is war.*
>
> The IRA wasn't throwing snowballs or just kicking people during the Conflict. We killed people too and people who were involved in the IRA died. The IRA had to take responsibility, not the individual. The IRA had to take responsibility for its actions. We killed family members. We killed fathers, sons, mothers, daughters and so on. So you really have to deal with it in that context. *There's no hierarchy of victimhood.* While you have the state trying to declare that there's a hierarchy of victimhood. I mean, I think in general everybody accepts that the reason for people taking up arms was due to the conditions within the North. (Emphasis in original)

As this ex-combatant insists, the key to the reintegration of ex-combatants in Northern Ireland is not to lay blame but, rather, to understand the armed struggle in the context of that society (Rolston 2006).

Joined Up Thinking: Peace Building Between and Within Communities

> The ex-prisoners are at the forefront or the coalface of building peace. So now there's a recognition that we are at the forefront of peace building. We have people from the Loyalist community come in here to do training. If

you had said that 10 years ago, that they would feel comfortable to come into a Republican ex-prisoners' thing to get training on security and things like that, or counselling. I wouldn't have believed you.

Recognising the need to deal with the consequences of imprisonment and the pain of war, 'politically motivated' former prisoners have formed their own organisations to assist with the reintegration process, dealing with a range of matters from employment to counselling to challenging discriminatory legislation.[3] The focus on the reintegration of ex-prisoners was because they were the most visible and tangible representatives of the ex-combatant community. In contrast to armed struggles elsewhere, combatants in Northern Ireland generally did not leave their communities or families and continued to live and participate in society largely unobserved, unless they were forced to go on the run or were imprisoned. In such a context, these ex-combatants needed, first, to be released and, second, to deal with the consequences of incarceration and the impact of war.

We've a group in there now who are doing counselling and there's people from the Loyalist community in there, and these are great things to happen.

Formative dialogue established between some Republicans and Loyalists during their incarceration has also encouraged future cross-community relations and contributed to further engagement. Carolyn Gallaher (2007, p. 46) notes, 'it is logical to assume … prison planted the early seeds of peace by allowing enemies to meet one other on neutral terrain and to see their commonalities'. McAuley et al. (2009, p. 35) have also argued that the experience of imprisonment enabled the 'awareness of common class status, support for the concept of peace and the development of a new post-conflict polity, that allowed for the development of relationships across divides to form'.

Their shared common experience of prison has enabled some ex-combatants to play a significant role in supporting, planning and par-

---

[3] Coiste na n-Iarchimí and Tar Anall.

ticipating in various components of the DDR process. On this road to recovery, many ex-combatants are beginning to address the economic, physical and psychological support needed.

Support After the Long War

I think when you look at the resources that have been provided from the British end of things, you see a very disproportionate approach to resources that have been provided for the former Republican prisoner community, that's in terms of resources around communities. But certainly in terms of providing support for projects like: Coiste na n-Iarchimí and Tar Anall, Tar Isteach[4] and a network of groups, but also in terms of resourcing, you know, support for communities around projects like this. I think it's something that could be proactively considered.

We are in a transitional phase and I think that hasn't been recognised and when you look at the amount of people, for example, who have died from the effects of CS[5] gas that came out of the burning of Long Kesh, and you look at the statistics around various reports that have provided information on the impact of imprisonment on both Loyalist and Republican former prisoners we see that there is a need for support at that level as well, and that's not being resourced. I feel it should. So I think pro-actively, you know, a proactive position on behalf of resourcing groups would go an awful long way to making a difference at that level.

I think we should be funded because of the work we do. I mean, where I live in North Belfast, lower North Belfast, the last 10 years there were bombings and riots and petrol bombs, it's all quiet now. It's very, very quiet because the former combatants on each side have sat down in rooms like this and have talked to each other.

Interviews from members involved in these projects stressed time and time again the importance of providing services within a framework

---

[4] Tar Isteach provides Counselling Advice and Services for Republican ex-prisoners.

[5] CS gas stands for chlorobenzylidene malononitrile anti-personnel riot gas. For military-based accounts, see Hamill (1985, pp. 36–39) and Barzilay (1977, pp. 11–16). See also Ó Fearghail (1970).

of trust, confidentiality and mutual support. There are many examples where ex-combatants have played a key role in facilitating the peace process at both local and structural levels, and have demonstrated how they can work to diminish political tensions and inter-communal hostility. Many studies have revealed indicators of social stress, which include difficulties in securing employment, social and familial dislocation, risks to both physical and mental health, addiction and longer-term effects of imprisonment and institutionalisation (Elder et al. 1994; Jamieson and Grounds 2002). These indicators of social stress are higher in areas where intense violence occurred showing the legacy of the Conflict and the personal troubles involved (Ferry et al. 2008).

> If I had a wish list one of the main things I would say would be is to deal with the issues in terms of ... particularly for those who are now at the stage of life where they're in their late fifties, sixties etc.
>
> In terms of a care package where people are helped through that sort of transition, I'm not talking about just people coming out from Long Kesh and trying to fit into society again and whatever else—all the illnesses they carry, some people suffer with Post Traumatic Stress Disorder and stuff like that. So I would like to see something in terms of helping our families, the likes of respite centres and stuff like that for people who can actually start dealing with some of the stuff without having to constantly have the debate about who's the perpetrator and who's the victim, because every time ex-combatants or ex-prisoners look for some sort of services like that the issue comes down to who deserves all this.
>
> Well, if you're involved in struggle we all deserve it. It's not about saying you were right and you were wrong. It's about saying we've come through struggle. The Good Friday Agreement was the agreement between opposing sides. So it's not about saying you were the perpetrators and we were right, it's about saying we've come through it. So what do we do with the people who actually came through it?
>
> And there are massive gaps in terms of support and I suppose, as a population, Republicans, I think that's a big issue in terms of how do you care for people who actually now need it, and the services aren't there? So if I had a wish list there would be care services, certainly, at the top of it.

The fact that former combatants in Northern Ireland have been instrumental in getting 'buy in' to the peace process from their communities illustrates that, as ex-combatants, they command remarkable social and personal resources, which can be called on in promoting peace-building initiatives. van der Merwe and Smith, suggested that:

> Ex-combatants are far more than simply fighters, they are often social activists with a strong understanding of the nature and cause of social injustice. They are often the *carriers of social memory of struggle* taking on the role of preserving the history of the struggle against injustice. (van der Merwe and Smith 2006, p. 15; emphasis in original)

It is this commitment to social justice that motivates ex-combatants to promote peace and social change. The Northern Ireland experience offers an example of how a society emerging from conflict can accommodate those who have been involved in violence and, simultaneously, enable them to contribute to the rebuilding and regeneration of a post-conflict polity. Thus, a political engagement continues to lead Northern Ireland into peace, albeit in a gradual and sometimes piecemeal manner reflecting at all times the fragility of the peace process. It is through the memoirs and narratives published by former ex-combatants that a space may be created in which meaning can be given to the past and to its place in the present. It is by making public private experiences of violence that one might hope that Northern Ireland might one day find a way to construct a narrative of the Conflict in which *all* can tell their stories and have their experiences of the Conflict recognised in the process of looking back, and looking forward to the future.

Looking Back: Looking Forward

While these reintegration projects have been driven by the ex-combatant community with no official national or international involvement, external finances are an obvious necessity. Since the start of the peace process, Northern Ireland has gained access to a significant level of funding to support peace-building and reconciliation projects, particularly through the European Union Peace and Reconciliation Fund (Aiken 2010). Since 1995, prisoner groups have received over £9.2 million, which supports over 60 community groups and 29 distinct projects working on prisoner reintegration and reconciliation (McEvoy and Shirlow 2009). Some funds have also been distributed by a local non-governmental organisation, such as the Community Foundation for Northern Ireland (Rolston 2007). The investment has supported former prisoners and their families in the areas of education, family breakdown, psychological and emotional support, trauma counselling, welfare and legal representation. The organisations may primarily be managed by and employ former combatants and their families but, although motivated initially by the need to generate reintegrative support for former combatants, many of these organisations also reach out to the wider community. In particular, they have become engaged in a range of conflict transformation projects which focus on various aspects of transitional justice, including anti-sectarianism, truth recovery, outreach to victim groups, working with young people at risk and restorative justice projects in the community (Rolston 2011). Of the 452 prisoners released under the Agreement, and almost 17 years after the Good Friday Agreement, fewer than 25 have returned to prison. Furthermore, various studies of the ex-combatant community have demonstrated the positive role many former combatants have played in the reintegration, reconstruction and transformation of Northern Ireland (Mitchell 2008). Their activities in leading community-based peace-making efforts, developing relations with previously opposing factions, participating in outreach work with victims and their families, and working in government are all indicators that the period of Conflict is well and truly over.

Conclusion

In concluding this journey, I was reminded of Brewer's (2010) *Peace Processes: A Sociological Approach*, where he begins with a quote by Archbishop Tutu, who remarked that 'South Africa had experienced a *negotiated revolution*' (2001, p. 14) and that all successful peace accords are like that.

In writing this and listening to the stories of the ex-combatants, and through the friendships that developed, it became clear that 'peace can be as costly as violence, as catastrophic as conflict. Giving up preferred first-choice options for the sake of a negotiated agreement asks as much of the protagonists as the original decision to fight. To die in war is sacrifice; to live, to make the peace is even a greater one' (Brewer 2010, p. 194). I would go further and argue that the question is not of which is the greater sacrifice, but of where the balance lies between the costs and gains involved in either course of action.

Despite the existence of a small body of studies and campaign literature regarding the treatment of female politically motivated prisoners in Northern Ireland (Brady et al. 2011; Corcoran 2006 Darragh 2012), women remain marginal in academic and first-hand accounts of the Conflict. Such accounts therefore capture neither the gendered specificity of their experiences or the complex interplay between their experience as gendered subjects socialised within a historically specific, politically shaped ethno-nationalist discourse of womanhood, nor their self-identification as soldiers in the struggle against an oppressive colonial state. By placing the voices of female ex-combatants themselves at the centre of this book, I have hoped not only to make visible their *agency* as both combatants and peace-makers, but also to illuminate the production and contestation of subjectivities and identities which were both a product and a key *site* of struggle and resistance in a war in which the prison experience of both women and men came to play a significant role.

It is by prioritising the voices of the women combatants that this book not only enables their re-positioning at the centre of the struggle and of the subsequent peace process, but also moves away methodologically from the more typical sole emphasis on structural conditions and political processes. Instead, prioritising the voices of the women combatants places the production of subjectivities and agencies at the centre, and explores their dialectical relationship to objective conditions and constraints. This enables a deeper and more complete understanding of the motivations and experiences involved in the Conflict and the subsequent peace process.

In the researching of the book, it became clear that the role of women as combatants has received little attention in the literature (with some notable exceptions in the feminist literature around the strip searches and so on). This may be attributable in part to stereotypical views of women primarily as either victims or as peace-makers.

While the literature regarding the Conflict has tended to be gender-blind, the conditions which gave rise to the Conflict were highly gendered in their impact on women's ability to carry out their traditional roles of primary responsibility for social reproduction. This has a bearing on the motivations of at least some of the women in joining the armed struggle and, subsequently, taking a committed role in support and reconciliation activities.

A dominant theme running through the book is the production of identities and subjectivities, both through historical circumstances and through the active agency of subjects. There is a tension between the idealised ethno-nationalist concept of womanhood and the determination of women participants to fight on equal terms with the men; it is in the intersection of their identities as women and as militarised defenders of an oppressed and colonised community that the construct of femininity becomes destabilised.

It is clear from the voices of the female combatants that the prison experience was marked specifically by assaults on their femininity, to which they were the more vulnerable due to the emphasis on sexual modesty within their socialisation and within the ethno-nationalist iconography of femininity. The aggression directed against them seems, in part, to have been a form of gender-based sexual violence in direct retaliation for the threat posed to gender norms by their assumption of the (ostensibly more powerful) role as combatants. They countered this by methods which foregrounded their collective identity as soldiers and their identification with their male comrades in 'the same struggle'.

It is clear from the voices of both female and male ex-combatants/ Volunteers that the role of the female combatant is not given but ambiguous, indicating a tension between different conceptualisations of societal security, where female combatants both fought against societal insecurity imposed by the state and contributed to placing constructions of femininity in dissent within their ethno-national groups. A theme running through the early chapters is the tension between the 'weaponising' of precisely those traditional constructions of womanhood, and the destabilising of those constructions through women's active and assertive roles in the struggle. Thus, for example, the women defending their communities from raids by the British military were both defending their ability to perform their traditional social-reproductive roles and 'weaponising' the tools of their reproductive work (the bin lids) and the leverage their 'femininity' afforded in being able to embarrass the soldiers. Yet, in the same moment, they were asserting a power and agency which contradicted received notions of feminine passivity and invisibility. Similarly, the Republican forces utilised the societal notions of feminine sexual modesty and non-violence which made it possible for women to 'pass' when carrying weapons. However, women's insistence on fighting on the same terms as men was often perceived as a threat, destabilising male as well as female identities and, ultimately, demanding a reconfiguration of the construct of femininity itself.

It was a particular feature of the Republican struggle in Northern Ireland that the struggles for political status of imprisoned combatants (both male and female) came to occupy a central place in the political manoeuvring and ideological contestations of the period. Thus, the struggle to survive the pains of imprisonment comes into view not simply as a matter of dealing with the deprivation of freedom and material comfort, but also as a struggle over the control of collective *identities* in which the very conditions of privation and assaults on the body became weaponised (most famously through the deaths of the male hunger strikers). It is in the chapters dealing with the experience of imprisonment and the fight for political status through the hunger strikes and the no wash protest that the gendered nature of struggle becomes the most apparent. The voices of the women poignantly reveal the outrage of the prison officers and British military at the offence against 'femininity' represented by the women's collective identity as combatants, and the punishment of this deviation through the arbitrary violence and the highly sexualised nature of the strip searches. Through these assaults, the prison authorities and state forces explicitly played on the objectification of the female body and the shame attached to its exposure which lie at the core of the (socially conditioned) subjective experience of womanhood; yet, in so doing, they necessitated the reclamation and reconfiguration of the meanings of the female body; for example, in the actions of women in decorating their cell-spaces with menstrual blood and through the shared political identities which enabled the collectivising of previously individualised shameful experiences of the body.

The most salient feature throughout the voices contained in these pages is that women performed a wide range of roles in both war and peace, and, in so doing, placed the construct of femininity in dissent (Callaghan 2002). It is clear that the women Volunteers were at the fore and central to the political struggle in creating the conditions for Northern Irish society to undergo a transition from war to peace. The United Nations Research Institute for Social Development states that:

> For more than a decade, the United Nations has proclaimed that women's needs deserve greater attention in the post-war context. Yet the problems, rights, abuses and programme shortcomings documented in many reports remain commonplace. (UNRISD 2005, p. 252)

The voices of the ex-combatants throughout this book emphasise women's involvement in the struggle as active agents, and challenges the myth of women as purely victims or peace-makers. Furthermore, in examining the commitment of these women ex-combatants to the reconstruction and reconciliation process, their testimonies serve to challenge the gendered dichotomy between combat and peace-building roles, instead serving to emphasise the continuity between the two and the way that participation in war has shaped the women's commitment to the peace process.

What this book clearly demonstrates is the role of resistance in identity formation, as the participants in the study reflect on who they were and who they have become. This book charts the twists and turns of the transitional journey from war to peace through the voices of Republican female and male ex-combatants. As Stanley and McCulloch (2012, p. 5) argue, 'both female and male ex-combatants have shown intention, opposition, communication and transformation'. The testaments of the Volunteers demonstrate that they are not merely victims of war, but are also agents of change (Sharoni 2000). The 'negotiated peace settlement in Northern Ireland may have stopped large-scale, indiscriminate use of violent force and terror … [T]he violence that remains is much lower in intensity, is different in form from terrorism, and played by rules that try to ensure it is controlled enough to avoid destabilising political gains and the overall peace process' (Brewer 2003, p. 2). This book is a testament to the role women played in political protest, the prison experience during the Conflict and the ongoing struggle for women to *speak and to be heard* (Spivak 1988). I hope that this book in some small way addresses the missing voices of women in the IRA and provides an informed commentary on the experiences of women's involvement, widening our understandings of the role female members of the IRA played in the Conflict and in the subsequent fragile road to peace.

References

Aiken, N. T. (2010). Learning to live together: Transitional justice and intergroup reconciliation in Northern Ireland. *International Journal of transitional Justice, 4*(2), 166–188.

Bairner, A. (1999). Violence, masculinity and the Irish peace process. *Capital and Class, 69*(3), 122–144.

BBC News. (2005, July). IRA statement.

BBC News. (2009, October 11). *Armed struggle is over – INLA.*

Belfast Telegraph. (2007, November 12). Key questions for UDA chiefs.

Brady, E., Patterson, E., McKinney, K., Hamill, R., & Jackson, P. (2011). *The footsteps of Anne: Stories of republican women ex-prisoners.* Belfast: Shanway Press.

Brewer, D. J. (2010). *Peace processes: A sociological approach.* Cambridge, UK: Polity.

Callaghan, H. M. (2002). Surveying politics of peace, gender, conflict and identity in Northern Ireland: The case of the Derry peace women in 1972. *Women's Studies International Forum, 25*(1), 33–49.

Cochrane, F. (2011). From transition to transformation in ethno-national conflict: some lessons from Northern Ireland. *Ethno-Politics, 11*(2), 182–203.

Darragh, S. (2012). *'John's Lennon Dead': Stories of protest, hunger strikes and resistance.* Belfast: Beyond the Pale.

Dwyer, C. D. (2007). Risk, politics and the 'Scientification' of political judgement: Prisoner release and conflict transformation in Northern Ireland. *British Journal of Criminology, 47*(5), 779–797.

The Economist. (2005, September 6). Now, IRA stands for *I Renounce Arms.*

Elder, G. H., Jr., Shanahan, M. J., & Clipp, E. C. (1994). When war comes to men's lives: Life course patterns in family, work, and health. *Psychology and Aging, 9*(1), 5–16.

Fegan, A., & Murray, R. (1995). *Collusion 1990–1994: Loyalist paramilitary murders in the North of Ireland*. Belfast: Relatives for Justice.

Féron, E. (2006). Paths to reconversion taken by Northern Irish paramilitaries. *International Social Science Journal, 58*, 447–456.

Ferry, F., Bolton, D., Bunting, B., Devine, B., McCann, S., & Murphy, S. (2008). *Trauma, health and conflict in Northern Ireland, a study of the epidemiology of trauma related disorders and qualitative investigations of the impact of trauma on the individual*. Belfast: Northern Ireland Centre for Trauma and Transformation and the Psychology Research Institute, University of Ulster.

Gallaher, C. (2007). *After the peace: Loyalist paramilitaries in post-accord Northern Ireland*. Ithaca, NY: Cornell University Press.

Gormally, B., Maruna, S., & McEvoy, K. (2007). *Thematic evaluation of funded projects: Politically-motivated former prisoners and their families*. Belfast and Monaghan: Border Action.

Green, T. M., Britt, T. W., & Castro, C. A. (2007). The stigma of mental health problems in the Military. *Military Medicine, 172*(2), 157–161.

Grounds, A., & Jamieson, R. (2003). *No sense of an ending: Researching the experience of imprisonment and release amongst republican ex-prisoners theoretical criminology, 7*, 347–362.

Hackett, C., & Rolston, B. (2009). The burden of memory: Victims, storytelling and resistance in Northern Ireland. *Journal of Memory Studies, 2*(3), 355–376.

Independent International Commission on Decommissioning. (2005, September 26). *Report of the Independent International Commissioning on Decommissioning*, published on the following website: http://www.nio.gov.uk/iicd_report_26_sept_2005.pdf

Integrated Disarmament, Demobilization and Reintegration Standards. (2006). http://cpwg.net/wp-content/uploads/sites/2/2013/08/UN-2006-IDDRS.pdf

Jamieson, R., & Grounds, A. (2002). *No sense of an ending: The effects of long term imprisonment amongst republican prisoners and their families*. Monaghan: Ex-Prisoners Assistance Committee.

Jamieson, R., Shirlow, P., & Grounds, A. (2010). *Ageing and social exclusion among former politically motivated prisoners in Northern Ireland*. Belfast: Changing Ageing Partnership.

Lawther, C. (2014). *Truth, denial and transition: Northern Ireland and the contested past*. London: Routledge.

Lundy, P., & McGovern, M. (2008). Whose justice? Rethinking transitional justice from the bottom up. *Journal of Law and Society, 265*, 265–292.

McAuley, J. W., Tonge, J., & Shirlow, P. (2010). Conflict, transformation and former loyalist paramilitary prisoners in Northern Ireland. *Terrorism and Political Violence, 22*(1), 22–40.

MacGinty, R., Muldoon, T. O., & Ferguson, R. (2007). No war, no peace: Northern Ireland after the agreement. *Political Psychology, 28*(1), 1–11.

McEvoy, K. (1998). Prisoner release and conflict resolution: International lessons for Northern Ireland. *International Criminal Justice Review, 8*(1), 33–61.

McEvoy, K., & McGregor, L. (Eds.). (2008). *Transitional justice from below: Grassroots activism and the struggle for change*. Oxford: Hart.

McEvoy, K., & Shirlow, P. (2009). Re-imagining DDR: Ex-combatants, leadership and moral agency in conflict transformation. *Theoretical Criminology, 13*(1), 31–59.

McMullin, J. (2004). Reintegration of combatants: Were the right lessons learned in Mozambique? *International Peacekeeping, 11*(4), 625–643.

Mendeloff, D. (2004).Truth-seeking, truth-telling and post-conflict and peace-building: Curb the enthusiasm? *International Studies Review, 6*(3). pp 355–380.

Mitchell, C. (2008). The limits of legitimacy: Former loyalist combatants and peace-building in Northern Ireland. *Irish Political Studies, 23*(1). pp 1–19.

Moore, L., & Wahidin, A. (2015). Transition, women and the criminal justice system in Northern Ireland. In C. O'Dwyer & M. McAlinder (Eds.), *Criminal justice in transition: The Northern Ireland context*. London: Hart.

Office of the First Minister and Deputy First Minister (OFMDFM). (2007). *Recruiting people with conflict- related convictions: Employers' guidance*. Belfast: OFMDFM.

Office of the First Minister and Deputy First Minister (OFMDFM). (2012). *Report of the review panel, employers guidance on recruiting people with conflict-related convictions: Employers' guidance*. Belfast: OFMDFM.

O'Malley, P. (2001). Northern Ireland and South Africa. In J. McGarry (Ed.), *Northern Ireland and the divided world*. Oxford: Oxford University Press.

Porto, J., & Parsons, I. (2003). *Sustaining the peace in Angola: An overview of current demobilisation, disarmament and reintegration*. Bonn: Bonn International Centre for Conversion.

Powell, J. (2008). *Great hatred, little room: Making peace in Northern Ireland.* London: Bodley Head.

Rolston, B. (2000). *Unfinished business: State killings and the quest for truth.* Belfast: Beyond the Pale.

Rolston, B. (2002). Assembling the jigsaw: Truth, justice and transition in the North of Ireland. *Race and Class, 44*(1), 87–106.

Rolston, B. (2006). Dealing with the past: Pro-state paramilitaries, truth and transition in Northern Ireland. *Human Rights Quarterly, 28,* 652–675.

Rolston, B. (2007). Demobilisation and reintegration of ex-combatants: The Irish case in international perspective. *Social and Legal Studies, 16*(2), 259–280.

Rolston, B. (2011). *Review of literature on republican and loyalist ex-prisoners.* Belfast: OFMDFM.

Sharoni, S. (2000). Gendering resistance within an Irish Republican prisoner community: A conversation with Laurence McKeown. *International Feminist Journal of Politics, 2*(1), 104–123.

Shirlow, P. (2001). *The state they are in.* Coleraine: University of Ulster and Social Exclusion Research Unit.

Shirlow, P., & McEvoy, K. (2008). *Beyond the wire: Former prisoners and conflict transformation in Northern Ireland.* London: Pluto.

Spivak, G. (1988). Can the subaltern speak? In C. Nelson & L. Grossberg (Eds.), *Marxism and the interpretation of culture.* Urbana: University of Illinois Press.

Stanley, L., & McCulloch, M. (2012). *State crime and resistance.* London: Routledge.

Tar Isteach. (2010). *Submission to the consultation on the bill of rights for Northern Ireland.* Belfast: Northern Ireland Office.

Tutu, D. (2001, November 6). *Dignity, equality and inalienable rights.* Lecture by Archbishop Desmond Tutu, Belfast. Belfast: Committee on the Administration of Justice.

United Nations General Assembly. (2011). *Disarmament, demobilization and reintegration: Report of the secretary-general* (A/65/741). 21 March 2011.

UNRISD. (2005). *Policy report on gender and development: 10 Years after Beijing.* New York: United Nations Research Institute for Social Development.

van der Merwe, H., & Smith, R. (2006). Ex-combatants as peacebuilders: Opportunities and challenges. In H. Van der Merwe & R. Smith (Eds.), *Struggles in peacetime, working with ex-combatants in Mozambique: Their work, their frustrations and successes.* Amsterdam: Netherlands Institute for Southern Africa.

Glossary of Terms

An Poblacht/Republican News The name of a weekly newspaper of the Republican movement. 'An Phoblacht' is an Irish term meaning 'The Republic'.

Army Council The seven-member ruling body of the IRA determines the organisation's military strategy.

Comms Prisoners and visitors smuggled communications or 'comms' in a variety of body cavities including rectums, foreskins, navels, mouths and noses. Things smuggled included cigarette papers, pens (used for smoking and writing), camaras and a number of quartz crystal radios designed for the blanketmen and the Armagh women by a Swedish technician (Feldman 1991, p. 199).

Criminalisation This is a model of prison management that referred to a period between 1976 and 1981 which conterminously ties in with Ulsterisation. It was part of a broader political and military strategy designed to deny any implicit or explicit acknowledgement of the political character of the conflict, to reframe terrorist violence as a 'law and order' problem, rather than a political one. In the prisons, this entailed an end to internment and the refusal of de facto political status to paramilitary prisoners. It required forcing prisoners to conform to the same regime as ordinary criminal prisoners and accept the tangible symbols of ordinary imprisonment, such as the wearing of prison uniforms and the carrying out of prison work—a plan designed to reduce the role of the British Army, giving security primacy to the RUC. As Bowyer Bell (1993, p. 429) argues, during 1974 there were signs of the beginning of an 'unarticulated strategy ... a typical British response; no theory, only practice, unarticulated values, personal experience and self-interest shaped by an Irish exposure'.

Cumann na gCailini From the Irish, translated literally as 'Girl's Club', it was the female equivalent of the Fianna or junior IRA. It is believed to have gone out of existence in the 1970s. The female junior wing of Cuman na mBan.

Cumann na mBan Meaning 'Club of the Women', this was the title of the women's IRA. Illegal in both parts of Ireland, its members played a significant role in IRA activities at all levels, with at least one woman having been a member of the Army Council. With the adoption of a cell-based structure, it was subsumed into the main IRA in the 1970s.

Managerialism After 1980/1981 to the present day, managerialism characterised the management of prisons in Northern Ireland. The distinct features of this model included an increased acceptance that the prison system could not defeat political violence and a tendency to view the management of paramilitary prisoners as a technical, rather than ideological, endeavour. The second feature of managerialism within the prisons mirrored the development of policies and practices in other aspects of political and public life in Northern Ireland, which increasingly came to see conflict and sectarian division as a feature which required management, rather than resolution (McEvoy 2001). It was characterised by ongoing attempts to demarcate and limit the power of paramilitaries within the prisons. Managerialism was not surrender; rather, it involved a more careful choice of battlegrounds and more subtle ways of undermining paramilitary influence. Such strategies included the opening of Maghaberry Prison in 1987.[1]

Official IRA A republican paramilitary group, it has remained largely dormant since declaringa ceasefire in 1972 after splitting with the Provisional wing.

Provisional Irish Republican Army Generally known as the IRA and by the security forces as PIRA, it is the largest of the republican paramilitary groups. Following the split with the Official IRA in 1969, its military campaign proceeded virtually unbroken for more than two decades. Known in Irish by the Republicans as Óglaigh na hÉireann, in August 1994 it declared a ceasefire which was later broken and then later restored.

---

[1] The female part of Maghaberry Prison opened the previous year in early 1986 and the prison at Armagh that had formerly housed female prisoners was closed (NIPS 1987, p. 1).

Reactive Containment Reactive containment characterised the management of prisons between 1969 and 1976 in Northern Ireland. It is described as a crude military model for the management of paramilitary prisoners and response to political violence. It was also a response to the broader conflict in Northern Ireland. The outbreak of violence in Northern Ireland was perceived in political and security circles in Britain as a quasi-colonial insurrection similar to that which had been faced in Kenya, Malaysia, Cyprus, Aden and Omar (Dewar 1985; Kitson 1991). To contain the violence, terrorist suspects were interned without trial, the criminal justice system was amended to process large numbers of terrorist cases through the jury-less Diplock Courts and convicted prisoners were granted de facto prisoner of war status while the government sought to negotiate with the paramilitary leaders to seek a political solution.

References

Bowyer Bell, J. (1993). *The Irish troubles: A generation of violence 1967-1992.* Dublin: Gill and Martin.

Dewar, M. (1996). The British Army in Northern Ireland. Weidenfeld Military; 2nd edition.

Feldman, A. (1991). *Formations of violence: The narrative of the body and political terror in Northern Ireland.* Chicago: University of Chicago Press.

Kitson, F. (1991). *Directing operations.* London: Faber and Faber.

McEvoy, K. (2001). Paramilitary Imprisonment in Northern Ireland: Resistance, Management, and Release. Oxford: Oxford University Press.

Index

© The Editor(s) (if applicable) and The Author(s) 2016
A. Wahidin, *Ex-Combatants, Gender and Peace in Northern Ireland*,
DOI 10.1057/978-1-137-36330-5